*A publication
sponsored by the
American Association of Colleges
for Teacher Education*

Diversity
in
Teacher
Education

Mary E. Dilworth, Editor

Diversity in Teacher Education

New Expectations

Jossey-Bass Publishers · San Francisco

For sales outside the United States, contact Maxwell Macmillan International Publishing Group, 866 Third Avenue, New York, New York 10022.

Manufactured in the United States of America

 The paper used in this book is acid-free and meets the State of California requirements for recycled paper (50 percent recycled waste, including 10 percent postconsumer waste), which are the strictest guidelines for recycled paper currently in use in the United States.

Library of Congress Cataloging-in-Publication Data

Diversity in teacher education : new expectations / Mary E. Dilworth, editor. — 1st ed.
    p.   cm.—(The Jossey-Bass education series) (The Jossey-Bass higher and adult education series)
  Includes index.
  ISBN 1-55542-472-4 (alk. paper)
  1. Teachers—Training of—United States. 2. Minorities—Education—United States. 3. Minority teachers—United States—Recruiting. 4. Pluralism (Social sciences)—United States.
I. Dilworth, Mary E. (Mary Elizabeth), date. II. Series.
III. Series: The Jossey-Bass higher and adult education series.
LB1715.D55   1992
370.15′4—dc20
        92-20123
        CIP

FIRST EDITION
HB Printing   10 9 8 7 6 5 4 3 2 1   *Code 9269*

Contents

Preface   xi

The Editor   xvii
The Contributors   xix

1. Restructuring for a New America   1
    Carlton E. Brown

2. Preparing Teachers for Culturally Diverse Classrooms   23
    Antoine M. Garibaldi

3. Countering Parochialism in Teacher Candidates   40
    Nancy L. Zimpher, Elizabeth A. Ashburn

4. Understanding the Dynamics of Race, Class,
    and Gender   63
    Donna M. Gollnick

ix

5.   Making Teacher Education Culturally Responsive   79
        Jacqueline Jordan Irvine

6.   Learning to Teach Hispanic Students   93
        Ana Maria Schuhmann

7.   Recruiting and Retaining Asian/Pacific
     American Teachers   112
        Philip C. Chinn, Gay Yuen Wong

8.   Accommodating the Minority Teacher Candidate:
     Non-Black Students in Predominantly Black Colleges   134
        Johnnie Ruth Mills, Cozetta W. Buckley

9.   Tapping Nontraditional Sources of Minority
     Teaching Talent   160
        Richard I. Arends, Shelley Clemson,
        James Henkelman

10. Changing School Culture to Accommodate
     Student Diversity   181
        Linda F. Winfield, JoAnn B. Manning

11. Diversifying Assessment: A Key Factor
     in the Reform Equation   215
        Leonard C. Beckum

12. Restructuring for Diversity: Five Regional Portraits   229
        Sharon S. Nelson-Barber, Jean Mitchell

     Name Index   263

     Subject Index   269

Preface

There is widespread recognition in the educational community that racial and ethnic diversity is a reality and must be accommodated in numerous ways and on many fronts. The dismal academic performance of many children of color, the economic imperative for a qualified work force, and the need for immediate and necessary resolution of domestic and international social problems all require dramatic adjustments to the manner in which we conceptualize and practice teaching and learning.

Heretofore, our approach to the growing racial and ethnic diversity in the nation's schools has been narrow, unimaginative, and, in some instances, punitive. However, we still have learned from this experience. For instance, we have come to realize that a single multicultural education course is insufficient preparation for prospective teachers to effectively understand and teach children of different cultural backgrounds. We also recognize that a critical mass of African, Hispanic, Asian, and Native American teachers is essential, not only to serve as role models for students from these groups but also to provide greater variance in knowledge and skills for those who will teach. Further, we are beginning to acknowledge that the training and assumptions propagated in schools, colleges, and departments of education (SCDEs) often run counter to the realities of many culturally rich but economically poor classrooms.

Diversity in Teacher Education is framed with these understandings. It attempts to clarify the challenges that we face and the context in which we must operate, and it offers meaningful directives for restructuring the teacher education enterprise. We wrote this book in response to the numerous and often desperate requests of teacher educators and policy makers for information about how best to prepare prospective teachers for the culturally, racially, and linguistically diverse classrooms of today and tomorrow.

Intended Audience

It is our sense that most readers of this book are familiar with statistics regarding the increasingly multicultural school population and the homogeneous teaching force. Harold Hodgkinson (1986, 1991) and the American Association of Colleges for Teacher Education (1990) have done much to describe, in concrete terms, the demographic imperative. This book seeks to move beyond the data by focusing on the reasons for the dilemma, because in this manner we are better able to move toward resolution.

This book should be instructive for faculty and staff with the responsibility of designing teacher education programs and curriculum and for practicing teachers seeking guidance on the equity reform agenda. There is much to be learned in *Diversity in Teacher Education*, even by the most informed teacher educator and administrator. While there is an increasing body of literature that focuses on teacher education reform, the knowledge base for beginning teachers, minority teacher recruitment and retention, and the education of "at-risk" youth, very little of this literature attempts to tie these issues together in a coherent and meaningful way. We hope that our readers will find the information presented here thought provoking and, more important, viable. Indeed, most of the prescriptions and models presented here require faculty and administrators to have broader visions rather than larger operating budgets. Practitioners may also find this book informative in terms of how new expectations for teaching differ from those that they have experienced in the past.

All of the contributors to *Diversity in Teacher Education* are recognized for their grasp of good educational practice and how it is best implemented in schools and in academia. When the contributors were asked to relate their knowledge and experience to issues of diversity and teacher education, interesting constructs emerged, each showing promise for the development of better programs, better teachers, and, most certainly, better education for all children.

Overview of the Contents

Challenges

In Chapter One, Carlton E. Brown leads us on a brief historical journey that explains how restructuring for diversity is not a new mission but one that is simply now more compelling than ever before. He discusses foundational theories and concepts of education, teacher education, and multiculturalism that inform current efforts. He then draws inferences for the new policies and future initiatives advanced by the contributors to this book.

As Antoine M. Garibaldi discusses in Chapter Two, there are many challenges in designing a teacher education experience that is sensitive to student diversity and effective. Tasks range from infusing pertinent information into the knowledge base for beginning teachers to revising textbooks to reflect what we know about learning differences between and among groups.

Perhaps the greatest challenge to the aggressive infusion of diversity throughout the teacher education process is what Nancy L. Zimpher and Elizabeth A. Ashburn, in Chapter Three, term *countering parochialism*. Most children of color are taught by white women who are unfamiliar with their students' cultural backgrounds and communities. According to Zimpher and Ashburn, much of this parochialism may emanate from absence of "an appreciation of diversity, a valuing of cooperation, and a belief in a caring community" in the society at large and in SCDEs. Consequently, not only teacher education students but also faculty must confront their own prejudices, a difficult task given the cultural insularity of the education professoriate.

In Chapter Four, Donna M. Gollnick advances a broad definition of diversity that considers gender and class, along with race and ethnicity, as intervening variables that influence the educational process. In her discussion, she points out both clear and subtle offenses to equitable instruction and learning opportunity.

Context

The foundations, methods, and field experiences that form the core curriculum of teacher education programs are designed by mainstream faculty for mainstream teacher education students and are presumed to be effective for students from mainstream America. The problem is that there has been a distinct shift in what is mainstream, particularly in the classrooms of urban and suburban communities. In short, teacher education programs, students, and faculty must view what is considered to be good practice in a new context—a heterogeneous context that takes into consideration the diversity of the nation's school population and that is formulated and executed by a diverse group of faculty and practitioners.

Chapters Five through Eight describe this new context and the practitioners who operate within its boundaries. Jacqueline Jordan Irvine, in Chapter Five, focuses on cultural variations in instructional strategies and social styles that are typically absent in education programs but that influence the learning process. She calls for structural and ideological changes in the teacher education process. While an understanding of these issues would obviously be facilitated and enhanced by a diverse teaching community, the racial and ethnic compositions of faculty and of the prospective teacher population offer few consultants. Minority teacher recruitment programs have yielded less than impressive results, and Ana Maria Schuhmann (in Chapter Six) as well as Philip C. Chinn and Gay Yuen Wong (in Chapter Seven) offer a number of likely causes. By describing socioeconomic factors such as religion and family structure for Hispanic and Asian Americans, they help us to better understand how culture influences both the learning process and the decision to teach.

Once minority students and faculty are interested in and recruited to SCDEs, there must be a conscious effort to retain them with an amiable environment. It is commonly known that historically black institutions train some of the best and brightest teachers and other professionals. What is not apparent to those outside of these institutions is the great extent to which such colleges and universities are culturally diverse in student body and faculty. Johnnie Ruth Mills and Cozetta W. Buckley, in Chapter Eight, use the experience of white students and faculty on black campuses to explain campuswide issues that should be addressed in making a culturally responsive learning environment.

Directives for Diversity

The task of putting theory into practice is a tremendous undertaking. In Chapter Nine, Richard I. Arends, Shelley Clemson, and James Henkelman describe a nontraditional university-based program of bright nontraditional candidates and thus help us to understand how program design, curriculum, field experiences, and students mix to create a culturally responsive teacher education program. In Chapter Ten, Linda F. Winfield and JoAnn B. Manning note that even the best prepared of these new teachers will need school orientation beyond that provided in SCDEs. They cite problems inherent in the public schools that naturally impede equitable educational progress—issues that only restructured schools, programs, and policies can begin to alleviate.

In addressing the task of assessment, Leonard C. Beckum, in Chapter Eleven, also notes that there is little congruence between the K–12 sector and the SCDEs, particularly in regard to policy development. He notes that "it is increasingly important for educators to refocus the discussion from piecemeal approaches to reform to the synthesis of design, implementation, and evaluation of effective education for students and teachers." Winfield and Manning, as well as Beckum, posit that reform in teacher education must be deliberately, not coincidentally, tied to school reform.

A number of SCDEs have begun to restructure for diversity. In Chapter Twelve, Sharon S. Nelson-Barber and Jean Mitchell describe how five SCDEs have infused cultural sensitivity into their programs, using newly developed assessment prototypes of the National Board for Professional Teaching Standards as guides. Nelson-Barber and Mitchell's presentation of actual experience adds validity to the call of all of the authors to pursue reform within a cultural context.

Diversity in Teacher Education offers numerous perspectives on the issue of diversity in teacher education, and yet all voices blend on how to achieve it. The contributors call for a holistic approach that directs attention to all phases of education and to the individuals who deliver and experience it.

Acknowledgments

This book represents the combined efforts of many individuals. The American Association of Colleges for Teacher Education (AACTE) Board of Directors provided initial and spirited support for its development. David G. Imig, AACTE chief executive officer, offered constructive comments on the framework and early drafts, and the thoughtful critiques of Carl Grant (University of Wisconsin, Madison) and G. Williamson McDiarmid (Michigan State University, East Lansing) helped to fine-tune the manuscript. Special thanks are extended to AACTE staff member Deborah Rybicki, who coordinated the very essential function of organizing many different materials into a single volume, and to Judy A. Beck, who lent her editorial expertise to this effort.

Washington, D.C.   Mary E. Dilworth
August 1992

References

American Association of Colleges for Teacher Education. (1990). *Teacher education pipeline: Schools, colleges, and departments of education enrollments by race and ethnicity.* Washington, DC: American Association of Colleges for Teacher Education.

Hodgkinson, H. L. (1986). Here they come, ready or not. *Education Week, 5,* 13–37.

Hodgkinson, H. L. (1991). Reform versus reality. *Phi Delta Kappan, 73,* 1.

The Editor

Mary E. Dilworth is senior director for research at the American Association of Colleges for Teacher Education (AACTE), a national voluntary organization of colleges and universities that trains the nation's teachers and other educational personnel. Dilworth is also director of the ERIC Clearinghouse on Teacher Education. She received a B.A. degree (1972) in elementary education and an M.A. degree (1974) in student personnel administration in higher education from Howard University, and her Ed.D. degree (1981) in higher education administration from Catholic University, Washington, D.C. Prior to joining AACTE, Dilworth was a research fellow with the Institute for the Study of Educational Policy at Howard University. She is the author of *Teachers' Totter: A Report on Teacher Certification Issues* (1986) and of the monograph *Reading Between the Lines: Teachers and Their Racial/Ethnic Cultures* (1990). She currently serves on numerous national boards and committees, including the National Center for Research on Teacher Learning, National Urban League Education Programs, American Educational Research Association-Division K, and the Task Force on Teacher Training and Assessment of the National Association for the Advancement of Colored People.

The Contributors

Richard I. Arends is dean of the College of Education and Professional Studies at Central Connecticut State University. He received his B.A. degree (1959) in social studies education from Casten College in Oregon, his M.A. degree (1961) in American intellectual history from the University of Iowa, and his Ph.D. degree (1972) in the social psychology of education from the University of Oregon, where he was also on the faculty from 1975 to 1983. Prior to his current position, Arends was a professor at the University of Maryland, College Park, and a classroom teacher. He has authored or contributed to over a dozen books on education, and his text *Learning to Teach* (3rd ed., 1993) is used widely in teacher education programs in the United States and abroad. The recipient of numerous awards, Arends was selected in 1989 as the outstanding teacher educator in the state of Maryland and in 1990 received the Judith Ruskin award for outstanding research in education given by the Maryland Association for Supervision and Curriculum Development.

Elizabeth A. Ashburn is senior research associate in the Office of Educational Research and Improvement, OERI, U.S. Department of Education, where she is responsible for development of the teacher education research agenda and oversight of related programs. She received her B.A. degree (1968) in English from the University of New Hampshire and her M.Ed. (1975) and Ph.D. (1979) degrees in educational psychology from the State University of New York, Buffalo. She has been the director of research as well as director of the ERIC Clearinghouse on Teacher Education at the American Association of Colleges for Teacher Education, where she was instrumental in the initial development of the Research About Teacher Education studies. She has taught high school students, prospective teachers, and experienced teachers.

Leonard C. Beckum is university vice-president and vice-provost, and a professor in the Program in Education at Duke University. He received his B.A. degree (1969) in interdisciplinary social sciences from San Francisco State University and his Ph.D. degree (1973) in psychological studies in education from Stanford University. From 1985 to 1990, Beckum was dean of the School of Education, City College, City University of New York. His research has focused on cognitive and social psychological factors that influence teaching and learning. Much of this research has focused on how learning styles influence the ability to acquire computer programming capability, how social-pscyhological influences have an impact on cognitive development, and the influence of contextual characteristics of the teaching and learning environment on how teachers and students learn. Beckum has published widely on these topics.

Carlton E. Brown serves as the dean of the School of Liberal Arts and Education at Hampton University. He received his B.A. degree (1971) in English and American studies from the University of Massachusetts, Amherst, to which he later returned to earn his Ed.D. degree (1979). Brown is currently engaged in a national study of the education of black males and has engaged in a number of educational research and development projects in his career, including Teacher Corps and a major research and development effort on disproportionate minority student involvement in school disciplinary actions in Norfolk, Virginia.

Cozetta W. Buckley recently retired as associate dean at Jackson State University, Jackson, Mississippi, where she has held numerous positions since 1967. She received her B.A. degree (1948) in elementary education from Jackson State University, her M.A. degree (1960) in English from Mississippi College, and her Ph.D. degree (1978) in library science from the University of Michigan. Buckley has contributed to many publications and has received numerous honors and awards for her work in public schools and the community.

Philip C. Chinn is a professor and chairperson of the Division of Special Education, California State University, Los Angeles (CSLA). He is also the director of the CSLA Center for Multicultural Education and directs a federally funded project to prepare teachers to work with handicapped Asian students. He received his B.A. degree (1959) in history and religion from Baylor University and his M.A. (1963) and Ph.D. (1967) degrees in special education from the University of Northern Colorado. He is the coauthor (with D. M. Gollnick) of *Multicultural Education in a Pluralistic Society* (3rd ed., 1990). He has authored and coauthored numerous chapters, monographs, and articles related to multicultural education and culturally diverse exceptional children. Chinn is the former special assistant to the executive director for minority concerns, the Council for Exceptional Children.

Shelley Clemson is director of the Office of Laboratory Experiences at the University of Maryland, College Park. She received both her B.A. degree (1969) in history and her M.Ed. degree (1974) in curriculum from Pennsylvania State University and her Ph.D. degree (1985) in educational administration from the University of Maryland, College Park. She is responsible for the coordination of six teacher education centers and professional development centers that are collaboratively run by school systems and the University of Maryland. Clemson has been directly involved in the planning, implementation, and evaluation of experimental teacher education programs in several colleges and universities in the Maryland-Virginia-District of Columbia region. She is a vigorous advocate of efforts to diversify the teacher pool and to make teacher education more culturally sensitive and responsive.

Antoine M. Garibaldi is vice-president for academic affairs and professor of education at Xavier University of Louisiana, in New Orleans. He received his B.A. degree (1973) in sociology from Howard University and his Ph.D. degree (1976) in education psychology from the University of Minnesota. Garibaldi is nationally recognized for his work in the areas of equity in teaching and teacher education. He is the editor of *Black Colleges and Universities: Challenges for the Future* (1984) and *Teacher Recruitment and Retention* (1989), a coeditor of *The Education of African-Americans* (1991), and the author of *The Revitalization of Teacher Education Programs at Historically Black Colleges* (1989) and *Educating Black Male Youth: A Moral and Civic Imperative* (1988).

Donna M. Gollnick is vice-president of the National Council for Accreditation of Teacher Education in Washington, D.C. Previously, she was director of professional development at the American Association of Colleges for Teacher Education. She received her B.S. (1966) and M.S. (1974) degrees from Purdue University in home economics education and her Ed.D. degree (1986) from the University of Southern California in education foundations. Her publications and work in the areas of multicultural education have been used as bases for national teacher education guidelines. Gollnick is the coauthor (with P. C. Chinn) of *Multicultural Education in a Pluralistic Society* (3rd ed., 1990). She also serves on the board of the National Association of Multicultural Education.

James Henkelman is associate professor of education at the University of Maryland, College Park, where he is also the associate director of the Office of Laboratory Experiences. He is actively involved in the development of alternative teacher education and graduate staff development programs. He received his B.S. degree (1954) and his M.Ed. degree (1955) from Miami University in mathematics education and his D.Ed. degree (1965) from Harvard University in mathematics curriculum. In addition, he received an M.A. degree (1981) in applied behavioral sciences from Whitworth College.

Jacqueline Jordan Irvine is professor of education in the Division of Educational Studies at Emory University. She received both her B.A. degree (1968) in political science and her M.A. degree (1970) in student personnel administration from Howard University and her Ph.D. degree (1979) in educational leadership from Georgia State University. Her book *Black Students and School Failure* (1990) was selected as a 1990 CHOICE Outstanding Academic Book, and in 1991 she received the Outstanding Writing Award of the American Association of Colleges for Teacher Education.

JoAnn B. Manning is assistant superintendent of the William Penn School District, Pennsylvania, and senior research associate in the Center for Research in Human Development at Temple University. She received her B.S. degree (1967) in history from Central State University, Ohio, and both her M.Ed. degree (1976) and her Ed.D. degree (1987) in educational administration from Temple University. Currently, she is director of the Pennsylvania Leadership Educational Institute, which is funded by the U.S. Department of Education. She is the coauthor of *Educational Leadership Development and the Implementation of Innovative Schooling Practices* (1989).

Johnnie Ruth Mills is dean of the School of Education and professor of education at Jackson State University, Jackson, Mississippi. She received her B.A. degree (1964) in elementary education from Florida A&M, her M.Ed. degree (1970) in elementary education and multicultural education from the University of Miami, and her Ph.D. degree (1978) in elementary education, teacher education, and instructional design and development from Florida State University. Mills has authored and coauthored numerous books, including *Improving Teacher Education: A Conscious Choice* (1989).

Jean Mitchell is research associate at the Far West Laboratory, where her project, funded by the National Board for Professional Teaching Standards, is the development of instrumentation for the valuation of teachers. The project is studying ways to assess how well teachers address educational matters that arise from student diversity in the classroom. She received her B.A. degree (1970) in secondary education from Antioch College and her Ph.D. degree (1991) in curriculum and teacher education from Stanford University. Her research interests are in the cognitive psychology of mathematics problem solving.

Sharon S. Nelson-Barber is acting assistant professor of anthropology at Stanford University. She received her B.A. degree (1974) in history and Russian civilization from Mount Holyoke College, her M.S. degree (1977) in disorders of communication from the University of Vermont, and her Ed.M. (1981) and Ed.D. (1985) degrees in human development from Harvard University. She serves on numerous national advisory boards and steering committees on teaching in culturally diverse settings and is former associate director of the Teacher Assessment Project at Stanford.

Ana Maria Schuhmann is dean of the School of Education and professor of education at Kean College of New Jersey in Union. She received her B.A. degree (1963) in English as a Second Language from the Profesorado en Lenguas Vivas in Buenos Aires, Argentina, and her M.Ed. (1977) and Ed.D. (1984) degrees in language education from Rutgers University. She is well known for her work with special programs and projects on the Hispanic presence in higher education.

Linda F. Winfield is principal research scientist in the Center for Research on Effective Schooling for Disadvantaged Students at Johns Hopkins University. She received her B.A. degree (1975) in psychology, her M.A. degree (1981) in human development, and her Ph.D. degree (1981) in educational psychology, all from the University of Delaware. Her recent works include *Resilience, Schooling, and Development in African American Youth* (1991) and "Lessons from the Field: Case Studies of Evolving Schoolwide Projects" (1991). She is currently co-director of the Special Strategies for Educating Disadvantaged Students, a federally funded, congressionally mandated study of promising practices to inform the reauthorization of Chapter 1 of Elementary and Secondary Education.

Gay Yuen Wong is assistant professor in the Division of Curriculum and Instruction at California State University, Los Angeles (CSLA). She received her B.A. degree (1973) in Chinese studies from the University of Southern California and her M.A. degree (1984) in bilingual education from CSLA. She is currently a Ph.D. candidate at the University of Southern California, where she is completing her dissertation research on Asian bilingual teacher education programs in California universities. Prior to joining the faculty at CSLA in 1989, she worked for fifteen years in the Southern California area as a Chinese bilingual teacher, bilingual program evaluator, bilingual curriculum writer, staff development specialist, and bilingual administrator.

Nancy L. Zimpher is associate dean of external relations and a professor in the College of Education at Ohio State University. She received her B.A. degree (1968) in English and speech, her M.A. degree (1971) in English, and her Ph.D. degree (1976) in teacher education and administration, all from Ohio State University. She has authored and coauthored a number of books and articles, including the *Research About Teacher Education* series. Zimpher has received numerous awards and honors, including the Adams Professorship at Indiana State University (1990), Distinguished Research Award of the Association of Teacher Educators (1990), and Leadership Award of the South-Western City School Teachers Association (1990).

Diversity
in
Teacher
Education

1

Restructuring for a New America

Carlton E. Brown

The agenda for restructuring education and teacher education is under development, based on directives from a variety of sources. Government officials and politicians are fully engaged in the rhetoric of restructuring and reform, and nearly every professional organization in education has also joined the fray. From concerns about our national ability to compete with the Japanese and Europeans in economic and technical spheres to concerns about increasing the number of high-quality teaching professionals, it is clear that major changes in education and teacher education are on the horizon. The authors of this volume have recognized the necessity of injecting a new and critical element into this discussion—the complex set of needs related to the increasing diversity of our national population.

There seems now to be broader acknowledgment that enabling schools and colleges to better meet the needs of minority students is more than a simple issue of equity in treatment and recruitment. Both the increasing diversity of the nation and the radical shifts under way in science, technology, and industry mean that the continuation of traditional results in the education of minority and poor students will lead to a reduction in economic power

1

for the nation at best, and serious international economic and political realignment at worst (National Alliance of Business, 1986;
and Education Commission of the States, 1983). Thus, issues related
to diversity take on a national priority status in the current climate
that exceeds the status of minority educational needs in the past.

Historical Antecedents to Restructuring

Most of the current literature related to reform and restructuring
date the movement from the period 1983–1984, with the publication
of *A Nation At Risk* (National Commission on Excellence in Education, 1983). While this publication helped to bring key educational issues to the forefront of public consciousness, we need to
remind ourselves that the concerns with which we are presently
occupied are not new. Indeed, they are simply contemporary manifestations of historical tensions and issues in society and education
that have frequently surfaced in moves toward reform and change
throughout this century.

John Dewey's many prescriptions and admonitions for
teaching and teacher education can be shown to be precursors to the
contemporary notion of "learning community." Dewey repeatedly
articulated his view of mass urban society. At its best, urban society
could become a democratic dialogue of communities oriented to the
improvement of society. The schools, in Dewey's vision, were to be
the central institution from which this dialogue would proceed,
where the many groups to which each individual belonged would
interact, and where experience could be shared and shaped through
scientific reasoning (Itzkoff, 1969).

Interpretations of his work by at least two of his disciples
brought Deweyan notions directly into multicultural education (Itzkoff, 1969). Both Horace Kallen and I. B. Berkson argued that the
many newcomers primarily from southern and eastern Europe had
an implied democratic right to retain their ethnic and cultural affiliations and not to suffer because of their exercise of this right
(Itzkoff, 1969). Much of their thought was in direct response to the
nativism that was often rampant during the early part of this century. The dominant position was that the United States needed to
do something to Americanize the large waves of recent southern and

eastern European immigrants and to break up the enclaves forming in many of the nation's larger cities.

From another vantage point, Carter G. Woodson, W.E.B. DuBois, and Booker T. Washington voiced positions on the issue of appropriate education for former slaves. Washington believed that the best development of these former slaves would be as industrial, skilled, and domestic laborers. He eschewed the classical education advocated by others for full equality under the law, feeling that this would only come as a result of the industrial and business development of the race (Washington, [1895] 1965). He suggested on more than one occasion that agitation for social equality was pure folly, and that neither the seeking of elected public office nor political protest would aid the elevation of the race.

DuBois, in expressing his concerns about transforming the nation to eradicate second-class citizenship and to foster equality, demanded in 1935 that the education received by African Americans be primarily constructed along classically liberal lines so that former slaves and the sons and daughters of former slaves would be able to become full participants in American society and develop a "talented tenth" to provide leadership and protection for the masses (Lester, 1971).

Woodson (1933) articulated a vision of the needs of the black community itself. Both Woodson and DuBois recognized the necessity of studying the history of African Americans and the needs of the African American community. Woodson, however, declared that the DuBoisian notion of an education for the talented tenth was inadequate. He also declared that the program advocated by Washington had failed in that it merely created obsolescence. In Woodson's view, the only remaining alternative was the pooling of resources in minority communities to build business and industry. Contemporary versions of this same debate are occurring during school board meetings and in college classrooms around the nation today. Neither the nation as a whole nor any minority community has ever settled on a single perspective to guide the education of its people.

Relevant federal legislation dates from the 1954 Supreme Court decision in *Brown* v. *Board of Education*. The language of this decision is too often ignored. Much of the wording centered on the fact that African American people could not develop in a situation in which separate meant inherent inequality. The justices cited research in which separate education was identified as a lack of access to experiences that enable individuals to function in the mainstream of society.

The consequent articulation of the concept of Black Power by Carmichael and Hamilton (1967) led to grass-roots calls for a uniquely black education. The operating premise of these efforts was that the education provided by public schools was inherently antithetical to the educational and developmental needs of the black community, a position reminiscent of the ideas of both Woodson and DuBois. Elements of other minority groups quickly took up the same banner and sought educational programs uniquely suited to their own developmental concerns.

This movement reached its full blossom in the late 1960s and early 1970s. Street academies, alternative schools, curricular changes in public schools, and minority-operated private schools flourished during this time period in New York City (Urban League, 1975) and Washington, D.C., and throughout the West Coast.

The late 1960s and early 1970s define a period of great national introspection. Some of this introspection was brought on by the high level of activity of minority groups and others in the continuing struggle for equal rights and cultural recognition. Eventually, white ethnic groups—most notably, eastern and southern Europeans—began to examine their own unique experiences in the United States and concluded, correctly, that much of their own histories and cultures was ignored in American education. Thus, they joined the movement toward culturally relevant education, but they were a largely conservative entity.

A legislative press toward multicultural education began in 1972. A significant portion of education and education-related legislation at the federal and state levels contained provisions relating to multiculturalism. In 1972, Congress passed the Ethnic Heritage Studies Act (Title IX of the Elementary and Secondary Education Act [ESEA]), which provided for the study of cultural and ethnic heritages in public schools. An assumption stated in the legislative history of this act is that the theory of the melting pot was never operative.

Also in 1972, Congress passed Title IV of the Emergency School Aid Act, which provided support for "a program of instruction of all children from all racial, ethnic and economic backgrounds, including instruction in the language and cultural heritage of minority groups."

In 1973, Congress passed the Bilingual Education Act (Title VII of ESEA). This act provided funds to support the bilingual and bicultural instruction of students with limited proficiency in English. Ten states followed these congressional initiatives with their own legislative support of multicultural, bilingual, and ethnic education (Giles and Gollnick, 1977). In addition, forty states charged a person, department, or division in their respective departments of education with responsibility for such matters.

Professional educational organizations also responded to multicultural issues during this time period. The statement of the American Association of Colleges for Teacher Education (1974) was followed by statements from a Kettering Foundation commission (Brown, 1974) and preceded by statements from the short-lived National Coalition for Cultural Pluralism (1971). But the end of the Vietnam War, recession, the oil crisis, and the ushering in of the back-to-basics movement and a generally conservative mood once again pressed multicultural issues into the background of educational concerns.

Issues related to organization and structure that are currently under discussion are also not new. While issues of organizational control have been present in American education since its inception, states' rights and local control are the standing conventions. Even in relatively homogeneous communities that seem to exercise democratic control over the schools given the sparcity of opposition in viewpoints and needs, bureaucratic controls still dominate most decisions. Indeed, bureaucratic controls are viewed by many scholars as a means that the schooling profession invented to prevent true involvement in decision making by those with other than status quo concerns and thus to reduce the possibilities of change (Katz, 1971).

The late 1960s and early 1970s also witnessed a great deal of experimentation and political action related to issues of organization and control. In response to the demands of minority communities and the work of educational reformers, several school systems temporarily established alternatives to the traditional public school. These designs often included new formats for the involvement of parents and the local community in critical school affairs, not in purely supportive or fund-raising roles characteristic of the Parent-Teacher Association. The new organizational designs were mostly the result of extreme feelings of alienation from schools and schooling experienced by minority and many other poor communities and the consequent press for power that characterized the period (Ornstein, Levin, and Wilkerson, 1975).

The 1960s and 1970s also saw a rebirth of Deweyan ideas about teaching and learning, a quest for methods of teaching that could enhance the thinking and affective skills of all students. In teacher education, U.S. Teacher Corps was a major innovator of the period. Preparation was largely at the master's degree level with extended and enhanced clinical and field experiences. Community involvement and community service were requirements for all interns.

This brief review of historical events relative to the contemporary reform movement shows that many elements of reform are the products of long-developing historical trends and tensions that have remained largely unresolved. However, as those of us who have been involved in the arenas of reform over the past fifteen to twenty years can attest, school district administrators believe that they have in fact responded to the concerns of minority groups. Most superintendents have reported that their curricula are multicultural, that they have substantial parental involvement, and that their school systems provide an appropriate education for all students. We should not assume from these responses that these individuals are seriously disconnected from reality. Rather, the point is that school systems have incorporated only minor, inconsequential, and non-controversial elements of reform. The fact that educational outcomes for most students, but for minority students in particular, have remained largely unchanged over the past twenty years is evidence that the reforms instituted have not impacted central elements of schooling.

The status of teacher education has not appreciably differed from the schools in terms of reform. Many teachers are able to meet all national accreditation standards of review related to multiculturalism, as well as those elements of their own state-approved program standards related to multicultural education. Yet, teachers are no better prepared to meet the needs of or to understand minority students and poor students.

Most teacher education programs include early field experiences as well as other practica. Many even require that at least half of all student teaching assignments take place in urban schools. Teacher candidates have completed these requirements for years, yet outcomes for minority students under the guidance of teacher education programs have remained largely unchanged.

The Restructuring Agenda

The restructuring agenda is still in its formative stages. A wide variety of changes in schooling and teacher education are advocated under the guise of restructuring. For example, a recent issue of a leading periodical (Association for Supervision and Curriculum Development, 1990) illustrates a full range of ideas already implemented in schools, from the elimination of bells to differentiated staffing, to site-based management, to outcomes-based education. While these and many other elements must be a part of the restructuring agenda, it is curious that this entire issue contains only brief mention of the central issue in the success or failure of restructuring—the increasing diversity of America's schoolchildren. These children are religiously invoked as a part of the rationale for restructuring, yet they are frequently omitted from the discussion of what will be restructured and its probable impact.

Nonetheless, based on the literature, it is now possible to outline the fundamental components of restructured schools and to forge a description of restructured teacher education. Restructured K–12 schools will operate initially in a climate of relief from a number of state regulations that can stifle innovation (Holmes Group, 1990). A site-based management scheme will allow for degrees of administrative, personnel, and budgetary flexibility to respond to specific needs identified for each school's population (McDonnell, 1989). Restructured schools will exhibit some form of differentiated staffing, either Holmesian (Holmes Group, 1986) or a mode advocated by other innovators. Most, if not all, classes will be heterogeneously grouped. Tracking in most of its forms will not be present, or it will be seriously debated in the schooling environment (Holmes Group, 1990; Braddock and McPartland, 1990). There will be a strong focus on enabling students to achieve higher-order thinking and to master the basic concepts and skills of science and technology. Finally, the restructured school will be characterized by a new kind of environment that raises expectations, establishes a success orientation, creates an academic press, and builds a sense of community (Holmes Group, 1990; Association for Supervision and Curriculum Development, 1990).

Restructuring and Diversity

The present volume adds much to the restructuring picture. Zimpher and Ashburn, in citing the ideas of Maxine Greene, note that one responsibility of schools is to overcome alienation and draw people into a public place. The environment and sense of community in restructured schools must be deliberately designed to provide experiences of inclusion, particularly for poorer members of the nation's many minority groups. Cultural changes in schools—that is, changes in the core assumptions, understandings, and implicit rules of the schools—are required for such inclusion to take place.

The inclusion of teachers in the school decision-making process is a necessary but insufficient condition for creating a true community. Parents and key community members must also be included in the process (Winfield and Manning, this volume). To leave this factor of inclusion to the goodwill of school administrators is to leave the door open for a change-resistant return to the status quo. Lest we forget the lessons about organizational and institutional change gleaned from educational efforts during the 1960s and 1970s, the Rand Corporation's study of educational innovation and change (McLaughlin, Mann, and Greenwood, 1974) and Sarason's (1971) work serve to remind us that changes in any aspect of the institution can only survive if supported by other consequent or related changes in structure and behavior. The Rand study, in particular, demonstrates that without fundamental changes in organization, the institution tends to return to its initial equilibrium.

As Schuhmann (this volume) and Chinn and Wong (this volume) point out, the element of inclusion may be more critical to some minority parents and communities than it is to others. Cultural communities with a strong focus on and tradition related to the family as a major element of culture may benefit to a greater extent than will others from measures designed to include family involvement in school decision making.

The access of all students to critical knowledge necessary for full participation in an information- and technology-driven republic must be a key element in the restructuring process (Goodlad, 1983). Thus, the position of some researchers, including Braddock and McPartland (1990), that modifications to tracking (such as limiting the number and types of courses that can be tracked and improving the distribution of resources to lower tracks) are more likely than its outright elimination must be reconsidered. There is evidence that tracking is a great deal more deleterious than beneficial to students (Oakes, 1983). Tracking inevitably results in limited access to knowledge for too many students as well as in racial, cultural, class, and gender resegregation. Tracking is thus much more dangerous to the future of the nation as a democratic and egalitarian society than its absence can ever be.

The most compelling examples of success in the education of poor and minority students indicate that context matters (Nelson-Barber and Mitchell, this volume). There are significant differences in our lives, cultures, and settings that make a difference in education (Cole and Griffin, 1987). The literature and lore of teaching and teacher education are loaded with examples of deviations from traditionally accepted instructional strategies and schemes that achieve high rates of success with diverse populations. Although, at present, cultural and contextual codes and clues may be immediately understood by teachers who are members of the targeted community, demographic projections for the next century make clear that all teachers will be instructing students with whom they do not share contexts. Teachers in restructured schools will, therefore, necessarily have to extend their role beyond the school into the community (Nelson-Barber and Mitchell, this volume). Further, as these teachers develop greater knowledge and understanding of their students and their students' respective communities, they will have to develop pedagogies that are responsive to the contexts and cultures encountered (Mills and Buckley, this volume).

Restructured schools will also involve interaction among school personnel and community members about cultural and community contexts and issues. Research and reflection will be needed to devise ever-improving instructional, relational, and motivational strategies to respond to students as whole human beings. Irvine (this volume) states that we simply do not yet know enough about the relationships between culture and teaching and learning to formulate definitive strategies. Asa Hilliard and others have made similar statements based on their research (Beckum, this volume). Research conducted in restructured school settings will help to expand our knowledge about culturally responsive strategies and the importance of cultural content and the context of teaching and learning.

The manner in which we gauge teaching and learning in the restructured environment is also critical. Beckum (this volume, p. 220) has taken the assessment issue head on: "If the characteristics of acceptable performance are developed within a diverse and stimulating framework, then the distinction between curriculum and assessment will blur." Clearly, the historical response of assessment architects to issues of diversity has always been an attempt to accommodate student diversity within a preexisting framework designed from a mainstream perspective with little or no regard for diversity. Restructured schools will be major participants in the design of new assessment procedures that more readily reflect actual teaching and learning processes in schools. In addition, such assessment will be more meaningful in processes of curriculum development and modification.

Restructuring Teacher Education

The process of restructuring schools, colleges, and departments of education must, to a significant extent, be informed by a vision of restructured schools and the activities of teachers within them. From the picture developed here thus far, it can be seen that teachers in restructured schools will require competencies far in excess of the traditional bodies of knowledge in teacher education. Teachers must be provided with the tools needed to adequately understand ethnic and racial relations in the United States, including structural conditions in the economy (such as school funding disparities), political structure (power alignments), and social norms (such as belief in the idea of personal responsibility) that affect the role of schooling in particular communities and the milieus in which teaching and learning take place. Teachers must master the fundamentals of systematically and reflectively studying culture in action.

Teachers must develop the ability to facilitate higher-order thinking through the establishment of stimulating and supportive environments and powerful curricula. They must be prepared to become involved in students' lives for the purpose of using these personal relationships to enhance learning. To achieve this kind of involvement, teachers must develop the ability to reflect on their own actions, observations, and responses to experience and to apply these reflections and their academic knowledge to the design and implementation of new approaches to teaching. Cross-cultural communication skills are clearly required.

Teachers in restructured schools must possess a wide array of instructional strategies and perspectives. They also must recognize the need to continuously hone their abilities to select and implement these strategies across diverse contexts of teaching and learning over the course of their professional lives.

Teachers must have a reasonable acquaintance with research, research skills and strategies, and modes for incorporating research findings into instruction and instructional perspectives. Further, a healthy respect for inquiry integrated with reflections on one's experience must be developed. Finally, and perhaps of greatest importance, teachers in restructured schools must have a professional commitment to service under difficult circumstances, a belief that the finest applications of their capabilities are in the most challenging situations. This commitment must be combined with the participant-anthropologist's mind-set that however uncomfortable or disturbing the experiences, the more powerful they are, the greater the possibility of seminal or deep learning. This type of belief and commitment is a very tall order for any profession, let alone a mass public profession so frequently maligned and with so few material rewards.

The beauty of the reform process is that one enters a powerful praxis. Each thought leads to a new action, which reveals additional knowledge leading to a new action, and so on. The current resurfacing of reform fever began in the early 1980s as a conservative public demand that teachers improve the quantity and quality of their teaching (National Commission on Excellence in Education, 1983). In the view of many, the primary goal was to better prepare teachers in subject matter because students were lacking subject matter competence and high levels of literacy. This view led to a renewed focus on the content of the college major and on general and liberal education.

In the meantime, scholars also began to focus again on the teaching of thinking, which inevitably led to issues of pedagogy (Berliner, 1988; Shulman, 1987). These issues soon included discussions of the increasing diversity in American society. Then came the focus on extended teacher preparation programs and the need for teacher education students to major in academic disciplines.

This reexamination of the structure and organization of schools and teachers' work lives stemmed directly from the realization by teachers that much of what they needed to do could not be achieved effectively in schools as presently structured. The problem of teacher education is that it has rarely, if ever, overcome the parochialism that characterizes the enterprise (see Zimpher and Ashburn, this volume; Irvine, this volume). Teachers have historically been conformist, utilitarian, and status quo in outlook. The vast majority of teachers in the foreseeable future will continue to be white, middle-class females prepared in conventional programs. Change in the preparation of teachers is thus unlike change in any other profession. At the outset, teacher education programs must counter over twelve years of intense socialization in which teacher candidates have developed their conceptualizations of teachers, teaching, and schools. In other words, all teacher candidates have met with reasonable success as students in the very same schools that we now have concluded cannot usher us effectively into the next century or even meet our present needs. These candidates want to help; they want to be good teachers. But many believe, as have generations of teachers before them, that they know, at the point of program completion, all that is needed to be effective with students.

Unfortunately, this attitude is reflected in the current condition of our schools.

As Arends, Clemson, and Henkelman (this volume) state, teacher education programs, even those redesigned on the basis of the tenets of 1980s reform, are not powerful enough interventions in the lives of teacher candidates to help them become effective and reflective practitioners. We have not found a training paradigm powerful enough to significantly influence teachers' attitudes. Even if many of the education program designs currently advanced by reformers can create a major paradigm shift, we are still left with the problem of transforming a collective of professional teacher educators who, on each campus and across campuses, operate from as many perspectives and theories as there are faculty. Several of the contributors to this volume call for a retraining of education faculty to implement advocated designs. Yet, the history of efforts directed at transforming faculties in teacher education, as elsewhere in academe, does not bode well.

Nonetheless, the battle must be engaged. But, first, we must conceptualize at least the rudiments of what a new paradigm should contain. Education faculties will have to mirror the faculties conceived for restructured schools. If these schools are to operate as learning communities, then teacher socialization toward this goal must begin in schools, colleges, and departments of education (SCDEs). The professional members of a learning community must share at least some views and assumptions in order to create an environment with consistent goals and expectations of learning as well as of communication and affect. While some K–12 schools have been able to accomplish this with guidance from effective schooling premises of the 1970s, as Zimpher and Ashburn (this volume) note, such commonality and articulation do not emanate either from the knowledge base of teacher education or from our faculties with their many specializations and divergent training and experience.

Gollnick (this volume) states that the restructuring of SCDEs must begin with critical self- and institutional introspection. Retraining must be informed by conscientious, thorough study of projects and teachers who are successful with a diverse range of students, including minority and poor children. Gollnick makes the additional point that in order to construct adequate teacher education curricula, we must reach a bit wider into academe for a knowledge base in general education and in the major disciplines. After all, we have been saying for some time that teacher education is a universitywide responsibility; now we must take this issue to its next logical steps.

In discussions of a new knowledge base for diversity, we must consider the work developed over the past thirty years by James Banks (1987), Carl Grant (1977), Geneva Gay (1987), and others. In addition, systematic documentation of teachers such as Jaime Escalante properly constitutes part of this new knowledge base

Clearly, however, the design of teacher education programs around these concepts covers new ground. As Arends, Clemson, and Henkelman (this volume) assert, we need to find ways to encourage prospective teachers to think and talk about teaching as they pass through their preparation, much as law students learn to "talk law" and medical students learn to "talk medicine." One major difficulty is that we have not fully developed a conceptual vocabulary for teaching and are often apologetic for specialized language. Specialized language will enable teacher education to engage in the "schema busting" required to eliminate the parochial and conventional conceptions of schools, students, and teaching that teacher candidates bring to us from the totality of their previous lives.

Restructured SCDEs will need strong thematic organization (Arends, Clemson, and Henkelman, this volume) to prevent the internal dissonance currently found in teacher education programs. As Garibaldi (this volume) notes, presently, in too many teacher education programs, instruction in one course or one program in clinical or field experience has no bearing or even conceptual connection to another course or program. We thus invite the student to rely on the only consistent framework available—that developed over twelve or more years of prior education.

As Mills and Buckley (this volume) observe, teacher education must strongly impact the cultural baggage that students bring to the institution. They also state that multicultural education in all institutions, including historically black colleges and universities, must be explicit and dominant in all professional coursework, case studies, and clinical and field studies. Regardless of ethnicity or background, teachers now are and will continue to be charged with the education of a greater diversity of students than that for which their personal experiences have prepared them.

A dominant multiculturalism in teacher education can be achieved in part through the establishment of the kinds of community service or community involvement concepts last used by Teacher Corps. Nelson-Barber and Mitchell (this volume) have advocated the addition of these programs to teacher education as a way to extend the teacher's role beyond the classroom walls. However, to be useful, a community service requirement—in fact, any field or clinical requirement—must be accompanied by systematically guided reflection.

Other aspects of new training paradigms must also have a strong presence in teacher education programs. Nelson-Barber and Mitchell have stressed the importance of personal relationships in the training process, the critical interrelationship between personal growth and professional growth in teaching, and the use of strategies that help to develop self-esteem and create awareness of how cultural differences influence instructional interactions. Additionally, we must attend to Schlechty's (1990) call for the establishment and use of rituals, rites of passage, ceremonies, and celebrations in teacher education. These are elements of culture that bind individuals as a group and create group identity. There is probably no greater power than a new identity and new, powerful affiliations to create new schemas and new perspectives. The formation of cohort groups that pass through rituals, rites, and ceremonies together intensifies mutual identity. This, too, was a lesson of Teacher Corps.

With respect to Beckum's (this volume) call for a new synthesis of design, implementation, and evaluation of teacher education, we must include new relationships with K–12 schools as well as schools of arts and sciences. Just as the restructuring of schools calls for new relationships and power allocations, so too does the restructuring of SCDEs. The traditional school, college, or department of education may not be the appropriate vehicle to deliver reformed teacher education. Already, colleges and universities are attempting to establish new internal arrangements. The graduate college of education advocated by many is only one possible design. In some institutions, a graduate school of education may effectively bar teacher educators from any substantial impact on the character and quality of undergraduate liberal arts and sciences. In other institutions, it may be just the tonic that provides the status necessary to have a critical voice in university decision making.

At least one institution has evaded traditional organizational arguments altogether by dissolving the school of education and creating a Center for Educational Excellence, the administrators of which report directly to the vice president for academic affairs. This center draws universitywide attention to the issues of teacher preparation. As chronicled by Yinger and Hendricks (1990), many Holmes Group institutions have established new organizational designs. Prominent among these are the State University of New York at Buffalo Research Institute on Education for Teaching, in which individuals research, design, and evaluate models of teaching; the Rochester Educational Council, a consortium of institutions and organizations in education that designs professional development schools; and the University of Missouri at Columbia, where outstanding faculty in the Department of Curriculum and Instruction and in arts and sciences departments receive joint appointments.

At many institutions, designs will be fairly eclectic as efforts develop to fit restructuring with particular institutional needs. At my own institution (Hampton University), we have restructured by combining the Divisions of Arts and Humanities, Social and Behavioral Sciences, and Education into the School of Liberal Arts and Education, with a teacher educator appointed dean. A major goal of the new structure is to pursue high levels of interdisciplinary collaboration on research and issues related to education and teacher education. Also, we have for some time maintained high levels of collaboration with the physical and life sciences, operating joint programs, providing joint appointments for faculty, and designing programs. Collaboration will intensify across campus under this new design.

In addition to arrangements internal to the university, we must also address changes in our relationships with the K–12 sector. Again, innovations such as the Rochester Education Council (Yinger and Hendricks, 1990) and the University of Maryland College Park/Montgomery County Public Schools Collaborative (Arends, Clemson, and Henkelman, this volume) are examples of the kinds of new arrangements required. The professional development school concept developed by the Holmes Group (1990) is also a major conceptual innovation. Some states and institutions are also in the early phases of developing clinical faculty programs that provide master teachers as adjunct faculty with strong support and training roles in teacher education.

However, no matter the arrangement or structure, teacher educators will do well to retain the idea that a more powerful training paradigm, based on more than intra- and interinstitutional connections, is required. As teacher educators, we must confront the fact that not only are we a major part of the problem of teacher education but so too are the colleagues with whom we desire connections. Academic programs are not always the powerful sources of intellectual transformation claimed by their architects and advocates. As McDiarmid (1990) suggests, we should not so readily assume that prospective teachers will develop a "connected conceptual understanding" of subject matter in their liberal arts courses, even in extended teacher education programs requiring an arts or sciences major.

The schools with which we must forge new relationships are the same ones that have historically "desocialized" teacher candidates from even our best teacher education programs during the student teaching experience. These are the schools that continue to have a negative impact on minority students, as indicated in part by their dropout and failure rates and disproportionate suspension and expulsion rates, and that continue to respond through predominantly monocultural modes to all students.

For true reform, it is necessary that teacher education programs engage new paradigms openly and boldly as they forge new relationships within and outside of academia. Without such bravado, we run the risk of compromising the depth of restructuring necessary to radically alter teacher education, education, and educational outcomes during the next century. By whatever mode of organization, teacher education is the clear linchpin in the movement to reform education. Schooling as a public institution and teacher education as a formal state-sanctioned process are both so new and so haphazardly developed that we need to cease to award them or

our conceptions of their processes and knowledge bases the sanctity
that is awarded time-honored institutions and notions.

Conclusion

In the immediate future, we must make a major effort to develop
a knowledge base for education and teacher education in regard to
diversity. Grant and Sleeter (1988) point out that though there is a
rich literature for multicultural education, there is virtually no research in classrooms or schools. While there is a growing body of
research relative to culturally determined learning styles, cognitive
styles, and related areas, very little of this research is directly useful
in developing the agenda proposed in this volume. Multicultural
education and related fields must finally grow up, solidify their
conceptions, and develop their own bases of research.

The symposium on minority teacher recruitment and retention sponsored by the American Association of Colleges for Teacher
Education (AACTE) and Metropolitan Life Foundation in January
1990 produced two items of note: AACTE's Next Level statement
(AACTE, 1991) and the concept "culturally responsive pedagogy."
Major attention must be paid to the development of this concept
through substantive and defensible research.

Researchers must begin to document idiosyncratic successes
of teachers or schools both in diverse settings and in single-race
settings. Both bodies of data will be extremely useful in restructuring and in refining responsive pedagogy. Personal experiences and
values must be set aside as these data are collected and examined.
At this juncture, we cannot reliably predict the direction from
which the next glimmer of light will emanate.

If case studies and structured clinical experiences in schools
and communities are to become a vital part of restructured teacher
education, teachers and scholars focused on issues of diversity must
become major contributors to the literature. Without their impact to
add balance to the work of those who now dominate the research world,
all good intentions will not achieve the necessary restructuring.

As collaborative action research with master teachers and
clinical faculty gains prominence, the teachers and scholars focused
on issues of diversity must find ways to involve teachers in action

research in this volatile, political arena. Again, without widespread participation and support the reform agenda will fail.

We also must begin to find ways to involve creative social scientists and humanities scholars in the building of this agenda. While many of these individuals have been the nemesis of teacher educators on many campuses, in the current climate they could easily become our staunchest allies. Moreover, our professional organizations must begin to listen to nontraditional voices: those of poor and minority parents, seriously beleaguered teachers, and any other groups that, historically, have not been heard at our conferences and in our publications.

If the nation continues down the path to true reform, there are a number of concerns that must be openly addressed and accepted. Issues related to diversity and raising the level of excellence in education across the population must now be joined and never again separated.

Restructuring for the new century, the new America, requires change of a magnitude to create trauma among all parties. We will be confused and fearful more often than we will be clear. A definite model of restructured education neither currently exists nor will exist for some time. Therefore, experimentation is the order of the day. We must allow for the development of multiple models, each open for examination. Many designs will fail to accomplish the desired ends. We must refrain from hiding these failures and instead use them as important lessons. Any period of reform will create disjunctions for a period of time—disjunctions between good teacher education and terrible schools, terrible teacher education and great schools.

Success will prove the truth of the national mythology that the United States changes in response to the true needs of its citizens and its institutions. Failure at reform means the acceptance of second-tier status in the world economically, politically, and morally. It also means that we are no different from the other great civilizations of history—we, too, can become a civilization of the past.

References

American Association of Colleges for Teacher Education. (1974). *No one model American: A statement on multicultural educa-*

tion. Washington, DC: American Association of Colleges for Teacher Education.

American Association of Colleges for Teacher Education. (1987). *Minority teacher recruitment and retention: A public policy issue.* Washington, DC: American Association of Colleges for Teacher Education.

American Association of Colleges for Teacher Education. (1991). *Minority teacher supply and demand: The next level. National symposium proceedings and policy statement.* Washington, DC: American Association of Colleges for Teacher Education.

Association for Supervision and Curriculum Development. (1990). Restructuring: What is it? *Educational Leadership, 47*(7), 4–90.

Banks, J. A. (1987). *Teaching strategies for ethnic studies* (4th ed.). Needham Heights, MA: Allyn & Bacon.

Berliner, D. C. (1988). *The development of expertise in pedagogy.* Washington, DC: American Association of Colleges for Teacher Education.

Braddock, H. J., and McPartland, J. A. (1990). Alternative to tracking. *Educational Leadership, 47*(7), 76–79.

Brown, B. F. (ed.). (1974). *The reform of secondary education: A report of the Kettering Commission on the Reform of Secondary Education.* New York: Morrow.

Carmichael, S., and Hamilton, C. V. (1967). *Black power: The politics of liberation.* New York: Vintage.

Cole, M., and Griffin, P. (1987). *Contextual factors in education: Improving science and mathematics education for minorities and women.* Madison: Wisconsin Center for Education Research.

Education Commission of the States. Task Force on Education and the Economy. (1983). *Action for excellence.* Washington, DC: Education Commission of the States.

Gay, G., and Barber, W. L. (eds.). (1987). *Expressively black: The cultural basis of ethnic intensity.* New York: Praeger.

Giles, R. H., and Gollnick, D. M. (1977). Ethnic/cultural diversity as reflected in state and federal educational legislation and policies. In F. Klasson and D. M. Gollnick (eds.), *Pluralism and the American teacher: Issues and case studies.* Washington, DC: American Association of Colleges for Teacher Education.

Grant, C. A. (ed.). (1977). *Multicultural education: Commitments, issues, and applications.* Washington, DC: Association for Supervision and Curriculum Development.

Grant, C. A., and Sleeter, C. E. (1988). *After the school bell rings.* Philadelphia: Falmer.

Goodlad, J. I. (1983). Access to knowledge. *Teachers College Record, 84*(4), 787–800.

Holmes Group. (1986). *Tomorrow's teachers: A report of the Holmes Group.* East Lansing, MI: Holmes Group.

Holmes Group. (1990). *Tomorrow's schools: Principles for the design of professional development schools.* East Lansing, MI: Holmes Group.

Itzkoff, S. W. (1969). *Cultural pluralism and American education.* Scranton, PA: International.

Katz, M. B. (1971). *Class, bureaucracy, and schools: The illusion of educational change in America.* New York: Praeger.

Lester, J. (ed.). (1971). *The seventh son: The thoughts and writings of W.E.B. DuBois.* New York: Vintage.

McDiarmid, G. W. (1990). The liberal arts: Will more result in better subject matter understanding? *Theory into Practice, 29*(1), 21–29.

McDonnell, L. M. (1989). *Restructuring and the American schools: The promise and the pitfalls.* ERIC Clearinghouse on Urban Education Digest, No. 57.

McLaughlin, M. W., Mann, D., and Greenwood, P. (1974). *Federal programs supporting educational change. Vol. 3.* Santa Monica, CA: Rand Corporation.

National Alliance of Business. (1986). *Employment policies: Looking to the year 2000.* Washington, DC: National Alliance of Business.

National Coalition for Cultural Pluraliam. (1971). *Policy Statement* (source unknown).

National Commission on Excellence in Education. (1983). *A Nation at risk: The imperative of educational reform.* Washington, DC: National Commission on Excellence in Education.

Oakes, J. (1983). Tracking and ability grouping in American schools: Some constitutional questions. *Teachers College Record, 84*(4), 801–820.

Ornstein, A. C., Levin, D. U., and Wilkerson, D. A. (1975). *Reforming metropolitan schools.* Pacific Palisades, CA: Goodyear.

Sarason, S. B. (1971). *The culture of the school and the problem of change.* Boston: Allyn & Bacon.

Schlechty, P. C. (1990). *Reform in teacher education: A sociological view.* Washington, DC: American Association of Colleges for Teacher Education.

Shulman, L. S. (1987). Knowledge and teaching: Foundations of new reform. *Harvard Educational Review, 57*(1), 1–22.

U.S. Office of Education. (1972). *Ethnic heritage studies centers.* Washington, DC: U.S. Office of Education.

Urban League. (1975). *New York street academy system.* New York: Urban League.

Washington, B. T. [1895] (1965). The Atlanta Address. In R. S. Blaustein and R. L. Zagrando (eds.), *Civil rights and the American Negro.* New York: Washington Square.

Washington, B. T. (1899). *The future of the American Negro.* New York: Small, Maynard.

Woodson, C. G. (1933). *Mis-education of the Negro.* Washington, DC: Associated Publishers.

Yinger, R. J., and Hendricks, M. S. (1990). An overview of reform in Holmes Group institutions. *Journal of Teacher Education, 41*(2), 21–26.

2

Preparing Teachers for Culturally Diverse Classrooms

Antoine M. Garibaldi

Schools, colleges, and departments of education must assume the responsibility of preparing all teachers, regardless of race, to teach in culturally diverse classrooms. The framework of these revisions must be comprehensive and holistic and include much more than a single course on multicultural education or human relations. Given changes in the demographic composition of the teaching force in the next decade, as well as the diversity already evident in school populations, this chapter addresses some fundamental recommendations for revising the curriculum and structure of preservice teacher education programs so that all teachers will be qualified to teach every child in any situation.

Undergraduate academic preparation of teachers is extremely important, and it is critical that individuals be exposed to a wide variety of liberal arts and science courses during their undergraduate training. The latter core requirements are essential for every preservice teacher since it is that substantive knowledge that must be conveyed to elementary and secondary students. Once such knowledge has been mastered by prospective teachers, they are then ready to learn and apply the general and specific foundations and behavioral aspects of teaching. However, as they acquire this professional knowledge and become familiar with a variety of methodological techniques, they must also learn that the practice of teaching is influenced by many contextual factors. These determinants include such factors as racial and cultural backgrounds, the ability and motivational levels of the students, the setting of the school (for example, rural, urban, or suburban), adequacy of instructional resources (for example, textbooks, equipment, laboratories, and so on), class size, and so on. For those reasons, the professional preparation of preservice teachers must include additional academic knowledge related to diversity and multicultural contexts that can be incorporated into their professional education curricula and their clinical teaching experiences. With that supplemental knowledge base, novice teachers will be better equipped to successfully teach children who come from culturally, racially, and socioeconomically diverse backgrounds.

Revising the Preservice Teacher Education Program

Because of the challenges created by adverse social and economic conditions in many communities today, tomorrow's cohort of teachers will need to be more proficient in many more skills than are teachers who were trained over the last two decades. More children—particularly in public schools—come from poorer backgrounds, and many more live in families where the head of the household is a single parent. Because of smaller budgets in most school districts, class size is larger today, which places greater responsibilities on teachers who must work with limited resources. And most public schools are not adequately funded to provide the essential (and supplementary) instruction that their students will need to enter a changing technological society. Thus, teachers of the future will have to be creative and resourceful educational leaders who are independent thinkers, applied researchers, and individuals who can detect flaws in their own instructional practices.

Besides being knowledgeable in many content areas, future teachers must also become more competent in a variety of methodological techniques so that they can adapt and modify those skills to meet the individual needs of their students. Traditional approaches to teaching will still be useful to beginning teachers, but these individuals must also be flexible (and knowledgeable) enough to use alternative instructional practices when their students are not progressing satisfactorily. Thus, the teachers of today's culturally diverse classrooms must understand that there are differences between the sociological dimensions of "culture" and "class" as they prepare to teach; know how to plan and organize effective instructional situations, how to motivate students and manage their classrooms, and how to motivate students, in addition to being competent in the assessment of the academic strengths and weaknesses of all children; and learn how to encourage the cooperation of their students' families and communities in the conduct of their daily responsibilities. Each of these principles, as well as other related issues, are discussed in this chapter from the perspective of how they can be appropriately incorporated into the teacher education curriculum.

Understanding the Difference Between Culture and Class

One of the first areas to which preservice teachers need more exposure concerns the cultural differences that exist between and among students. This is an important dimension since a great deal of research over the last decade has shown that children from culturally diverse backgrounds do indeed exhibit learning differences and that other factors such as parental support, encouragement, and feedback positively affect their motivation, aspirations, and achievement (Banks, McQuater, and Hubbard, 1979; Boykin, 1979; Hale-Benson, 1986; Clark, 1983; Oakes, 1985; Willis, 1989). Overall, this research demonstrates that the successful academic performance of nonwhite children is both possible and the result of the influence of a variety of external factors. Moreover, the majority of researchers who have focused on the academic functioning of culturally diverse children disprove the notions that cognitive deficiencies and heredity are the primary causes of low performance by these youth.

Teachers of culturally different children, therefore, must recognize that learning distinctions are prevalent and that environmental influences can mediate academic success. But, as Hilliard (1989) has warned, the teacher must not confuse the meaning of "culture" with that of "race" or "social class." In his view, more emphasis needs to be placed on the aspect of social culture that affects learning the most, namely, style. According to Hilliard (1989, p. 67), style is the "consistency in the behavior of a person or a group that tends to be habitual—the manifestation of a predisposition to approach things in a characteristic way." Hilliard stresses, though, that teachers must recognize that styles are not innate but are learned and can be changed. Moreover, everyone (and particularly students) can learn to use more than one style and can alternate styles according to context.

For Hilliard, as well as for other educators and researchers, however, stylistic differences do not in and of themselves explain why so many minority students fail to perform at high levels. Instead, his research indicates that they fail "primarily because of systematic inequities in the delivery of any pedagogical approach" (Hilliard, 1989, p. 68). Thus, a fundamental implication of Hilliard's work is that preservice teachers must receive more training in creating novel pedagogical techniques to accommodate the varied learning styles of their pupils. This recommendation is supported by much of the related research cited in the remainder of this chapter.

A variety of techniques have been used in schools, colleges, and departments of education to increase education majors' awareness of and sensitivity toward students of different racial, cultural, and ethnic backgrounds. But as Cazden and Mehan (1989, p. 47) note, exposure of education students to the particular characteristics of the cultures of different groups is "both impossible and potentially dangerous. . . . It is impossible because there may be too many cultures represented in the classroom; it is dangerous because limited knowledge can lead to stereotypes that impede learning." Cazden and Mehan argue that the beginning teacher must take a holistic approach to learning and use educational research in sociology and anthropology to fully understand the importance of context, code, classroom, and culture. Their fundamental premise is that children must learn (and be taught) the culture of the classroom in order for them to effectively participate in learning. According to Cazden and Mehan (1989, p. 50), classroom behavior, which is also a culturally based behavior, "is guided by rules and norms established by convention, which means they are implicitly taught, tacitly agreed upon, and cooperatively maintained." Thus, if the children understand and learn the appropriate expected behaviors for different classroom contexts (for example, a lesson, taking a test, individual or group activities, or recess), communication and interaction between the teacher and students should increase.

A salient implication of Cazden and Mehan's work for beginning teachers, especially those who teach in pluralistic settings, is that the classroom culture is different from most children's out-of-school environments. But the culture of the classroom can be easily taught, and instruction can be more effectively conveyed. The authors recommend that teachers make use of those factors that are under their control rather than blame school failure on student characteristics that the school (or the teacher) cannot change. The teacher-control model is a much more healthy approach to teaching since it minimizes a teacher's reliance on cultural-deficit models to explain why culturally different students do not succeed on classroom tasks and it promotes the use of alternative teaching (and grouping) practices to maximize student learning.

Since learning and stylistic differences exist in pluralistic school settings today, it is important to acknowledge here that there is debate about whether teachers' perceptions of culturally different children can be changed as a result of exposure to multicultural courses, seminars, or courses that include a unit on multicultural issues. According to the research of McDiarmid (1990), who has evaluated the utility of multicultural seminars of extended duration (that is, as a form of orientation and as a practice throughout the school year) in a large urban district, as well as multicultural courses taken by preservice teachers, those teachers who were exposed to this information were no more inclined to reject stereotypes of students than they were before the training or the course. However, another small study of an experimental program designed to prepare teachers to work with culturally diverse, learning-handicapped students indicated that changes were obvious as a result of limited instruction and applied practical experiences (Burstein and Cabello, 1989). In one of the experimental courses designed to show the influence of culture on student performance and how culture affected frequently misunderstood school behaviors related to motivation, social interaction, and learning styles, Burstein and Cabello (1989) found that the majority of teachers who received training and worked with these students were much more inclined to attribute pupils' general school performance not to their cultural deficiencies but instead to their cultural differences. Moreover, the preservice teachers in this experiment overwhelmingly noted the importance of motivation and effective reinforcement techniques (that is, verbal praise and nonverbal, immediate, and extrinsic reinforcement) in increasing these students' learning.

Despite the difference in results in these two studies, there is much to be learned from what happens to teachers in these training situations. McDiarmid (1990) strongly suggests, for example, that teachers should interact more with each other during the sessions (especially since presenters "talked" three-fourths of the time in the activities that were evaluated) and discuss how they might handle particular problems. Moreover, like Cazden and Mehan (1989), he cautions that teachers' overgeneralizations about particular groups of children as a result of their exposure to multicultural information are a potential danger and may strengthen rather than diminish stereotypical beliefs. Thus, McDiarmid (1990, p. 18) emphasizes that it is important to treat students as individuals rather than "as instances of a set of general characteristics attributed to the group of which they are a part." Maintenance of a balanced approach in the presentation of multicultural information is therefore critical to the success of orientations, in-service seminars, and courses that are designed to influence teachers' attitudes toward culturally different children.

Planning and Organizing Instruction

To be effective educators, teachers must be highly competent in planning and organizing instruction as well as in managing the classroom environment if their students are to be academically successful. Some of these management skills are learned in methods courses, others are developed in educational psychology and social foundations of education courses, and still other expertise is derived from exposure to classroom situations in schools through clinical practical experiences.

As noted earlier, recognition and understanding of contextual factors are extremely important in successful teaching practices, and those factors influence the planning and organization of instruction. An interorganizational report of the American Association of Colleges for Teacher Education, the American Federation of Teachers, the National Council on Measurement in Education, and the National Education Association identifies four key skills that teachers must possess prior to engaging in instruction: "understanding students' cultural backgrounds, interests, skills, and abilities as they apply across a range of learning domains and/or subject areas; understanding students' motivations and their interests in specific class content; clarifying and articulating the performance outcomes expected of pupils; and planning instruction for individuals or groups of students" (*Standards for Teacher Competence in the Educational Assessment of Students,* 1989, p. 2).

Effective instructors who are knowledgeable in the subject matter areas that they teach are better able to establish objectives and goals for themselves and their pupils than are teachers who are less proficient in academic content. Thus, planning alone cannot overcome the knowledge deficit of a teacher in a particular subject area, and it is unrealistic to think that such an individual can explain underlying concepts or develop reasonable learning goals for students. These objectives or goals must be further transformed into appropriate lesson plans, as well as into flexible (and alternative) instructional strategies that can be used if students do not master the material on the first try. Instructional strategies are extremely important for teachers who already work or will work in culturally diverse settings since there is an unfortunate tendency for teachers to erroneously blame these children's low performance on their cognitive abilities rather than to admit that the material was not communicated adequately or not taught effectively. Because very few homogeneous classrooms exist in schools today and since no ethnic, racial, or cultural group is monolithic, all teachers must be prepared to use a variety of instructional practices and be aware of the limitations of strategies derived from traditionally ethnocentric research.

Preservice teachers must, therefore, be trained to employ approaches and modalities that accommodate the distinctive learning styles of students from different racial and cultural groups. While traditional approaches may be useful in some settings, teachers must be able to adapt or select the pedagogy that is most appropriate for their pupils and that will not only increase their students' intellectual abilities but also enhance their self-concepts. For example, research on cooperative learning practices indicates that students achieve more when working in groups rather than when working individually or in competitive situations (Johnson and Johnson, 1987, 1989; Slavin, 1986; Garibaldi, 1979). Moreover, Banks, McQuater, and Hubbard (1979) have shown that the academic motivation of African American children is influenced by task interest or task liking; and Boykin (1979) has postulated and demonstrated that African American children possess a unique adaptive style known as "psychological-behavioral verve" whereby they tend to engage in "high energy level" activities in and out of the classroom. Thus, the teacher must be able to modify the traditional teaching method into movement-oriented, participatory, and exploratory activities for children (for example, through laboratory or group exercises, discussion sessions, or instructional uses of music and the visual and dramatic arts), especially when those pedagogical techniques promote more student involvement, interest, and higher academic performance. Teachers must be highly creative and be able to communicate to children not only through the traditional modes used in society but also in contemporary forms that they may understand even better. However, teachers must be careful not to overgeneralize or to assume that all children will benefit from (or enjoy) a novel instructional approach (for example, memorization using "rap" music styles).

Educational Assessment

In addition to learning how to plan and organize instruction, tomorrow's teachers must also become more proficient in educational assessment. Expertise in educational assessment is critically important for teachers since their teaching skills are significantly enhanced when they know how to monitor students' academic progress and to diagnose their strengths and weaknesses. Keeping in mind students' stylistic learning differences due to their varied cultural backgrounds, teachers must develop comprehensive criteria for assessment and they must not allow their personal expectations of students to interfere with their academic evaluations of them.

Given the large numbers of nonwhite students who drop out, are suspended and expelled, are placed in special education classes, and do not perform at high academic levels, we cannot discount the obvious fact that low teacher expectations contribute in large part to the disproportional representation of nonwhite children in those negative categories. Whether intentional or subtle, teachers must not allow self-fulfilling prophecies or limitations in their assessment skills to affect the amount and quality of instruction that their students receive.

Teachers also must be reminded that their own effectiveness will be judged by the academic progress of all of their pupils. Irvine (1990, p. 48), like Hilliard (1989) and Oakes (1985), posits that a lack of "cultural synchronization" exists between students and teachers and contributes to negative teacher expectations. She further asserts that teachers' beliefs, attitudes, behaviors, and perceptions influence the level and type of communication and classroom interaction, the quality and rigor of instruction, and the affect that they show toward their students. More attention should be devoted to the critical relationship that exists between educational assessment and teacher perceptions since sufficient evidence exists to demonstrate that many students are treated and judged inequitably because of teachers' beliefs and attitudes rather than objective measures of student performance.

Classroom Management

The teacher who bases lesson planning on his or her desired educational goals and objectives, who is highly organized, and who varies learning strategies has very few classroom discipline problems. As Boykin (1979) has noted, schools need not be "unstimulating, constraining, and monotonous" places where children are usually bored; thus, teachers must channel students' high energy levels into productive, task-oriented activities.

Teachers in culturally diverse classrooms must be careful not to use double standards in the administration of discipline or to reduce the amount of classroom teaching time in their conscious or unconscious desire to appeal to their students as fair and understanding authority figures. As Grant (1989, p. 767) states,

Teachers let students know—sometimes explicitly, sometimes not—that if they work quietly for 40 minutes of a 55-minute period, they may use the remaining classroom time to talk quietly with their classmates (Grant and Sleeter, 1986). This arrangement lets teachers feel good for having kept their students on task for a sizable portion of the class period, and it lets students feel good because they have finished their work and thus deserve to be rewarded. The students don't realize that, later in their lives, this wasted time will come back to haunt them. Their knowledge and skills will be inadequate to allow them to take advantage of other educational opportunities. The teachers don't realize that they are unconsciously extending the cycle of poverty and low achievement to another generation of urban students.

Teachers must use the entire class period for every subject that they teach, and they must be firm, fair, and consistent in their disciplinary practices. Transmission of false messages of justice to children is the ultimate transgression and must be avoided by all teachers, especially by those who teach in urban and culturally diverse settings. When this transgression occurs, not only do teachers lose respect and control but also students interpret wrongs and socially inappropriate behavior as inconsequential. The teacher must accept the responsibility to communicate the importance of rules, norms, equity, discipline, and morality in our society to all children and in the same way.

Motivational Techniques

Conventional wisdom as well as research indicate that all individuals, and especially students, become more eager to learn when they have been successful and when their achievement has been acknowledged. But while recognition for academic achievement is expressed in many classrooms, teacher education students receive very little applied training in motivational techniques. The skills of motivating children, making learning exciting and interesting, and reinforcing children when they succeed deserve more attention during preservice training since they correlate directly with academic achievement.

Similarly, teachers must learn how to handle situations where students are not academically successful. Negative reinforcement generally does not motivate students to keep trying. Supportive comments (for example, indicating where mistakes have been made rather than simply telling them that they were wrong) are much more likely to keep students interested in learning. But teachers must be careful that students do not develop a false sense of their own abilities. Nevertheless, by providing appropriate and consistent reinforcement and motivation in the classroom, teachers can help children raise their own academic expectations and develop more confidence in their abilities.

Clinical Experiences in Schools

Although human relations classes have been incorporated into many teacher education programs since the early 1970s, in addition to in-service cultural and racial awareness seminars for novice and veteran teachers in school districts, the best way for teachers to learn about their diverse students is through real situations (Goodwin, 1990). Education majors, therefore, must be exposed to a variety of students and schools as early as their first semester of preservice education. They should be assigned to different schools and classrooms every semester of their four- or five-year programs so that they can both observe and participate in the daily activities of teachers in varied school situations. Moreover, students in methods courses should be required to tutor and to perform microteaching in classrooms and schools so that they can "reality test" the suitability of particular instructional approaches with children of exceptional, average, and below-average abilities.

Teacher education majors, therefore, should be required to have a minimum of twenty hours of combined one-on-one tutoring, group or classroom instruction, and specific methods courses so that they can practice teaching content to students while simultaneously applying varied instructional techniques. Even more important, serious consideration should be given to extending student teaching experiences to an entire year rather than one semester or, at the very least, to increasing the amount of required clock hours during the semester in which they perform their student teaching. A more extended student teaching experience should help academically proficient preservice teachers to become more efficient planners and organizers of instruction, as well as better classroom managers.

When prospective teachers have the opportunity to assess for themselves how schools with numerous resources, and those with inadequate materials, actually function, they experience realistic situations in which they may find themselves early in their careers. These kinds of experiences also emphasize to the prospective teachers that they must constantly be able to vary pedagogical techniques since there are few ideal, homogeneous classrooms where one instructional approach will always work.

Textbook Selection

Another area in which teacher education programs must become more sensitive is the selection of professional education textbooks that address issues pertinent to multicultural populations. Even though a great deal of educational research has been conducted on students of different races, much of that research does not appear in basic education and psychology textbooks. Teacher educators must therefore demand that authors and textbook publishers include the basic and applied research that has been conducted on children of different races. In many cases, faculty members who are aware of this glaring absence have incorporated supplementary readings into their courses so that students receive a broader perspective on why some children respond differently from others to certain kinds of instruction. This kind of information should be in all textbooks so that education majors recognize that all theories do not apply to every group of individuals.

Competing educational philosophies need to be discussed more in teacher education courses, and faculty members should specifically indicate how sampling limitations reduce the generalizability of popular theories and instructional practices. Because so many textbooks lack this kind of information, teacher educators must take the responsibility to selectively choose professional education materials that devote ample attention to multicultural differences and related issues of diversity. Moreover, the theoretical and applied work cited should be recent and comprehensively covered throughout the textbook, rather than solely in those areas where nonwhite students are traditionally (and often erroneously) discussed, for example, classroom management, psychological testing, and high-risk students.

Home, Community, and School Collaborations

Preservice teacher education programs must also devote more attention to the important roles that the home, parents, and community play in the effective education of children, especially those who come from inner-city and rural communities. Few school systems have successfully brought schools and communities close together, even though history, especially the experiences of immigrants, clearly demonstrates that the academic success of previous generations of students was largely due to the combined involvement of and encouragement by teachers, parents, and the community.

Young teachers must be trained how to communicate better and work more closely with the parents of their students. Parents can become more effective partners in the educational process when teachers know how to tell them about their children's academic strengths as well as weaknesses. These types of balanced evaluations give teachers the opportunity to suggest to parents ways in which their children might develop better study skills, more self-confidence, and more constructive uses of their time after school. Emphasis on the positive characteristics of children, even when their abilities are below average, is a very constructive way of demonstrating to parents their role in encouraging, assisting, and monitoring more closely the academic performance of their children.

The support and involvement of religious, civic, and community-based organizations as well as businesses are also critical to the success of schools that serve culturally diverse students. These community partnerships must be revived or strengthened where they currently exist. Otherwise, fatalistic approaches to these opportunities will only continue to bring about the same negative educational results that prevail in too many metropolitan school districts. Teachers and administrators can take the lead in this effort by showing parents and other segments of the community that they can directly and effectively motivate and reinforce their children for academic success.

Conclusion

Preservice teacher education programs must be restructured to accommodate the diverse learning and cultural styles of elementary and secondary school populations. This goal cannot be accomplished with one course focusing on multicultural populations, through orientation and in-service seminars, or through a single field experience in an inner-city or rural school. A holistic approach to teacher training must be developed that recognizes the strengths of different cultural orientations and that places less emphasis on cultural-deficit models to explain low performance by children of particular backgrounds. Teachers must also take into consideration the context of the school and the diversity of their students in planning and organizing instruction and use pedagogical techniques that are most appropriate for the grade and subject matter that is being taught.

Teachers must also learn more about educational assessment, classroom management, and motivational techniques during their preservice years so that children can develop appropriate social skills and personal confidence, in addition to their academic talents. But teachers must be afforded more opportunities to practice these skills, and in varied settings, through more clinical experiences throughout their undergraduate training. Furthermore, teacher education programs must take an active role in demanding that publishers develop textbooks that address issues relevant to and inclusive of multicultural populations. Finally, students who will teach must learn how to communicate more closely with the parents of their children and learn how to effectively use churches as well as civic and community-based organizations to motivate, encourage, and reward children's academic performance.

In conclusion, prospective teachers must be trained to believe that all children, regardless of race and social class, can learn and succeed. Society and the environment in which they live influence young persons' conceptions of themselves and of what they are able to accomplish. However, all teachers, regardless of their own racial or ethnic backgrounds, must realize the important role that they can (and often do) play in shaping culturally different students' career aspirations, their academic and personal expectations, and their life chances. While there is much that we still need to know to maximize student learning in varied situations and with culturally different children, teacher training institutions, master teachers, and local schools must begin to cooperatively develop solutions for an American educational system whose population will be thoroughly multiethnic by the year 2000 and beyond.

References

American Association of Colleges for Teacher Education. (1988). *Teacher education pipeline: Schools, colleges, and departments of education enrollments by race and ethnicity.* Washington, DC: American Association of Colleges for Teacher Education.

Banks, W. C., McQuater, G. V., and Hubbard, J. L. (1979). Toward a reconceptualization of the social-cognitive bases of achievement orientations in blacks. In A. W. Boykin, A. J. Franklin, and J. F. Yates (eds.), *Research directions of black psychologists.* New York: Russell Sage Foundation.

Boykin, A. W. (1979). Psychological/behavioral verve: Some theoretical explorations and empirical manifestations. In A. W. Boykin, A. J. Franklin, and J. F. Yates (eds.), *Research directions of black psychologists.* New York: Russell Sage Foundation.

Burstein, N. D., and Cabello, B. (1989). Preparing teachers to work with culturally diverse students: A teacher education model. *Journal of Teacher Education, 40*(5), 9–16.

Cazden, C. B., and Mehan, H. (1989). Principles from sociology and anthropology: Context, code, classroom, and culture. In M. C. Reynolds (ed.), *Knowledge base for the beginning teacher.* Elmsford, NY: Pergamon Press.

Clark, R. (1983). *Family life and school achievement: Why black children succeed or fail.* Chicago: University of Chicago Press.

Garibaldi, A. M. (1979). Affective contributions of cooperative and group goal structures. *Journal of Educational Psychology, 71,* 6.

Garibaldi, A. M., and Zimpher, N. (1989). *1988 National survey of students in teacher education programs.* Washington, DC: American Association of Colleges for Teacher Education.

Goodwin, A. L. (1990). Fostering diversity in the teaching profession through multicultural field experiences. Paper presented at the Next Level Symposium, American Association of Colleges for Teacher Education, Tampa, FL.

Grant, C. A. (1989). Urban teachers: Their new colleagues and curriculum. *Phi Delta Kappan, 70,* 10.

Grant, C. A., and Sleeter, C. E. (1986). *After the school bell rings.* Philadelphia: Falmer Press.

Hale-Benson, J. E. (1986). *Black children: Their roots, culture, and learning styles.* Baltimore, MD: Johns Hopkins University Press.

Hilliard, A. G. (1989). Teachers and cultural styles in a pluralistic society. *NEA Today, 7*(6), 65–69.

Hodgkinson, H. (1991). Reform versus reality. *Phi Delta Kappan, 73,* 1.

Irvine, J. J. (1990). *Black students and school failure: Policies, practices, and prescriptions.* Westport, CT: Greenwood Press.

Johnson, D. W., and Johnson, R. T. (1987). *Learning together and alone: Cooperation, competition, and individualization.* Englewood Cliffs, NJ: Prentice Hall.

Johnson, D. W., and Johnson, R. T. (1989). *Cooperation and competition: Theory and research.* Edina, MN: Interaction Book.

McDiarmid, G. W. (1990). *What to do about differences? A study of multicultural education for teacher trainees in the Los Angeles Unified School District.* Research report 90-11. East Lansing: National Center for Research on Teacher Education, Michigan State University.

National Education Association. (1987). *Status of the American public school teacher, 1985–86.* Washington, DC: National Education Association.

Oakes, J. (1985). *Keeping track: How schools structure inequality.* New Haven, CT: Yale University Press.

Slavin, R. (1986). *Cooperative learning in student teams: What re-*

search says to the teacher. Washington, DC: National Education Association.

Standards for teacher competence in the educational assessment of students. (1989). Washington, DC: American Association of Colleges for Teacher Education, American Federation of Teachers, National Council on Measurement in Education, and National Education Association.

Willis, M. G. (1989). Learning styles of African American children: A review of the literature and interventions. *Journal of Black Psychology, 16,* 1.

3

Countering Parochialism in Teacher Candidates

Nancy L. Zimpher
Elizabeth A. Ashburn

Profiles of prospective teachers at the undergraduate level depict a population of students strikingly similar in demography, experience, and career aspirations. Questions abound concerning the capacity of preservice programs to create experiences that expose teacher candidates to unfamiliar or unacknowledged diversities sufficient to transform their thinking and responses. We start with the assumption that to ensure effective professional growth of a largely homogeneous clientele, teacher educators must foster "global" training programs. This chapter discusses the nature of our current population of teacher candidates and the parochialism that is likely embedded in their homogeneity. In addition, we offer a perspective on diversity that we believe, if made a stronger part of extant teacher education programs, could potentially counter parochialism. More specifically, we propose that teacher educators must first examine their own thinking for its parochial nature. Further, we explicate three among a number of possible beliefs that ought to be embedded

Note: This chapter serves to promote the exchange of ideas among educators, researchers, and policymakers. The views are those of the authors, and no official support by the U.S. Department of Education is intended or should be inferred.

in any program that seeks to counter parochialism among prospective teachers, grounding those beliefs in extant theory and research.

Parochialism Among Teacher Candidates

Over the past several decades, the characterization of the teacher work force has remained remarkably stable. The typical teacher is a white, forty-year-old married mother of two children; she is not politically active, and she teaches in a suburban elementary school (Feistritzer, 1983). Four years of data describing today's preservice teacher candidates (American Association of Colleges for Teacher Education [AACTE], 1987, 1988, 1989, 1990) provide a profile of future cohorts that is similar to the current profile of teachers. These findings from a random sample of teacher education programs stratified by institutional type show that the average preservice student is typically a white female from a small town or suburban community who matriculates in a college less than one hundred miles away from home and intends to return to small town America to teach middle-income children of average intelligence in traditionally organized schools.

Specifically, 76 percent of the students are female and 91 percent are white; nearly half speak no language other than English (Zimpher, 1989). In the Research About Teacher Education (RATE) III study (AACTE, 1989) of elementary teacher education students, the number of female candidates pushed 90 percent, 33 percent were married, less than 7 percent were people of color or of international descent, less than 25 percent came to college from over one hundred miles away, and over 75 percent reported wanting to return to their suburban or rural hometowns to teach. Even among the 8 percent who came from major urban settings to attend college, only 33 percent would have considered returning to those cities to teach. Recent case studies of six midwestern institutions that prepare teachers (Howey and Zimpher, 1989) reveal a similar profile. These prospective teachers largely were reared in small towns or suburban settings and in middle- or working-class families, and they viewed their education as teachers as essentially a matter of fulfilling a vocational need to go to work. That is, although teacher candidates revealed a high degree of altruism about their career choice (as helping children grow and learn), they also reported a high degree of confidence that they would find jobs in the field of teaching.

It is not surprising that the demographic profiles of most teacher education faculties mirror the total student bodies in their homogeneity. Here again, 91 percent of education professors responding to the AACTE surveys are white, and more than 70 percent of the faculty are white males (Ducharme, 1988). With regard to social demographics, Lanier and Little (1986) observe that a disproportionately large number of faculty teaching teachers have come from lower middle-class backgrounds. So goes the description of most teacher education graduates as well.

These descriptions of both preservice faculty and students suggest a degree of insularity pervasive among the central actors in the teacher education enterprise. Lanier and Little (1986, p. 535) advance the following view of the education professoriate: "It is very likely that [the faculty] obtain conformist orientations and utilitarian views of knowledge from their childhood experiences at home, educational opportunities in school, and restrictive conditions of work as teachers before coming to higher education. Thus the teacher educators closest to schools and prospective and practicing teachers often assume professional work assignments and routines that demand minimal intellectual flexibility and breadth and require, instead, conformity and limited analysis." The student population reflects the same limits of experience. In interviews with faculty about the nature of the students' backgrounds, Howey and Zimpher (1989) collected a set of descriptions characterizing students who were "first-generation college enrollers . . . [who] have limited travel and, in many ways, limited cultural experiences," who are "very good kids," "hard-working, polite and courteous," and "remarkably homogeneous" (p. 128). As one professor observed, "They aren't so much different than we are to begin with. . . . Everyone's blonde-haired around here" (p. 20).

Many generalizations surfaced with regard to the local nature of the populations served in several of the institutions studied by Howey and Zimpher (1989). For instance, sites reported that their students mostly came from the surrounding counties, or all from the same state. Such localism might be expected and in fact was borne out at one regional campus of a large state system campus. More surprising are the observations about students at larger research institutions that attract students from around the world and where a more cosmopolitan student cohort might be expected. These two contrasting types of sites generated a single profile. First, from a small state system campus, the following observations were reported: "The typical student, and by typical I mean well over 30 percent of the students on this campus, comes from a community smaller than 10,000. They either grew up in a small town or on a farm. Typically, they've lived in one family. They are first-generation college students; their parents have not been in college. Often, they're the first ones in their peer group to go to college. They've not travelled. . . . They know no minorities. In fact, many have never met one" (1989, p. 128). The following observations are from a large multiversity: "I was surprised that they [the students] were parochial. I thought coming to a big university that these kids would be worldly and cosmopolitan and appreciative of other cultures and understanding of ethnic groups. And I don't find that, generally speaking. There are a few exceptions in each group but I was surprised" (p. 168).

Although this profile might be expected of a midwestern student population, the AACTE survey data suggest that such parochialism characterizes the mainstream of the teacher candidate population. Mainly, this typification rests on issues of gender, ethnicity, and class, but other attributes suggest parochialism as well: a common age cohort among prospective teachers, a provincialism marked by little geographical mobility or travel experience, an inability to communicate fluently with non–English speaking people or to offer basic instruction in other languages, a pervasive lack of interest in teaching in the major urban areas of this country, and a general lack of acknowledgement of "otherness."[1]

Compelling data gathered through the several iterations of the RATE studies portray a largely female, white, monolingual, and locally raised group, who associate on campus with like groups of students and who prefer to teach average ability, middle-class pupils. However, we do not have specific attitudinal data that would warrant an absolute determination that our students represent any of the definitional properties identified above.

We can, however, draw from the literature on adult development wherein an individual's ability to perceive and cope with the complexities of their environment (in this case, the diversity within it) are tempered by the degree to which students are exposed to "otherness" (Perry, 1968), that is, to individuals whose social, ethnic, cultural, and even geographical backgrounds differ from their own. Thus, the extent to which teacher candidates are culturally insular may be a function of limited access to diversity and little tolerance toward difference.

Role of Teacher Education in Countering Parochialism

To counter the phenomenon of parochialism, major initiatives must be launched to recruit more men and women into teaching who have breadth and depth in cultural diversity. Recruitment alone, however, is an insufficient strategy. We must look as well to the nature of the teacher preparation program as a way to broaden the learning and awareness of our current students, particularly since they do not yet reflect the diverse teacher population that we ultimately seek to establish.

There is little evidence to date that schools, colleges, and departments of education, and the programs that they maintain are, or can be, a force for freeing students from their parochialism. Two observations from the Howey and Zimpher (1989) study capture this difficulty. First, one midwestern dean observed that "I'm not so sure how well our students would fare in many of the school systems if they had been exposed to more radical thinking. . . . The fact is that if you take a student who comes from a family that has a long history of a certain value system and they're first-generation college students . . . , I mean they aren't rebellious people. They are very cooperative; they tend to do what they are told. Superintendents and principals love them" (1989, p. 58). Second, another college administrator remarked that "you send your kid here because of the inculcation of values that you hope they will come out with, and in many cases they're the ones the parents believe in themselves, whether they went here or not. They see a set of values here that to them means something and they are willing to pay for that. I'm not at all convinced that the teachers that we prepare here will cut it on 49th and Halstead in Chicago—down in the meat-packing section. I doubt that. . . . You've got to value this college and what it represents . . . which to me is a solid conservative liberal arts background" (p. 43).

This limited cultural milieu and frequently conservative orientation reflects what Howey and Zimpher (1989) refer to as the "closed-loop" problem in the majority of our teacher training institutions. It appears that program recruiters and architects hold modest expectations for attracting a more diverse population to teaching and, in addition, have modest plans for changing the orientations of these students. One might hypothesize from the above observations that the faculty appear to encourage parochialism, since it satisfies the students' parents and those who seek to hire program graduates. Such an approach to teacher education may hold serious consequences, some of which we are not yet aware. As Goodlad (1986, p. 424) claims, "To derive one's world view from the parochial perspective almost always emerging from such limited participation in the human conversation is dangerous—for oneself and for those who live just beyond one's experiential neighborhood."

Recruitment of diverse individuals into teaching is an incomplete strategy. Membership in a cultural minority group, for example, does not automatically bring an openness and understanding of diversity or knowledge of the pedagogical implications of diversity. While recruitment of individuals who are aligned with program goals (see, for example, Zeichner, 1991) may increase the possibility of program effectiveness, we must also look to the nature of the teacher preparation program as a way to broaden the learning and awareness of our current students, whoever they might be. We must redesign teacher education programs, starting with a learner-centered conception of teaching, often derived from the learner's prior knowledge and experiences (Barnes, 1989). Since our learners' purview as surmised from a sociodemographical perspective appears severely limited, our charge as teacher educators must be to expand our students' range of vision.

We acknowledge the difficulty of such a task. Even those programs that are designed to change prospective teachers' beliefs about teaching may have little success. Evidence from programs that address diversity issues in particular is disheartening. McDiarmid (1990, p. 17) points clearly to the dilemma inherent to multicultural programs: "Describing cultural groups requires the use of generalizations. Yet, a universal purpose of the multicultural curriculum is to expose the logical and moral problems inherent in prejudging individuals on the basis of their membership in a particular group." Zeichner (1991, p. 23) reports that research on a decade of program development at the University of Wisconsin-Madison, which has centered on helping students incorporate different cultural and intellectual perspectives into their teaching, shows that the transformation of their students "into those who are able to competently practice 'culturally relevant' teaching . . . is still a long way from accomplishment." Difficulty of the task and lack of evidence of effectiveness, however, are no excuses for ignoring the goal. The conditions of our existence today bespeak a moral imperative to expand the conversations and dispositions of prospective teachers.

Reconceptualizing Teacher Education Toward Diversity

For many reasons, recent attempts at expanding the prevailing views of future teachers have produced less than promising results. A host of scholars have offered advice on how to organize our curricula to effect a more cosmopolitan, global perspective (Cogan, 1977; Goodlad, 1986; Evans, 1987). Banks (1977) offers the following reasons for the limited effects of these attempts to initiate a cultural revolution in our teacher education programs.

First, we have looked at the curricula of these programs as largely additive. That is, ethnic heroes and cultures have been inserted into school curricula (Cuban, 1968) without adequate thought or teacher preparation to properly integrate these "new" understandings into current instructional approaches and materials. Some teacher educators complain that certain of these concepts are irrelevant, while others worry that the insertion of discrete lessons, modules, units, and programs on "worldly" topics dislodges other curriculum "tenants." Thus surfaces the perennial problem in teacher education of curriculum life space.

Another reason for limited effects of curriculum change is that new formats for teaching about differences have been developed largely through the eyes of mainstream scholars and historians (Garcia and Goebel, 1985). As a consequence of this mainstream perspective on diversity, the "others"—those not in the main-stream—have remained invisible. As Greene (1983, p. 84) has so poignantly observed, "There seems to be so little recognition of those who are strangers (and there are so many strangers today); and, yet, it is recognition that grants individuals the moral equality that is their due."

Finally, we have been constrained in attaining a global perspective largely because our responses have been masked by our own cultural ideology. As we have moved nationally through images of the melting pot and cultural assimilation, we have not been able as a society to provide for the full participation of all of our citizenry in an open society. Partly, or some would say mainly, schools have not been an instrument of positive social change; they function largely as vehicles for the *reproduction* of society in its own image, not as conduits for the *production* of a new global society (Katz, 1975; Bowles and Gintis, 1976).

Beyond Banks's (1977) analysis, yet another unsuccessful approach to establishing a global perspective among teacher candidates involves the recommendations that beginning teachers try to learn details about the cultures of different groups. As Cazden and Mehan (1989, p. 54) observe,

> This is both impossible and potentially dangerous. . . . The limitations come from the practical impossibility for beginning teachers to learn about the many cultures that may be represented in their class. The dangers come from the likelihood that such knowledge will contribute only stereotyped categories and labels that then become barriers to understanding the behavior of a particular child working on a particular school task, and contribute to lowered expectations about that child's possible achievement. Moreover, such information is likely to be considered controversial, even racist, by adult members of the groups described, and any action that undermines trust between home and school is, by that fact alone, detrimental to children's learning.

Instead, they offer a context-specific view of human behavior as associated with teaching, learning, and schooling. This stance requires more understanding by both teachers and students of the cultural context (that is, expected ways of perceiving, thinking, and behaving within the classroom, school, and community) and a process of mutual accommodation achieved through increased understanding of and respect for pupil differences, greater access to parents, and integration of the community culture into the classroom. Zeichner (1991) draws similar conclusions from research conducted on the Wisconsin program.

There are numerous proposals for curriculum changes, in teacher education particularly, that hold promise in countering the parochial perspectives characterized here. Traditionally, these proposals have been instrumental in nature, including suggestions for adding courses or infusing courses with global understandings, and for changing the nature of field experiences to expose our students to culturally diverse school settings. We propose that a more appropriate beginning point is an in-depth examination of a notion of diversity that is fundamental to curriculum designs in teacher education.

Barnes (1987) suggests that curriculum designs based on diversity must be an outgrowth of shared conceptions of teaching and learning among faculty who develop and offer programs. This aspect of program cohesion is also reflected in Howey and Zimpher's (1989) case studies. Essentially, the argument is that in instances where program architects share common perspectives on the nature of effective teaching, the conditions that foster pupil growth and development, and the sociocultural aspects of schooling, these shared views are likely to foster well-articulated programs that inform and extend the shared conceptions (Howey and Zimpher, 1989).

These conceptions emanate from various knowledge bases of teaching and learning, such as the array of perspectives in Reynolds (1989), which has a sociocultural focus, as well as the ideas about multiculturalism and global education now advanced by a sizable group of scholars. However, if teacher education is to increase teacher candidates' exposure to differences, we must draw a value perspective on diversity that has the potential of countering perceived parochialism. As such, we assume that, based on an explicit set of values and beliefs about teaching and schooling, teacher educators are working to develop diversity-sensitive dispositions toward teaching that can be imbued in teacher candidates. These dispositions, or "trends toward teacher actions" (Katz and Raths, 1985; Green, 1964), reflect the ways in which teacher education programs influence the perspectives of future teachers. Thus, in addition to documenting the common demography of our teacher candidate population, we present in this chapter a value perspective on diversity that can inform the design of teacher education programs and potentially expand the horizons of a demographically homogeneous population.

Our notion of an appropriate diversity perspective for teacher education curriculum design is based on the concept of global education, which has been a topic of research for nearly twenty years. The term *global* does not have the same meaning as *multicultural, intercultural, cross-cultural,* or *multiethnic* (for definitions of these and related terms, see Banks, 1977; Montero-Sieburth, 1988; Sleeter and Grant, 1987). The National Council for the Social Studies has defined global education as "a perspective of the world which emphasizes the interconnections among cultures, species, and the planet . . . [and the development of] knowledge, skills, and attitudes needed to live effectively in a world possessing limited natural resources and characterized by ethnic diversity, cultural pluralism, and increasing interdependence" (Montero-Sieburth, 1988, pp. 11–12).

Our aim here is to broaden the conceptualization of "globalness" in relation to education. We define *worldview* as a system of values and beliefs that make meaning and sense of life experience. These values and beliefs underlie one's conceptions of education and of the knowledge, capacities, and dispositions that teachers exercise in classrooms (Zimpher and Ashburn, 1985). We conceive of the global worldview as the penultimate "ism," the sine qua non for significant education in the world today. We argue that the beliefs and values that characterize a global worldview, and that could become more deeply embedded in teacher education curricula, include but are not limited to an appreciation for diversity, a belief in the value of cooperation, and a belief in the importance of a caring community.

First Priority: Appreciation of Diversity

Diversity has been a cornerstone of American society. That it is increasing is a recognized fact (Hodgkinson, 1983); that it is valued is highly questionable. A view expressed almost twenty years ago addresses this lack of valuing of diversity: "We fight it [diversity]. Instead of rejoicing in the fact of the existence of individual differences and enjoying the uniqueness of one another, we are most apt to wish others were more like us—or at least more alike—and we run our schools accordingly" (Parker, 1970, p. 244). Paine's (1988) research on prospective teachers at the National Center for Research on Teacher Education suggests that this provincial perspective persists; diversity is perceived by teacher candidates as a problem rather than as a neutral phenomenon or a potential resource.

More broadly, the current reform movement appears to eschew diversity. Metz, a sociologist at the National Center for Research on Effective Secondary Schools, claims that the reform movement is based on assumption of homogeneity—with reform garments coming in "one size which will fit all" (1988, p. 2)—when in fact the body of evidence to the contrary is sizable. Based on her research in eight high schools, she points out the important dichotomy between public discourse and reality: "In the formal elements of social, physical, and temporal structure, and in the official curriculum, the schools were alike. . . . There was wide variation [however] in the meaning of the temporal, physical, and social structures and the curricular practices . . . , in their impact on the tasks of teaching and learning, and in the overall experience of both staff and students at the different schools. While the social structures might be the same, cultural meanings were different. Academic learning was also different" (1988, pp. 5–6). She also notes that the basis for this homogeneous view is culturally embedded: "The assumption that a school is a school and a student a student, that all are fundamentally alike, has a long history in American educational discourse. It reflects our national image of public schools as all essentially the same, a national ritual experience, which provide us a common background" (p. 20).

While there have been arguments in education for valuing diversity across a range of participants and activities, the arguments have usually been focused on cultural diversity, and the pedagogical response has been "multicultural education." Sleeter and Grant (1987) reviewed the literature in this area and concluded that most of it focuses on race and ethnicity as the primary form of human diversity.

Other forms of pedagogically relevant diversity exist in addition to cultural diversity. Diverse capacities for learning constitute an important category. Gardner's (1985) theory of multiple intelligence is one new perspective on this type of diversity. He has redefined intelligence as "the ability to solve problems, or to create products, that are valued in one or more cultural settings" (1985, p. x), and he has described evidence and operational modes for seven different types of intelligence. His notion about pedagogical responses to these types is that "if we can discover an individual's profile of intelligences, we can make more informed decisions about which program of education to follow if we want to play from strength or if we want to shore up weaknesses" (p. 278).

Another diversity important to teacher education is multiple approaches to good teaching. Fenstermacher and Soltis (1986), for example, present three basic approaches to teaching as a heuristic scheme that teachers might use in pursuing their own individual beliefs about the purposes of teaching. Other diversities that are important to teacher education include ways of learning, handicapping conditions, ways of effective schooling, interests and attitudes of students, levels of entering knowledge (general, specific, academic skills), felt needs for learning, and language skills.

The consequences of failing to value diversity are serious. Bilingual education advocates argue that disregard for language differences is a barrier to equal educational opportunity ("Cultural Differences in the Classroom," 1988). Self-concept and desire to learn may be affected (Drucker, 1968), dropout rates may increase (Parker, 1970), and social responses to diversity among students, which tend to be stereotypical as well as pedagogical responses (Paine, 1988), may perpetuate patterns of cultural inequalities. Since there have been few research studies in this area (Sleeter and Grant, 1987), we understand little in a systematic way about these serious consequences. A valuing of diversity does not suggest that cultural inequalities, the source of diversity, should be valued. Patterns of inequalities may be acknowledged while valuing the diversity that results by appropriate pedagogical and socializing responses.

Teacher education programs have typically treated diversity as an "add-on"—usually with a course in multicultural education that is designed to change attitudes. True valuing of diversity implies an understanding of the broad array of differences among people and how these differences interact with subject matter and with teaching. It is in responding to these diversities through continuing examination and discourse that they become valued; disregard of them leads to social alienation and perpetuation of the existing parochialism.

The practice of truly embracing diversity as a cornerstone of teacher education programs holds at least two important possibilities. First, we can counter what appears to be our own likeness—our own parochialism—by discovering a host of previously unacknowledged diversities among ourselves. Second, by exposing ourselves to our own differences, we become more receptive to the differences in others. These revelations can lay the groundwork for more globally infused programs. A third possibility emerges from McDiarmid's (1990, p. 18) analysis of a program in Los Angeles: "Given that our knowledge of how to teach culturally different children is, at best, speculative, uncertain, and contentious, a pedagogy that enables teachers to talk together about the kinds of problems they encounter and the various ways they might address these seems appropriate. In such an arrangement, teachers educators . . . would use their expertise less as 'knowledge bases' from which they dispense information and more as 'places' from which to view the teacher trainees' experiences and from which to ask questions about those experiences and the lessons teachers draw from them."

Belief in the Value of Cooperation

A discussion of cooperation requires a simultaneous consideration of competition, since it is the opposite as well as the predominant of the two values in our culture. Kohn (1986) documents the destructive role of all forms of competition in our society and shows through extensive and compelling evidence and argument that it is not the source of achievement in any arena. Kohn points out that we have been socialized to compete and to believe in the value of competition to such a degree that we fail to think about other alternatives, such as cooperation. Our misinformation about competition is based on four myths: Competition is part of human nature; it motivates us to do our best and be productive; it is the way to have a good time; it builds character and self-confidence. He refutes each of these myths by reviewing research across a number of academic arenas, from sociology to evolutionary biology. While the emphasis of his book is on the negative aspects of competition, it also, as a corollary, makes a strong case for cooperation.

The nature of competition, according to Kohn, is both external and internal; situations are structured within a win-lose framework, and individuals have intentional desires to win. The consequence of competition is that success can be had only at the cost of the failure of others. Cooperation, on the other hand, is

> an arrangement that is not merely noncompetitive but requires us to work together in order to achieve our goals. Structural cooperation means that we have to coordinate our efforts because I can succeed only if you succeed, and vice versa. Reward is based on collective performance. Thus, a cooperative classroom is not simply one in which students sit together or talk with each other or even share materials. It means that successful completion of a task depends on each student and therefore that each has an incentive to want the other(s) to succeed. . . . Cooperation is a shrewd and highly successful strategy—a pragmatic choice that gets things done at work and at school even more effectively than competition does [Kohn, 1986, pp. 6–7].

Slavin (1983) defines cooperation in four different ways: (1) cooperative behavior (for example, helping others), (2) cooperative incentive structures (where group rewards are based on all group members' performance), (3) cooperative task structures (group work not associated with performance rewards), and (4) cooperative motives (a predisposition to choose cooperative behavior over competitive or individualistic behavior). Research shows that the benefits of cooperation for school learning are multiple. As Slavin (1983, p. 121) noted, "About two-thirds of the cooperative learning studies that investigate any positive outcome find a significantly positive effect on it." Johnson and Johnson (1981) conducted the definitive metanalysis of 122 studies examining the results of competition and cooperation on achievement and performance; cooperation promoted higher achievement than did competition in 65 studies, and higher achievement than did independent work in 108 studies. Fewer than 10 studies found the reverse to be true; cooperation was superior for all ages and all subjects. Johnson and Johnson also concluded that students of medium and low-ability benefit especially from working collaboratively with students of all ranges of ability, and that high-ability students may benefit and definitely are not hurt. The results of competition compared to cooperation are even worse when the quality of performance is considered, above and beyond performance speed, amount of information recalled, or problems solved (Kohn, 1986).

According to Kohn's (1986) review of the literature, a broad range of behavior and attitudes are changed as a result of cooperative structures, and they are generalized to other aspects of one's life. For example, when we cooperate, productivity increases, as does our sense of fulfillment. Cooperation is a powerful motivator; a sense of accountability to others is established among those who are cooperating. Finally, cooperation enhances individuals' abilities.

Slavin (1983; 1986) and Johnson and Johnson (1983) have provided ways of incorporating cooperation into classroom activities and into relationships among teachers. The incorporation of cooperation into the curricula and interpersonal relationships of programs for teacher learning is important for countering the parochialism that competition fosters.

Belief in the Importance of a Caring Community

Many commentators on our culture (for example, Etzioni, 1983) have written about the alienation and isolation in American society—the opposite of a "caring community." The sense that parochial, excessively individualistic interests constitute an unchangeable cultural system may be so prevalent in our society that it may be difficult to believe in the possibility of a different kind of world (Greene, 1983; Peck, 1986). Etzioni, the foremost contributor to public policy analysis in the past decade, argues that "millions of Americans, the pillars of a vigorous and free economy, have been cut off from one another and have lost their effectiveness" (1983, p. 3). As a sociologist and student of Japanese business, Ouchi (1981) suggests that, unlike the Japanese, Americans believe that intimacy and mutuality should be supplied only from traditional sources such as the family and church, and that feelings do not belong in the workplace. In education, according to Noddings (1986, p. 499), "This way of thinking and speaking [about relationships and caring community] has almost disappeared from formal educational discourse. It occurs on the fringes . . . in almost embarrassed whispers."

Although the nature of a caring community has been described in a number of ways, it essentially involves a simultaneous consideration of the importance of both the individual and the group. Etzioni (1983, p. 21) says that the desirable kind of community is "much more integrated than an aggregate of self-maximizing individuals" and that it is characterized by "mutuality," the commitment "not for ego to sacrifice itself to other, or to a higher cause, but for both ego and other to attend to each other and to their shared world" (p. 27). According to Peck (1986), a community is by definition caring. It is defined by inclusivity, commitment, safety, and honest communication. He has discovered in his work that the development of a caring community follows certain specific steps and that these steps can be taught. Ouchi's (1981) description of the Japanese workplace points to trust and subtlety in human relationships as key elements in developing a sense of community. Noddings (1986) describes a caring community in teacher education as having four components: (1) teacher educators who model caring, (2) true dialogue to "produce people who will make autonomous decisions for the sake of their own students" (p. 504), (3) practice teaching as practice in sustaining an attitude of caring, and (4) confirmation of others by helping them to act on their own ideals. Noddings (1984, p. 159) elaborates on the idea of caring by defining "educational caritas" as "something very real. It is a force that can be the most powerful agent in the classroom, leave the most lasting impressions, and touch lives most deeply. . . . [It includes a] desire to become involved with the other person . . . a deep interest and even passionate commitment to the subject matter being taught . . . [and] a love of the acts of teaching and learning [which] . . . are in reality manifestations of the same drive to explore, discover, and share."

Greene (1983, p. 87) claims that it "is one of the responsibilities of the public school to . . . overcome . . . alienation, to draw persons into a public space, and to build a common world." The value of a caring community for the educational setting can be argued from several perspectives. First, it is necessary to survive as humans, both physically and emotionally. The psychological perspective is that we are social creatures who need each other for sustenance and meaning in our lives (for example, Peck, 1986). Sociologists have made the same claim for society as a whole: "Sociologists have long maintained that intimacy is an essential ingredient in healthy society. Once intimacy in a society begins to disintegrate, the process feeds on itself. . . . In the end, we will be a dust heap of individuals without connections to one another" (Ouchi, 1981, p. 8). Etzioni (1983, p. 33) summarizes this reason for community: "Individuals are not viable unless integrated into a web of mutual affection and respect. They must maintain human bonds—or be deformed."

Second, a caring community contributes to development and learning. Noddings (1984) describes three philosophical systems that have included love as an important part of education: Zen Buddhism and the philosophies of Johann Pestalozzi and Martin Buber. Pestalozzi's viewpoint and that of Zen "stress the importance of personal discovery and growth . . . and that these goals cannot be accomplished merely through logical thought processes but require the interaction of human beings and introspection" (1984, p. 162). Buber's message is that "the individual with whom we interact, whom we teach, or whom we are about, must be viewed and experienced directly, without the mediating and diluting influence of words or symbols that turn the *Thou* into an *It*. In the frequently overcrowded and occasionally impersonal setting of modern school, the distinction . . . is worth remembering, and the *I-Thou* relation-ship is worth cherishing" (p. 165). Noddings sums up the importance of love by saying that typical teaching "too often blunts the desire to learn," and that "without a love of teaching in the broadest sense, teachers can do little that is useful, and students who have lost the desire to learn will gain few benefits from any form of instruction" (p. 168).

Third, a caring community is important for productivity. According to Ouchi (1981), productivity will not increase through hard work but rather through addressing the social organization and learning how to work together more effectively; his theory sug-gests that "involved workers are the key to increased productivity" (1981, p. 4). He has described in detail the Japanese approach to building a work community based on trust and friendship, and he has provided evidence that this type of company community is more productive. In the school setting, productivity is often equated with achievement; there is evidence that membership in a supportive school community contributes to higher achievement (Purkey and Smith, 1985).

Conclusion

One group of institutions concerned about reform has directly con-fronted the task of challenging prospective teachers' parochial views. Project 30, sponsored by the Carnegie Corporation, has fo-cused on cultural diversity issues in particular, arguing that they are not peripheral or "add-on" matters but rather are "at the heart of the reform of the course of study in both education and the arts and sciences. . . . The charge that higher education is parochial and in-sensitive to international global matters as well as to matters of significance to the nation's many minority groups is fundamentally a charge that the curriculum is wrong" (Murray and Fallon, 1989, p. 28).

What we have outlined here in terms of beliefs suggests that not only can the substance of the curriculum be wrong but also the manner of implementing the curriculum. What are we teaching by how we *do* teacher education, beyond the content itself? If our teacher education programs are not caring and collaborative learn-

ing communities that foster continuous discourse about the pedagogical implications of diversity, how can we expect our white
middle-class students to believe or act differently from the ways in
which they were taught?

The value perspective on diversity advanced here is arguable
and incomplete. Yet, we have described a perspective that is already
developing, as evidenced by the work cited here. We hope that this
perspective will become more a part of the continuing dialogue on
the reformulation of teacher education programs.

The important question during the reconstruction of teacher
education becomes, How do these changes reflect our values and
beliefs? More specifically, How do they reflect the values of cooperation and a caring community? How do they express an appreciation of diversity? While we look forward to the impact of
recruitment strategies to diversify the teaching force, we are obliged
to concentrate on the task of expanding the views of a monocultural
population that is currently dominant in our teacher education
programs.

Note

1. Although we have chosen the term *parochial* to characterize the
   nature of the student population in teacher education, other
   terms are used somewhat interchangeably (however inappro-
   priately) in such characterizations as well. The *American Heritage Dictionary* (1977) defines parochialism as "narrowness of
   range or understanding," and *Webster's New Collegiate Dictionary* (1973) as "selfish pettiness or narrowness (as of interests, opinions, or views)." A second term, *provincialism,* is also
   used to describe teacher candidates and reflects these definitional properties: "(a) exclusive attachment to one's own pro-
   vince, region, or country; (b) indifference to what is alien,
   unfamiliar, or diverse" (*Webster's Third New International
   Dictionary of the English Language,* 1961); and "narrowness of
   outlook, attitudes, or loyalties" (*American Heritage School
   Dictionary,* 1977).

   Yet a third term, *ethnocentrism,* is also employed to typify our student population and is defined in this twofold

manner: (1) ethnocentric, "inclined to regard one's own race or social group as the center of culture"; and (2) ethnocentrism, "a habitual disposition to judge foreign peoples or groups by the standards and practices of one's own culture or ethnic group" (*Webster's Third New International Dictionary of the English Language,* 1961).

References

American Association of Colleges for Teacher Education. (1987). *RATE I. Teaching teachers: Facts and figures.* Washington, DC: American Association of Colleges for Teacher Education.

American Association of Colleges for Teacher Education. (1988). *RATE II. Teaching teachers: Facts and figures.* Washington, DC: American Association of Colleges for Teacher Education.

American Association of Colleges for Teacher Education. (1989). *RATE III. Teaching teachers: Facts and figures.* Washington, DC: American Association of Colleges for Teacher Education.

American Association of Colleges for Teacher Education. (1990). *RATE IV. Teaching teachers: Facts and figures.* Washington, DC: American Association of Colleges for Teacher Education.

American heritage school dictionary. (1977). Boston: Houghton Mifflin.

Banks, J. A. (1977). The social studies, ethnic diversity, and social change. *Elementary School Journal, 87*(5), 531–543.

Barnes, H. L. (1989). Structuring knowledge for beginning teaching. In M. Reynolds (ed.), *Knowledge base for the beginning teacher.* Elmsford, N.Y.: Pergamon Press.

Bowles, S., and Gintis, H. (1976). *Schooling in capitalist America.* New York: Basic.

Cazden, C. B., and Mehan, H. (1989). Principles from sociology and anthropology: Context, code, classroom, and culture. In M. Reynolds (ed.), *Knowledge base for the beginning teacher.* Elmsford, N.Y.: Pergamon Press.

Cogan, J. (1977). Global education in elementary schools: Teacher education. *Social Education, 41,* 46–49.

Coulson, J., Carr, C. T., Hutchinson, L., and Eagle, D. (eds.).

(1975). *The Oxford illustrated dictionary*. Oxford, England: Oxford University Press.

Cuban, L. (1968). Black history, Negro history, and white folk. *Saturday Review*, pp. 64-65.

Cultural differences in the classroom. (1988). *Harvard Education Letter*, *4*(2), 1-4.

Drucker, P. F. (1968). *The age of discontinuity: Guidelines to our changing society*. New York: HarperCollins.

Ducharme, E. (1988). Perceptions of faculty members about their teacher education programs. Paper presented at the annual meeting of the American Educational Research Association, New Orleans, LA.

Etzioni, A. (1983). *An immodest agenda: Rebuilding America before the 21st century*. New York: McGraw-Hill.

Evans, C. S. (1987). Teaching a global perspective in elementary classrooms. *Elementary School Journal*, *87*(5), 545-555.

Feistritzer, C. E. (1983). *The American teacher*. Washington, DC: National Center for Education Information.

Fenstermacher, G. D., and Soltis, J. (1986). *Approaches to teaching*. New York: Teachers College Press.

Garcia, J., and Goebel, J. (1985). A comparative study of the portrayal of black Americans in selected U.S. history textbooks. *Negro Educational Review*, *36*, 118-127.

Gardner, H. (1985). *Frames of mind: The theory of multiple intelligences*. New York: Basic Books.

Goodlad, J. I. (1986). The learner at the world's center. *Social Education*, *50*(6), 424-434, 435-438.

Green T. F. (1964). Teaching, acting, and behaving. *Harvard Educational Review*, *34*(4), 507-509.

Greene, M. (1983). Openings to possibility: The common world and the public school. In J. Frymier (ed.), *Bad times, good schools*. West Lafayette, IN: Kappa Delta Pi.

Hodgkinson, H. L. (1983). Challenge and response in the eighties. In J. Frymier (ed.), *Bad times, good schools*. West Lafayette, IN: Kappa Delta Pi.

Howey, K. R., and Zimpher, N. L. (1989). *Profiles of preservice teacher education: Inquiry into the nature of programs*. Buffalo: State Univerity of New York Press.

Johnson, D. W., and Johnson, R. T. (1981). Effects of cooperative, competitive, and individualistic goal structure on achievement: A meta-analysis. *Psychological Bulletin, 89,* 47–62.

Johnson, D. W., and Johnson, R. T. (1983). The socialization and achievement crisis: Are cooperative learning experiences the solution? In L. Bickman (ed.), *Applied social psychology annual.* Vol. 4. Newbury Park, CA: Sage.

Katz, M. B. (1975). *Class, bureaucracy, and schools: The illusion of educational change in America.* (Rev. ed.) New York: Praeger.

Katz, L., and Raths, J. (1985). Teachers' dispositions as goals for teacher education. Paper presented at the annual meeting of the American Educational Research Association, Chicago.

Kohn, A. (1986). *No contest: The case against competition.* Boston: Houghton Mifflin.

Lanier, J., and Little, J. (1986). Research on teacher education. In M. C. Wittrock (ed.), *Handbook of research on teaching.* (3rd ed.) New York: Macmillan.

McDiarmid, G. W. (1990). *What to do about differences? A study of multicultural education for teacher trainees in the Los Angeles Unified School District.* Research report 90-11. East Lansing: National Center for Research on Teacher Education, Michigan State University.

Metz, M. H. (1988). Some missing elements in the reform movement. *Educational Administration Quarterly, 24*(1).

Montero-Sieburth, M. (1988). Conceptualizing multicultural education: From theoretical approaches to classroom practice. *Equity and Choice, 4*(3), 3–12.

Murray, F. B., and Fallon, D. (1989). *The reform of teacher education for the 21st century: Project 30 year-one report.* Newark: University of Delaware.

Noddings, N. (1984). *Awakening the inner eye: Intuition and education.* New York: Teachers College Press.

Noddings, N. (1986). Fidelity in teaching, teacher education, and research for teaching. *Harvard Educational Review, 56*(4), 496–510.

Ouchi, W. G. (1981). *Theory Z: How American business can meet the Japanese challenge.* New York: Avon.

Paine, L. (1988). Orientations towards diversity: What do prospective teachers bring? Paper presented at the annual meeting of the American Educational Research Association, New Orleans, LA.

Parker, D. H. (1970). *Schooling for what?* New York: McGraw-Hill.

Peck, M. S. (1986). *The different drum: Community making and peace.* New York: Simon & Schuster.

Perry, W. (1968). *Forms of intellectual and ethical development in the college years.* New York: Holt, Rinehart & Winston.

Purkey, S. C., and Smith, M. S. (1985). School reform: The district policy implications of the effective schools literature. *Elementary School Journal, 85*(5), 353–389.

Reynolds, M. (ed.). (1989). *Knowledge base for the beginning teacher.* Elmsford, NY: Pergamon Press.

Slavin, R. E. (1983). *Cooperative learning.* White Plains, NY: Longman.

Slavin, R. E. (1989). *Using student team learning.* Baltimore, MD: Center for Research on Elementary and Middle Schools, Johns Hopkins University.

Sleeter, C. E., and Grant, C. A. (1987). An analysis of multicultural education in the United States. *Harvard Educational Review, 57*(4), 421–441.

Webster's new collegiate dictionary. (1973). Springfield, MA: Merriam-Webster.

Webster's third new international dictionary of the English language (unabridged). (1961). Chicago: Merriam-Webster.

Zeichner, K. M. (1991). Teacher education for social responsibility: The conception of teaching expertise underlying elementary teacher education at the University of Wisconsin-Madison. Paper presented at the annual meeting of the American Educational Research Association, Chicago.

Zimpher, N. L. (1989). The RATE project: A profile of teacher education students. *Journal of Teacher Education, 40*(6), 27–31.

Zimpher, N. L., and Ashburn, E. A. (1985). Studying the professional development of teachers: How conceptions of the world inform the research agenda. *Journal of Teacher Education, 26*(6), 16–26.

4

Understanding the Dynamics of Race, Class, and Gender

Donna M. Gollnick

Since 1978, when the National Council for Accreditation of Teacher Education began requiring the inclusion of multicultural education in teacher education, institutions have struggled with its meaning and implementation. This chapter proposes the need for serious attention to race and ethnicity, class, and gender as teacher education is reconceptualized for the future. It also includes specific recommendations for multiculturalization of the curriculum.

At a time that the percentage of students of color in the nation's schools is increasing and the cultural diversity within classrooms includes recent immigrants from Southeast Asia, Africa, Central America, and the Middle East, we can no longer afford for our schools to perpetuate only Western European values and norms (Banks, 1988). The ethnic, linguistic, religious, and class differences of students must be valued as we try to provide the best education for all students. While the provision of education that is multicultural is critical in culturally diverse communities, it is also important that students in communities with little cultural diversity learn that the nation's history and experiences are not theirs alone. It is just as important that these students learn to hear other voices and be able to view their community and the world from the perspectives of other cultural groups.

The task of understanding the dynamics of race and ethnicity, class, and gender is not easy. There is no recipe book that describes the educational strategies guaranteed to work with students from different cultural groups. Nevertheless, the scholarly work about women and different racial and ethnic groups can provide a valuable resource for letting us hear voices other than our own. The fiction and nonfiction stories written by persons from other cultural groups also help to expand our knowledge of multiple voices.

The study of racial and ethnic groups and of women is extremely important in expanding our understanding of each other. However, knowledge about students' racial and ethnic identities alone does not reveal who the students are. Class or gender or religion may be more important in their self-identities than ethnic membership, and the importance may change over time. It is the interaction of these dynamics—particularly race and ethnicity, gender, and class in our society—that determines cultural identity (Gollnick and Chinn, 1990).

The categorization of students, or of any individual, by a single microcultural membership and the expectation of certain behaviors in turn are inappropriate and often prove incorrect anyway. The interactions are complex and ever-changing. McCarthy and Apple (1988, p. 25) credit Emily Hicks with theorizing that the "operation of race, class, and gender relations at the level of daily practices in schools, work places, etc., is systematically contradictory or nonsynchronous." Further, "individuals (or groups) do not share similar consciousness or similar needs at the same point in time" (Hicks, 1981, p. 221). "The interaction of these relations can indeed lead to interruptions, discontinuities, attenuations, or augmentations of the original effects of race, class, or gender in a given social context or institutional setting" (McCarthy and Apple, 1988, p. 25).

Antagonism in relation to one or more of these cultural dynamics causes the lack of solidarity at certain times. For example, strong racial identity has sometimes prevented class solidarity across racial groups. Individuals sometimes feel pressured to identify themselves as women or Chicano first to show solidarity with one group over another. This identification is often based on the economic and political realities affecting a specific group at the time.

Within multicultural education, the study of the interaction of race and ethnicity, class, and gender within economic, political, and cultural spheres is essential. We cannot afford to fight racism and classism in schools and let sexism remain. Discrimination against all groups, including those defined on the basis of religion or disability, needs to be fought. In this effort, we need to remind ourselves constantly of existing biases. As part of this process, we should "expose to view the unstated norms or distinctions we usually rely on and challenge the views embedded in our institutional practices" (Minow, 1990, p. 25).

Central to the implementation of multicultural education is the integration of race and ethnicity, class, and gender issues throughout the curricula and activities of schools. Too often the focus has been solely on the revision of the curriculum to reflect the cultural diversity that exists in the United States and the world. Although the revision of curricula and textbooks is essential, the multiple voices of a culturally diverse community may continue to be ignored as the values and ways of the dominant society are promoted through the hidden curriculum, policies, and activities of the school.

The elimination of racism, classism, sexism, and discrimination against the disabled, children, and the elderly within society is the goal. The recognition and elimination of these behaviors within schools is the beginning. This task, though, requires a critical analysis of current practices and the courage to change them so that all students, regardless of their ethnicity, gender, or class, are valued. No longer can racist or sexist behavior be tolerated from administrators, teachers, or students in our schools. The school setting should become the model for human rights. In time, education should become transformative (Sleeter and Grant, 1988).

The task for teacher education is to help teacher candidates begin the process of critical examination of the practices of educators and schools. The writings of educational theorists who have analyzed schooling critically should be the focus of dialogues among candidates and faculty. In an examination of the interaction of race and ethnicity, class, and gender in the teaching and learning process, the radical critiques of culturists and poststructurists are extremely helpful.

As teacher education is restructured and transformed over the next decade, we must ensure that the culturally diverse nature of our nation is reflected in the curriculum, student body, faculty, and policies. Teacher educators should become models for instruction that is multicultural, and they should continue to provide support to graduates as they grapple with issues of race, class, and gender in their own classrooms. Together as professionals, we can learn to establish classrooms that affirm and value our cultural differences. This challenge is critical to the realization of equality in our schools.

Restructuring the Curriculum to Reflect
Race, Class, and Gender

Some proponents of multicultural education argue for a separate course on the topic. Others argue that the concepts inherent to multicultural education should permeate the teacher education curriculum. Both are probably necessary, especially at the early stages of restructuring the teacher education curriculum. This process should provide a unique opportunity to deliberately integrate issues of race, class, and gender throughout the curriculum.

A separate, required course for all teacher candidates should ensure attention to the importance of race and ethnicity, class, and gender in the teaching and learning process. A problem with this approach has been the variation in the content and focus of such courses. They are usually dependent on the background and experiences of the professor and on the textbooks used. They range across a spectrum that includes multiethnic studies, nonsexist and nonracist education, the at-risk student, bilingual education, and the exceptional child. In only a few cases have courses identified by institutions as multicultural critically examined race and ethnicity, gender, and class and the interactions of these dynamics in schools and society. Issues of institutional discrimination, prejudice, power, and the cultural dominance of the curriculum have received minimal attention in most professional education courses.

Some of these topics and issues are addressed in the general studies component of a candidate's program. Some courses in sociology, anthropology, ethnic studies, history, women studies, religion, and foreign languages provide knowledge, and even critical exploration, of cultural diversity and equality. Some of these courses provide perspectives of the world to which candidates have never before been exposed. The problem is that candidates are usually not required, or advised, to take these courses.

A criticism of the separate-course approach to multicultural teacher education is that the responsibility for addressing the impact of racial, ethnic, gender, religious, and class differences on schooling is often limited to the professor who teaches the course. The expert in the field becomes the only faculty member who has been charged with worrying about these issues. Other faculty are released from the responsibility for making their courses multicultural.

A better approach is the use of these cultural dynamics as an overlay for the total teacher education curriculum. The restructured program should guarantee the examination of race, gender, and class. It also should ensure opportunities to practice nonracist, nonsexist, and nonclassist teaching. One promising approach is the regular review of courses for currency with the profession's knowledge bases and the inclusion of multicultural issues and strategies. Not only should candidates be exposed to the multiple voices of different cultural groups, they also should have opportunities to explore difficult issues such as racism, sexism, classism, and institutional discrimination. They should learn to recognize these biases both in their own interactions and in the policies and practices of schools. Finally, they need to learn strategies for correcting discriminatory practices.

The goal should be that graduates of teacher education programs are actually able to transfer this knowledge and these skills to their own classrooms when they begin to teach. The record on this transfer is not good. Too often their behaviors are not significantly changed as a result of exposure to these topics in courses. Systematic attention to two areas would be helpful.

First, cultural dynamics should be integrated throughout all clinical and field experiences to reinforce their importance in the education process and to force candidates to attend to them. Candidates should be asked to observe or practice some aspect of multicultural education in each clinical setting. When these issues are limited to attention in only one or two courses, it is easier for their importance to be diminished than if they are continually included in assignments for clinical and field experiences. Open discussions related to the candidate's own and observed biases in these settings should establish an environment for continued reduction and eventual elimination of these behaviors. Multicultural education also should be designed to lead to the development of skills that will increase the potential for academic achievement of all students.

Second, the professional education program must be extended into the first years of practice by graduates. Seminars, visits to their classrooms, and dialogues at professional meetings should continue to reinforce the establishment of classrooms that are multicultural. Graduates should feel comfortable asking for assistance in their work with culturally diverse student populations and in their efforts to establish classroom environments that support the goals of equity and justice. An enlightened nation requires educators who can think critically about these cultural dynamics as teacher education and schools are restructured over the next decade.

Cultural Influences on Teaching and Learning

Assurance that teacher candidates learn what is known from research and practice about effective teaching is of foremost importance in restructuring the teacher education curriculum. A thorough understanding of the subject matter is just a beginning. Knowledge about how to impart that understanding and thirst for learning to students is key. As teacher educators determine what knowledge is essential within the conceptual framework that describes the professional education program, the impact of race and ethnicity, class, and gender on teaching and learning must be considered.

Teaching and learning are complex acts. What works with one student may be ineffective with another. Cultural influences can have a great impact on both how teachers react to students and how students react to the learning environment. If we believe that there are not inherent intellectual differences among ethnic, class, and gender groups, then overall academic performance across groups should be similar. The fact that there are differences in academic achievement presents us with the challenge to overcome those differences.

As the research that undergirds programs and courses is reviewed, teacher educators should become aware of the cultural groups and educational settings that were included in the studies. Effective practices in a middle-class suburban school may not be transferable to an inner-city school. In many cases, studies have not been replicated across cultural groups.

Educational research has found clear differences in the cultural backgrounds of both students and teachers. For example, teacher candidates should understand the influence of culture on their teaching style and on the learning styles of students. Oral and nonverbal communication patterns between students and teachers should be analyzed to increase the involvement of students in the learning process. Teacher expectations are sometimes based on the race, gender, or class of students, with a resulting impact on student learning. Cooperative learning appears to enhance the learning environment for minority students (Wilkinson, 1988). Poor, minority, and male students are more likely to be assigned to remedial and special education classes where their education is often stymied rather than enhanced (Oakes, 1985). Peer pressures in some communities involve devaluation of academic achievement in schools.

There are a number of projects that have produced amazing leaps in academic achievement by minority and poor children. Project SEED (a program that has been successfully teaching algebra and conceptual mathematics to elementary and middle school students from diverse backgrounds for twenty-seven years), Jaime Escalante's approach to teaching calculus in a Hispanic school, and other similar strategies should be studied and the methods practiced in teacher education laboratories and in classrooms. Candidates should have opportunities to observe and work with teachers who are effective in increasing achievement in minority, poor, and multicultural settings as well as with teachers in suburban, middle-class settings. Candidates should learn that there are teaching and management strategies that work with students who too often are perceived as nonachievers. Teacher candidates must add to their repertoires teaching and management strategies that eliminate, or at least reduce drastically, the differences in student performance that currently exist.

Multiple Voices and Perspectives

In reconceptualizing the curriculum, teacher educators must critically analyze the content to ensure that it reflects the diverse perspectives of the country's multicultural population. The multiple voices of students and communities must be incorporated. Multicultural education calls for teaching that starts from the students' life experiences, not the experiences of the teacher, or the experiences necessary to fit into the dominant school culture (Shor and Freire, 1987). In addition to reviewing the content of the total curriculum for the inclusion of multiple perspectives and voices, we need to consider how to help candidates bridge their own cultural backgrounds in order to hear others.

As new courses are developed and current ones revised, anthropological, sociological, philosophical, and educational research on values and norms in communities and schools should provide guidance. Teacher candidates should learn which groups' values and norms are reflected in schools and apprehend the resulting impact on students who are not members of the dominant groups. They should study the hidden curriculum and the messages sent to minority, poor, and female students. They should examine recommendations for changing education from groups that hold little or no power within the dominant society.

Courses in general studies can provide valuable background in understanding other cultural groups. There is value in requiring all teacher candidates to study at least one cultural group other than their own. Most campuses offer ethnic studies, women studies, foreign languages, anthropology, religion, linguistics, and sociology courses that could greatly expand candidates' knowledge about at least one group. The potential for learning from such courses is strengthened greatly if they are taught from a critical perspective that allows candidates to struggle with new information that may contradict their former perceptions of a cultural group. Even courses that focus on more facts to be learned to pass the tests could lead to a better understanding of a different group. The dilemma is that courses taught in this manner may only reinforce long-held biases rather than undermine them. Ideally, advisers of teacher candidates should identify the courses and professors that will help candidates learn and guide them toward the most valuable among these.

Professional education courses should then build on this background in the development of skills for hearing the voices of students and communities with different cultural backgrounds from those of the candidates. Work in educational foundations particularly should build on work in general studies. For instance, the study of education history would examine the schooling of girls and women, the poor, and ethnic groups. This study would include examination of educational strategies and policies during different historical periods for educating immigrant and migrant students, for supporting either segregation or integration, for encouraging or discouraging the use of second languages, and for handling differences between Protestants, Catholics, Jews, Muslims, and other religious groups. Whatever academic discipline is applied to the study of education, it should go beyond the presentation of the dominant view. The perspectives and voices of other cultural groups must be heard (O'Connor, 1988). Many times these can be heard in class discussions, supplementary readings written by members of different groups, and presentations by members of different groups.

Another discipline that deserves much more attention in teacher education is linguistics and communication. In order to hear the voices of teacher candidates and their students from cultural groups other than our own, teacher educators need to develop and model good cross-cultural communication skills. Candidates should study bidialectalism and multilingualism because they are likely to teach students who use different dialects or whose native languages are not English. Strategies for using communication skills effectively in teaching should be taught and practiced. Perhaps teacher candidates should be required to become fluent in at least one language other than English, especially since the United States is becoming increasingly multilingual. At a minimum, they should be familiar with programs on English as a Second Language. In addition, the teacher education program should help candidates become aware that cultural groups differ in their views of the content and delivery of education and that there are valid and understandable reasons for these differences. Many of us, especially those of us from the dominant group, have become encapsulated in our own cultural groups and have very little first-hand experience with members of other groups. The years spent in the teacher education program should provide the opportunity to expand both knowledge about and experiences with other cultural groups. This opportunity is particularly important for teacher candidates because many of them will have to move out of their communities, and even geographical regions, to find jobs. Even if they return to their respective communities, experiences with and knowledge about other groups should help them to expand the knowledge bases of future students.

Many institutions are in regions of the country where visible cultural diversity is limited. However, almost all regions have religious, class, and gender diversity that can provide laboratories for learning about diversity and practicing strategies for effectively teaching culturally different populations. At the same time, all candidates, no matter the location of the institution, should be provided the opportunity to work with students who are from racial and ethnic backgrounds different from the candidates. This goal may require exchange programs with institutions in more culturally diverse areas or field experience assignments in urban areas or on Native American reservations. Extended exposure to different cultures and accompanying feedback and discussion about those experiences are desirable.

Finally, the restructuring process should involve members of different cultural groups. This involvement could include representatives on advisory groups, consultants, and hearings in schools and communities outside of college and university settings. A key to incorporating other voices and perspectives in teacher education is to seek them out during the restructuring process.

Multicultural Issues

Most current practices do not provide the kinds of learning environments needed to help all students learn, regardless of their cultural backgrounds. The reasons for the continuation of these practices must be explored. Steps should be taken to ensure that cultural diversity is integrated throughout the curriculum. Candidates should be allowed and encouraged to think critically. The teacher education program should allow them "the freedom to ask questions and [provide] the tools to reason, liberating [one's] mind from unthinking prejudice, and promoting an appreciation for pluralistic democracy" (Starr, 1989, p. 107).

The separate study of race and ethnicity, women, and class is critical in documenting the history of various groups and their experiences as oppressed groups within our society. At the same time, membership in multiple groups must be recognized as we try to understand who students are. Erickson (1990, p. 35) proposed that "ethnic and language studies can be vital, provided that they link directly to and grow out of the lives of the actual students and their families in the school community. . . . But multicultural education cannot be simply nostalgic and uncritical. . . . It must be actively anti-racist."

At the same time that multicultural education is actively antiracist, it must be actively antisexist and anticlassist and work toward eliminating discrimination against the disabled and the aged. Overcoming one wrong, while allowing others to exist, is an anathema to the goals of multicultural education.

In addition to inclusion of information related to different cultural groups in the professional education program, issues pertinent to understanding race and ethnicity, gender, and class should be critically examined by teacher education candidates. These issues include racism, sexism, classism, power, prejudice, institutional discrimination, stereotypes, and oppression.

These issues are often controversial and sensitive for many individuals. Nevertheless, it will be nearly impossible for candidates to deal with these issues in their own classrooms and schools if they have not had the opportunity to study them. This study should include self-examination of the candidate's own prejudices and biases. It should provide serious and critical analysis of the discrimination that is inherent to society's institutions.

Much of the study in this area might be offered outside of professional education. This study would be enhanced by listening to speakers on campus and even by discussing movies that deal with these topics. It is important to expose candidates to these issues and to relate the issues to teaching and schools in professional education courses. Most helpful will be the opportunity to struggle with the meaning and existence of these conditions through critical dialogue with peers and professors of the same and different cultural backgrounds.

Knowledge about these controversial issues should encourage candidates to question current practices in schools that perpetuate inequalities among groups in the school setting. Professional education courses should include case studies, clinical experiences, and field experiences to examine current practices from this perspective. The next step would be the development of strategies and practices for eliminating the inequalities that exist in schools. Both teacher education faculty and teacher candidates together must tackle the challenge of changing our schools as part of the restructuring process.

Student-Teacher Interactions

The provision of multicultural education requires educators to reflect critically on their own interactions with students and with the communities represented in the schools. Erickson (1990, p. 34) warned that "a serious danger lies in treating culture traits in isolation, fragmentalizing and trivalizing our understanding of people's lifeways as we freeze them outside time, outside a world of struggle in concrete history." Teacher candidates need to be able to transfer their knowledge about cultural differences to their own classrooms with students who are members of different ethnic, class, and gender microcultures. They should be able to evaluate their own biases, overcome them in their teaching, and help all students learn.

The teacher education program should teach candidates to evaluate their own interactions with students to detect differences based on race and ethnicity, class, or gender. Although some differences may be appropriate, based on the individual needs of students, analysis of the interactions is important to determine unconscious or conscious biases. The teacher education program also should evaluate candidates' interactions with students who are culturally different in clinical and field experiences.

Racist, sexist, or classist behavior by candidates cannot be tolerated. When signs of inappropriate behaviors and interactions are found, the candidate should be counseled on how to correct them. If biases cannot be overcome, candidates should be counseled to enter a different profession. Individual and group feedback throughout the teacher education program, especially as part of clinical and field experiences, is important. The ability to spot discriminatory behavior, discuss it, and determine how to change it is very important in the delivery of multicultural education.

Expanding the Cultural Diversity of Teacher Education

If teacher education of the future is to model the positive incorporation of racial, ethnic, class, and gender diversity, its student bodies and faculty must become more culturally diverse. Members of most minority groups are not attending colleges and universities in numbers equal to their representation in society. Men are much less likely than women to select teaching, especially early childhood and elementary education.

The recruitment of candidates of color still focuses primarily on the traditional visits to high schools and has done little to overcome pending shortages. One promising improvement is to recruit more actively in community colleges, where many minority students, especially Hispanic students, begin their college work (American Association of Colleges for Teacher Education, 1989). In restructuring teacher education and recruitment, we need to encourage the involvement of nontraditional students as well as to begin our efforts in elementary and middle schools. Teacher education faculty and our graduates in K–12 settings should work together to overcome the academic deficiencies that have been allowed to exist in many of the nation's minority schools. We need to work more directly with community organizations and leaders to gain their support in these efforts.

We should continue to compete with the other professional schools for the brightest minority students. At the same time, we need to identify early those students with potential to become effective teachers who normally would not plan to attend college. Scholarships must be provided to these students and financial aid arranged to encourage them to enroll in teacher education. Nontraditional students are another rich resource for teacher education. The experience of these adults could be a valuable asset to schools.

In addition, universities should begin to attract more candidates of color into doctoral programs. The future professoriate will be drawn from these students, and it could become representative of the culturally diverse groups in society. At the time that greater diversity is being demanded in our institutions, the pool is dwindling. Incentives to encourage minorities to enter programs should be established. Financial commitments to recruit and to provide scholarships and graduate assistantships should be made. A restructuring plan must include strategies to ensure a culturally diverse teaching force at all levels, including the teacher education professoriate.

Conclusion

Multicultural education is complex. It entails much more than the addition of information about minority groups to the teacher education program. Because students and teachers are members of many interlinking microcultures that influence their individual and group cultural identities, those memberships and their roots need to be acknowledged and studied. The group memberships that have the greatest impact on our lived cultures are based on race and ethnicity, gender, and class. Other group memberships that can be very important to individuals are based on religion, geographical region, and physical or mental disability. The interaction of membership in these groups varies across individuals and is greatly influenced by the institutional discrimination that exists in society. A teacher cannot automatically expect specific student behaviors based on race or class or gender alone. The recognition of cultural differences and the ability to adapt teaching to provide a fair and equitable learning environment for all students are expected in multicultural education.

The preparation of candidates to teach in multicultural settings is a shared responsibility of faculty in colleges or universities. Many of the courses offered in arts and sciences can provide a knowledge base about cultural differences. It is the responsibility of teacher education to ensure that teacher candidates develop that background in general and preprofessional studies. The professional studies component can then help candidates apply their knowledge about race and ethnicity, gender, and class in classrooms and schools.

As teacher education is reconceptualized, these cultural dynamics should serve as an overlay for curriculum development to ensure that they are addressed. The goal is to integrate what we know about race and ethnicity, gender, and class in educational settings throughout the teacher education program. In the beginning it may be appropriate to include a course on multicultural education. Candidates should learn about cultural influences on teaching and learning, the importance of incorporating multiple voices and perspectives, and the impact of racism, sexism, and classism on schooling and society. They should learn how to monitor and overcome their own discriminatory practices, and they should have opportunities to observe and practice nonracist, nonsexist, and nonclassist teaching.

For teacher education to become a model of multicultural education, more than a restructuring of the curriculum is required. The student bodies and faculty also must reflect cultural diversity. This goal requires the development of multicultural recruitment and retention strategies. The importance of having a culturally diverse teaching force as a model for all students makes this goal an imperative.

References

American Association of Colleges for Teacher Education. (1989). *Recruiting minority teachers: A practical guide.* Washington: DC: American Association of Colleges for Teacher Education.

Banks, J. A. (1988). *Multiethnic education: Theory and practice.* (2nd ed.) Needham Heights, MA: Allyn & Bacon.

Erickson, F. (1990). Culture, politics, and educational practice. *Educational Foundations, 4*(2), 21–45.

Gollnick, D. M., and Chinn, P. C. (1990). *Multicultural education in a pluralistic society*. Columbus, OH: Merrill.

Hicks, E. (1981). Cultural Marxism: Nonsynchrony and feminist practice. In L. Sargent (ed.), *Women and revolution*. Boston: South End Press.

McCarthy, C., and Apple, M. W. (1988). Race, class, and gender in American educational research: Toward a nonsynchronous parallelist position. In L. Weis (ed.), *Class, race, and gender in American education*. Albany: State University of New York Press.

Minow, M. (1990). On neutrality, equality, and tolerance: New norms for a decade of distinction. *Change, 22*(1), 17–25.

Oakes, J. (1985). *Keeping track: How schools structure inequality*. New Haven, CT: Yale University Press.

O'Connor, T. (1988). Cultural voice and strategies for multicultural education. Paper presented at the annual meeting of the American Educational Studies Association, Montreal, Canada.

Shor, I., and Freire, P. (1987). *A pedagogy for liberation: Dialogues on transforming education*. Granby, MA: Bergin & Garvey.

Sleeter, C. E., and Grant, C. A. (1988). *Making choices for multicultural education: Five approaches to race, class, and gender*. Columbus, OH: Merrill.

Starr, J. (1989). The great textbook war. In H. Holtz, I. Marcus, J. Dougherty, J. Michaels, and R. Peduzzi (eds.), *Education and the American dream*. Granby, MA: Bergin & Garvey.

Wilkinson, L. C. (1988). Grouping children for learning: Implications for kindergarten education. *Review of Research in Education, 15*, 203–223.

5

Making Teacher Education Culturally Responsive

Jacqueline Jordan Irvine

As the twenty-first century rapidly approaches, schools, colleges, and departments of education (SCDEs) are facing a serious dilemma. The "typical" student for whom educators' pedagogy and prescriptions are designed is an endangered species. Highly motivated, achievement-oriented, white, middle-class students from two-parent families are becoming scarce in most school systems—rural, suburban, or urban. By the year 2000, these students will be even more atypical. Hodgkinson's (1988, 1989) and Coates and Jarratt's (1987) data confirm that divorce, delayed marriage, delayed childbirth, declining fertility rates among white middle-class women, increasing fertility among poor minority women, and the influx of immigrants from Mexico, Asia, and the Caribbean will dramatically change how we will administer schools and instruct students.

Unless SCDEs make significant reforms to accommodate these students, the future of school education is not promising. Nonwhite public school children will be instructed by white female teachers who were trained in conventional teacher education programs, many of which will have not significantly changed since the 1960s. The schools will operate with anachronistic administrative structures and hierarchies designed in the 1900s and will depend on the financial support of an aging, white, middle-class population.

Coupled with these dramatic demographic changes, there is evidence that present strategies for training teachers are less than promising. Law and Lane (1987) found that white preservice teachers had negative attitudes toward all American subcultures. More surprising, however, was the finding that these preservice teachers were more negative than were the preservice teachers in any of the previous six decades of national studies. Yoa (1985) found that Texas teachers who had multicultural coursework were still unprepared to teach culturally diverse students, and there is concern that inadequate or cursory multicultural training can lead to more, not less, hostility toward culturally different students (LeCompte, 1985).

How should SCDEs respond to this problem of the growing, at-risk, minority student populations, decreasing minority teacher pools, and culturally encapsulated, majority teacher education students? This chapter posits that if SCDEs are to significantly increase the number of culturally responsive teachers in the future, then major structural and ideological changes must be designed and implemented. SCDEs must begin to seriously ponder two critical questions: (1) How should the teacher education curriculum be revised in order to meet the needs of the twenty-first century? (2) How should SCDEs provide a model of cultural diversity on their campuses that sets an example for the teacher education students whom they seek to train?

The first question addresses the need for SCDEs to concentrate their teacher education research and training resources on the identification of effective pedagogy for minority, at-risk students. The cultural and social contexts of teaching and learning should become critical components of these research and training endeavors. The second question calls for SCDEs to become models of cultural diversity for the teachers and school systems that they train and serve. Minority faculty should be vigorously recruited and promotion, tenure, and faculty development policies reexamined for possible bias and disproportionate impact. In this chapter, I discuss these two questions and conclude with a call for research on, reconceptualization of, and new paradigms for the education and training of teachers in order to meet the challenges of the twenty-first century.

Revising the Teacher Education Curriculum

Part of the problem of teachers' inability to effectively teach minority students is the lack of well-documented research on effective pedagogy. SCDEs should direct greater attention to explication of those variables that contribute to the achievement of at-risk children in an effort to find ways to break the invidious cycle of "teachers teaching the way they've been taught" (Goodlad, 1984, p. 469).

There is evidence to support the position that effective teachers of mainstream students can be as effective with minority, at-risk students. Hilliard (1988, p. 201), for example, stated that "there is no special pedagogy for at-risk students. . . . Further, at-risk students fail to achieve because appropriate regular pedagogy has not been provided to them."

Effective teachers of minority, at-risk children do share some characteristics and teaching behaviors with all other effective teachers (Irvine, 1990): Both groups are competent in subject matter and have mastered standard usage of the written and spoken language. These master teachers provide all of their students—regardless of previous categorization or labeling based on standardized test scores, social class, or behavior—with access to high-status knowledge. These teachers understand that the job market of the next century will demand that all workers be critical thinkers and problems solvers, not merely students who have mastered minimum competencies in the basic skills. The practices of "drill and kill" and "chalk and talk" are not elements of these effective teachers' repertoires.

Effective teachers have appropriately high standards and expectations for their students. When their pupils do not initially master the materials, these teachers do not ascribe blame to external factors, such as the child's parents or previous teachers, nor do they impute negative characteristics to the child, such as an inability or unwillingness to learn. Instead, they restructure the learning activities, assuming that the child has not yet mastered the instructional objectives. As Brophy (1982, p. 527) has described, "If something is not learned the first time through, they teach it again."

All effective teachers concentrate on finding a match between a student's present achievement level and the assignment or task to be completed. The task is never so difficult that the student consistently fails or so easy that the assignment is meaningless or offers no challenge.

These findings on effective teaching appear to be sound, logical, and applicable to the instruction of all students, regardless of race, culture, or ability. However, educational researchers' present knowledge of effective instruction for minority, at-risk students is inadequate, and more research needs to be planned, implemented, and evaluated. For example, effective teachers of at-risk students, compared to effective teachers of privileged students, more often use interactive rather than didactic methods. That is, the teaching style involves acceptance of students' ideas, frequent feedback, demonstrations, explanations, questions, rephrases, reviews, summaries, drills, recitations, and the monitoring, individualizing, and reinforcing of students. The lesson's pace is brisk and the activities are varied.

Effective teachers of at-risk children employ many different methods, materials, and instructional strategies, but they also often ignore and sometimes violate the principles of effective teaching. In a study of effective, independent black schools, Lomotey and Brookins (1988) noted that classrooms were not always orderly, quiet, or high on "time on-task." Jaime Escalante, depicted in the movie *Stand and Deliver,* illustrates this point. This Hispanic teacher achieved impressive results with the Hispanic students in an inner-city school in Los Angeles. Before Escalante came to this school, there were no advanced-placement math classes; during his tenure at the school, he produced one-half of all Hispanic students who passed advanced-placement calculus. Escalante is obviously an excellent teacher, although some principles of the teaching effectiveness research are ignored in his classroom. He used the slang and dialect of his students, waited longer for his students to respond, spent time off-task to attend to students' personal concerns, and designed and implemented his own curriculum, ignoring mandates and directives concerning ability grouping, text coverage, and pacing.

Also, effective teachers of culturally diverse students use their students' everyday experiences in an effort to link new concepts to prior knowledge. This is a process of finding pertinent examples, comparing and contrasting, and bridging the gap between the known (students' personal cultural knowledge) and the unknown (materials and concepts to be mastered). I contend that Escalante and others like him are not just effective teachers. They are culturally responsive teachers who contextualize teaching by giving attention to the immediate needs and cultural experiences of their students.

The research on effective teaching provides a useful framework for the instruction of minority students. However, we still do not know enough about the attributes of culturally responsive instructional strategies or the nature of the cultural context of teaching and learning.

Cultural Context of Teaching and Learning

Culture and the cultural context of teaching and learning are often ignored or treated perfunctorily in teacher education programs. This omission can be corrected by revising the content of the curriculum of teacher education to address the instructional needs of minority students. In other words, both minority and majority teachers have to become culturally responsive to their students, and SCDEs must provide teacher candidates with appropriate instruction and training, as well as with field experiences in schools that serve minority students.

Culture is the sum total of ways of living (Hoopes and Pusch, 1979) that are shared by members of a population (Ogbu, 1988). Culture encompasses and is constituted by rites, rituals, legends, myths, artifacts, symbols, language, ceremonies, history, and "sense-making devices that guide and shape behavior" (Davis, 1984, p. 10). Culture is characterized by the statement "It's the way things are done around here" (Kilmann, Saxton, Serpa, and Associates, 1985, p. 5).

Byers and Byers (1972) have helped us to understand the implications of culture and race for teaching and learning. They investigated nonverbal communication between teachers and students by filming the interaction between a white teacher and two black and two white girls in nursery school. They found that one of the white girls was more active and successful than were the other children in getting the teacher's attention. For example, she looked at the teacher fourteen times and the teacher reciprocated eight times. On the other hand, one of the black girls looked at the teacher thirty-five times but caught the teacher's eye only four times. The researchers concluded that the black girl, unlike her white counterpart, timed her glances at inappropriate times, making inappropriate moves at crucial times and pulling when she should have pushed or pushing when she should have pulled. The black girl, unlike the white girl, did not share with the teacher an implicit understanding of cultural nuances, gestures, and timing, which resulted in frustration and missed opportunities. In contrast, the white girl's shared cultural and racial identity with the teacher produced many instances of shared expressed affection and created learning opportunities.

This research finding is but one explicit example of what occurs in schools when teachers and students lack cultural correspondence or are not synchronized culturally because of differences in race and class. The white teacher and the white child understood the stated rules and the subtleties of the majority culture's verbal and nonverbal communication processes. For the white child, interaction and learning with the teacher was productive and enjoyable; the black child had the opposite experience (Irvine, 1990)

In the following discussion, I illustrate three cultural conflicts, using one minority group, black students. The same types of conflicts are no doubt evident in schools that serve other minority groups, such as Hispanics and Native Americans (Bennett, 1986; Roberts and Akinsanya, 1976; Soldier, 1989). The three conflicts concern the (1) style or manner of personal presentation by black students, (2) use of black English, and (3) cognition or processes of knowing and perceiving (Irving, 1990). The examples were selected because they are so incompatible with white middle-class school norms.

Black children's, particularly black males', language, style of walking, glances, and dress have engendered fear, apprehension, and overreaction by many teachers and school administrators. The nonverbal and verbal communication style of black students baffles school personnel, especially white teachers, who fail to understand black students' expressive language. Verbal ability is valued as highly as physical ability among black males, and whenever black males, young and old, assemble, a boasting or teasing encounter usually ensues. The contest of words is an important male ritual in the black community. A typical example of nonverbal defiance is provided in Gilmore's (1985, p. 117) description of black students' stylized sulking: "Girls will frequently pose with their chins up, closing their eyelids for long periods and casting downward side glances. . . . A girl also will rest her chin on her hand with her elbow supported by the desk. . . . Striking or getting into pose is usually performed with an abrupt movement or a verbal marker like 'humpf.' . . . [Boys'] stylized sulking is usually characterized by head downward, arms crossed at the chest, legs spread wide, and desk pushed away."

Black students' language in school is a crucial variable. Like skin color, language is an obvious characteristic of individuals that teachers may use to separate and stereotype. Black students who speak standard English are perceived to have greater ability and to be more middle class than are black students who speak black English. According to Lightfoot (1978), the language of black children symbolizes social and cultural deviance and is the basis of teachers' (primarily white teachers) hostility toward black children.

Because black students' spoken language does not match standard English, successful black students must often translate to standard English before they write or speak. Teachers of these students must be, in a sense, bilingual. They should understand black English so that they can understand and communicate with their students. In addition, teachers must help black students translate black English into standard English, and they must discover how to salvage otherwise talented black students who fail because they cannot master standard English.

There is evidence that black and white children do not perceive the world and process and organize information according to classic Piagetian theory, and these differences in processing and organizing negatively affect black students' achievement. Hilliard (in Hale-Benson, 1986) posits that schools approach curriculum and instruction from an analytical versus a relational cognitive style. Black students are assumed to be relationally predisposed to a learning style characterized by freedom of movement, variation, creativity, divergent thinking approaches, inductive reasoning, and a focus on people. In contrast, schools favor an analytical learning style, characterized by rules and restrictions of movement, standardization, conformity, convergent thinking approaches, deductive reasoning, and a focus on things.

Shade (1982), in a comprehensive review of the literature on African American cognitive styles, concluded that more research is needed before definitive statements about thought processes can be made. However, she contends that "there does appear to be a racial difference in each of the dimensions subsumed under the cognitive style construct" (p. 226).

Differences in cognitive style do not imply a superiority or inferiority relationship between analytical and relational style. Nor does it argue that all black children possess a relational style. However, when teachers use only analytical teaching methodologies and ignore relational methods of instruction, they fail to capitalize on the respective strengths of children's different learning modalities.

Theories of cultural congruence in teaching and learning have been criticized by scholars (Kleinfield, McDiarmid, Grubis, and Parrett, 1983; Singer, 1988) who claim that this body of research lacks substantial evidence, deprives minority children of their culture, and does not explain the poor performance of minority children in culturally homogeneous schools. Other scholars fear that discussions of cultural differences lead to more stereotyping and further racial isolation and segregation. However, there is growing evidence that cultural variables are powerful in the teaching and learning processes, and SCDEs can help to provide the needed research and direction for continued exploration of these issues.

SCDEs as Models of Cultural Diversity

Finally, the litmus test for the ability of SCDEs to design culturally responsive teacher education curricula is whether they are successful in providing models of cultural diversity on their own campuses. If SCDEs are not able to recruit and retain minority faculty, how will they be able to provide an example of cultural diversity for their teacher education students? SCDEs have perhaps more opportunities than do other divisions of higher education institutions to have a racially representative faculty, since one-half of all black doctoral degree holders are in education (Thomas, Mingle, and McPartland, 1981). Yet, the faculties of SCDEs remain pitifully homogeneous: 96 percent of full professors, 92 percent of associate professors, and 89 percent of assistant professors are white (American Association of Colleges for Teacher Education, 1987).

The presence of minority faculty members in SCDEs attracts minority students. When minority students see minority faculty members, they conclude that SCDEs are interested and committed to equity issues and to minority group persons. Their feelings of isolation and inclusion are lessened, especially if the minority faculty members are tenured and visible as power brokers in the organization. Minority faculty serve as role models and advisers to minority students, visible and tangible examples of achievement. For majority students and faculty, the presence of minority faculty illustrates the nature of our multiethnic society and assists in countering negative stereotypes about minorities—stereotypes perpetuated by ignorance, isolation, and distortions in the media. Moreover, Blackwell's (1983) work informs us that the presence of minority faculty is positively related to minority student recruitment and retention. He concluded that the most salient and statistically significant predictor of black graduate students' enrollment and graduation is the presence of black faculty.

SCDEs must become introspective and reflective about how their climates, policies, and formal and informal practices may help to stifle and circumscribe the careers of their minority members. Questions to be seriously entertained by leaders of SCDEs include, but are not limited to

- How has the leadership of the institution communicated its commitment to recruiting and retaining minority faculty?
- Has the commitment been institutionalized by affirmative action goals, incentives for minority hiring, research funds for

junior minority faculty members, minority administrators in decision-making positions, and competitive salaries?

- Do senior faculty members mentor or sponsor minority junior faculty, including them in their professional networks and assisting them in their research?
- Are minority faculty members perceived as affirmative action hires, unqualified colleagues who were hired simply because they were members of a minority group?
- Are research issues related to equity and at-risk populations devalued or ignored?
- Are the minority faculty members overburdened with committee work in an effort to include a minority perspective?
- Does the organization recognize and reward the informal advisement that minority faculty perform for minority students?
- Does the organization recognize and reward minority faculty's contributions and service to the minority community?
- Are tenure and promotion committee members fair and receptive to a variety of educational issues, philosophies, and methodologies?
- Are tenure and promotion committee members familiar with minority-focused publications and minority scholars who might serve as external evaluators?

Conclusion

SCDEs must design, implement, and evaluate their programs to significantly increase the number of culturally responsive teachers. The programs must acknowledge the complexity of the problem as well as the need for multifaceted strategies, ranging from intervention in the schooling of at-risk elementary and secondary minority students to development of comprehensive recruitment and faculty development policies for minority faculty. The solutions should center around new paradigms and reconceptualizations related to the teacher education curriculum as well as to individual faculty research.

Reconceptualization of the teacher education curriculum should include issues such as the contextualization of instruction and teaching materials, reflection and critical inquiry in teaching, redefinition of the teachers' role, cultural immersion experiences, and interpersonal skills training. SCDEs cannot effectively address these concerns without the assistance of professional education organizations, such as the American Association of Colleges for Teacher Education. In addition, elementary and secondary teachers and school administrators can bring a wealth of experience, knowledge, and new perspectives to the issue of culturally responsive teaching. Cooperative arrangements and exchanges with school systems that allow school-based personnel to teach and consult in primary and secondary schools are called for. Similar exchange programs between historically black and predominantly white institutions have proved beneficial.

Concomitant with efforts to change the teacher education programs, SCDEs must work to restructure the schools in which their graduates eventually will work. Poor working conditions are impediments to teacher recruitment, retention, job satisfaction, and school morale (Metropolitan Life Insurance Company and Harris and Associates, 1988). For example, decisions concerning organizational structures, instruction arrangements and grouping, curriculum, and financial expenditures must be planned, implemented, and evaluated at the local school level with participation from administrators, teachers, parents, and the community.

The problem of culturally homogeneous teacher education will not be adequately addressed without long-term financial assistance from federal, state, and private sources. Funds are needed for programs of research and training related to the problem of preparing teachers for multicultural populations. Bold and courageous efforts are required if teachers are to meet the challenges of cultural diversity. It seems clear that the opportunities of the next century will be realized only if SCDEs and policymakers make the commitment to educate all of America's children.

References

American Association of Colleges for Teacher Education. (1987). *RATE I. Teaching teachers: Facts and figures.* Washington, DC: American Association of Colleges for Teacher Education.

Bennett, C. I. (1986). *Comprehensive multicultural education.* Needham Heights, MA: Allyn & Bacon.

Blackwell, J. E. (1983). *Networking and mentoring: A study of cross-generational experiences of blacks in graduate and professional schools.* Atlanta, GA: Southern Education Foundation.

Brophy, J. E. (1982). Successful teaching strategies for the inner-city child. *Phi Delta Kappan, 63,* 627–630.

Byers, P., and Byers, H. (1972). Non-verbal communication in the education of children. In C. Cazden, V. John-Steiner, and D. Hymes (eds.), *Functions of language in the classroom.* New York: Teachers College Press.

Coates, J. F., and Jarratt, J. (1987). *Future search: Forces and factors shaping education.* Washington, DC: National Education Association.

Davis, S. M. (1984). *Managing corporate culture.* New York: Ballinger.

Gilmore, P. (1985). "Gimme room": School resistance, attitude, and access to literacy. *Journal of Education, 167,* 111–128.

Goodlad, J. I. (1983). A study of schooling: Some findings and hypotheses. *Phi Delta Kappan, 64,* 465–470.

Goodlad, J. I. (1984). *A place called school.* New York: McGraw-Hill.

Hale-Benson, J. E. (1986). *Black children: Their roots, culture, and learning styles.* (2nd ed.) Baltimore, MD: Johns Hopkins University Press.

Hilliard, A. G. (1988). Public support for successful instructional practices for at-risk students. In Council of Chief State School Officers (ed.), *School success for students at risk.* Orlando, FL: Harcourt Brace Jovanich.

Hodgkinson, H. L. (1988). The right schools for the right kids. *Educational Leadership, 45,* 10–14.

Hodgkinson, H. L. (1989). *The same client: The demographics of education and service delivery systems.* Washington, DC: Institute for Educational Leadership.

Hoopes, D. S., and Pusch, M. D. (1979). Definitions of terms. In M. D. Pusch (ed.), *Multicultural education: A cross-cultural approach.* Yarmouth, ME: Intercultural Press.

Irvine, J. J. (1990). *Black students and school failure: Policies, practices, and prescriptions.* Westport, CT: Greenwood Press.

Kilmann, R. H., Saxton, M. J., Serpa, R., and Associates. (1985). Introduction: Five key issues in understanding and changing culture. In R. H. Kilmann, M. J. Saxton, R. Serpa, and Associates (eds.), *Gaining control of the corporate culture.* San Francisco: Jossey-Bass.

Kleinfeld, J., McDiarmid, G. W., Grubis, S., and Parrett, W. (1983). Doing research on effective cross-cultural teaching: The teacher tale. *Peabody Journal of Education, 61,* 86–108.

Law, S. G., and Lane, D. S. (1987). Multicultural acceptance by teacher education students: A survey of attitudes toward 32 ethnic and national groups and a comparison with 60 years of data. *Journal of Instructional Psychology, 14,* 3–9.

LeCompte, M. D. (1985). Defining the differences: Cultural subgroups within the educational mainstream. *Urban Review, 17,* 111–127.

Lightfoot, S. L. (1978). *Worlds apart: Relationships between families and schools.* New York: Basic Books.

Lomotey, K., and Brookins, C. C. (1988). Independent black school institutions: A cultural perspective. In D. T. Slaughter and D. J. Johnson (eds.), *Visible now: Blacks in private schools.* Westport, CT: Greenwood Press.

Metropolitan Life Insurance Company, and Harris, L., and Associates. (1988). *The American teacher.* New York: Louis Harris and Associates.

Ogbu, J. (1988). Cultural diversity and human development. In D. T. Slaughter (ed.), *Black children and poverty: A developmental perspective.* New Directions for Child Development, no. 42. San Francisco: Jossey-Bass.

Roberts, J. I., and Akinsanya, S. K. (1976). *Schooling in the cultural context.* New York: McKay.

Shade, B. J. (1982). Afro-American cognitive style: A variable in school success? *Review of Educational Research, 52,* 219–244.

Singer, E. A. (1988). *What is cultural congruence, and why are they saying such terrible things about it?* Report no. UD-026-083. East Lansing: Institute for Research on Teaching, Michigan State University.

Soldier, L. L. (1989). Cooperative learning and the Native American student. *Phi Delta Kappan, 71,* 161–163.

Thomas, G. E., Mingle, J. R., and McPartland, J. S. (1981). Recent trends in racial enrollment, segregation, and degree attainment in higher education. In G. E. Thomas (ed.), *Black students in higher education.* Westport, CT: Greenwood Press.

Yoa, E. L. (1985). Implementation of multicultural education in Texas public schools. Paper presented at the annual meeting of the American Educational Research Association, Chicago.

6

Learning to Teach Hispanic Students

Ana Maria Schuhmann

The Hispanic population in the United States is faced with an alarming high school dropout rate, low enrollments and graduation rates from college, and serious underrepresentation in the teaching force. This chapter discusses the roles that schools, colleges, and departments of education (SCDEs) should play in assuming the responsibility for both increasing the numbers of Hispanic teachers and preparing all teachers (majority and minority) to educate the increasing population of Hispanic students in the public schools.

Demographic Profile

The Hispanic population is currently growing nearly five times faster than the general public, with one out of every twelve Americans now of Hispanic background. There are twenty million Hispanics in the United States, with births and legal immigration expected to bring the number to twenty-five million by the end of the century. The term *Hispanic* is used in this chapter as a generic reference to such diverse communities as persons of Mexican descent, Puerto Ricans, Cuban Americans, and people from Central and South America. It is misleading to view Hispanics as a monolithic culture, since differences exist among the groups in citizenship, socioeconomic status, acculturation patterns, linguistic assimilation, years of schooling, and so on.

Although Hispanics comprise 8 percent of the total population of the United States, they represent less than 2 percent of the teachers in the public schools (American Association of Colleges for Teacher Education [AACTE], 1989). What is the reason for this serious underrepresentation? In order to become a teacher, one must first be a college graduate; however, Hispanics' most serious problem is undereducation. Only about one-half of Hispanic adults twenty-five years of age and over are high school graduates, compared to three-quarters of whites and more than three-fifths of blacks. Only about one in twelve Hispanics is a college graduate, compared to one in nine blacks and one in five whites. Depending on the measure used, up to 56 percent of Hispanic adults are functionally illiterate (McKay, 1988).

Hispanics are far more likely to drop out of school than are members of any other ethnic group. Nationally, at least one-half of Mexican American and Puerto Rican youth leave school without a high school diploma. Hispanics not only have higher dropout rates, but they also tend to leave school earlier than do blacks or whites. It has been estimated that about 40 percent of Hispanic dropouts leave high school before the spring semester of their sophomore years (McKay, 1988).

Dropout figures for Hispanic students are notoriously imprecise because of the difficulty of measuring transfers and migration. Studies put the dropout rate for these students in New York state at 62 percent, Texas at 45 percent, and Illinois at 47 percent (Applebome, 1987). The problem is magnified when one considers that, in cities such as Los Angeles, Hispanics already make up more than one-half of the students entering the first grade. Unless there is a dramatic improvement in the high school completion rate of Hispanic students, consequences could be devastating for both the Hispanic community and the entire nation. The findings of the Aspira Five Cities High School Dropout Study (Fernandez and Velez, 1989) suggest that the three most important factors in predicting whether a Latino student will stay in school are age, grades, and absences, all of which can be affected by school policies and practices. According to the Aspira study, the typical Hispanic dropout has the following profile: "He or she has repeated at least one grade in school, is over-age for the ninth grade (15.6 years old), had a 'D' grade average for school work, has missed an average of seventeen days of classes in a semester, and does not plan to go on to college" (Fernandez and Velez, 1989, p. 12).

Education experts agree that Hispanic attrition from high school is alarming, but few can pinpoint the causes for this crisis. Among the reasons given are alienation of Hispanic parents in the educational process, economic pressures to contribute financially to the family, language and cultural differences, failure of the system to identify students in danger of dropping out, and a shortage of role models, such as teachers and counselors, in the schools. The high dropout rate of Hispanics from high school accounts, in part, for the small number of Hispanics in the teaching force.

What are other factors that contribute to the declining numbers of Hispanics and other minority teachers? The reasons cited most often are (1) expanded career choices for women and minorities, (2) dissatisfaction with the teaching profession, (3) general decline in college enrollment and college completion among minority youth, and (4) impact of competence testing for teaching candidates (Baratz, 1986; Garibaldi, 1987, 1989; Rodman, 1985; Webb, 1986; Witty, 1982). Two of these factors are expanded on here as they affect the Hispanic teaching force: the general decline in Hispanic college enrollment and the impact of competence testing.

Hispanics continue to be one of the most underrepresented subgroups in four-year institutions of higher education. Chapa (1991) points out that although Hispanics have increased their presence on college campuses during the last decade, and degrees awarded to Hispanics have increased at all levels, these increases are an artifact of population growth that tends to mask actual declines in rates of high school completion and college participation. Of all eighteen- to twenty-four-year-old Hispanics, only 16 percent were enrolled in college in 1989. The changes in baccalaureate degrees conferred during the period 1976–1985 represent a major shift away from education and the social sciences. Hispanics received a smaller share of the degrees in education. At the graduate level, Hispanics earned more master's degrees in 1985 than in 1976 and continued the shift away from education and social sciences. As at the baccalaureate degree level, Hispanics also were proportionately underrepresented among master's degrees conferred in 1985. In 1985, Hispanics earned 3.3 percent of all master's degrees in education.

The reform movement in education and public concern over the quality of instruction in American schools have led to an increased emphasis on teacher competence testing. According to Anrig (1986), teacher testing is one of the fastest moving changes in this period of educational reform. Most states now require tests for entry into teacher preparation programs and/or for exit and certification. The single most important issue regarding teacher certification tests involves the high failure rates among minorities (Galambos, 1986). Widely published statistics show that failure rates for minorities are two to ten times higher than those for whites.

It is too early to predict whether competence testing will improve the quality of teachers for minority students. We do know, however, that the practice of using tests to improve teacher quality has reduced minority representation in the profession (Witty, 1982; Smith, 1984; Garcia, 1985; Cooper, 1986; Baratz, 1986; Smith, Chang Miller, and Joy, 1988). Castro (1989) argues that institutions should adopt alternative assessment procedures to replace standardized testing of prospective teachers. This would allow Hispanic and other minority students to demonstrate competencies in ways that reflect their unique cultural values and learning styles.

Recruiting and Retaining Hispanics in Teacher Education Programs

In order to increase the number of Hispanics in their teacher education programs, the first task of SCDEs is to intensify their efforts in identifying and attracting these students. Literature in teacher education describes the following populations as important targets for recruitment: (1) college-bound students (for example, high school students), (2) general population (such as current paraprofessionals), and (3) nontraditional teacher candidates (career changes, military and corporate retirees, and so on) (Middleton, Mason, Stilwell, and Parker, 1988).

In the case of Hispanic students, SCDEs should consider starting recruitment at an earlier age than the traditional last two years of high school. Preparation for a teaching career, or the possibility of one, should begin before the ninth grade, when many Hispanic students drop out. For instance, future teachers clubs and precollege programs could start in the middle schools for this population. Castro (1989) believes that partnership efforts among institutions of higher education and school districts should focus on early (such as junior high level) identification of potential teacher candidates and on monitoring of students' performance throughout their schooling.

In addition, recruitment of Hispanics into teacher education requires concentrated efforts by four-year institutions to work with community colleges, since more than one-half of all Hispanic postsecondary students are enrolled in two-year colleges. Furthermore, transfer rates for all students from two-year to four-year institutions are low.

In recruiting Hispanics into education programs, SCDEs should consider two important factors: financial concerns and family concerns.

The Hispanic population is poor. In 1987, the median U.S. family income was $30,900. No Hispanic groups achieved the national median; Puerto Ricans earned about one-half of the national average. Nationwide, about 13 percent of all families lived in poverty; for Hispanics the rate was 28 percent. Nearly 38 percent of Puerto Ricans lived at or below the poverty line (Quality Education for Minorities Project, 1990). It is not surprising, then, that finances influence the choice and pursuit of postsecondary education for Hispanics more than for students in general. Hispanic students are more likely than white students to attend colleges where they can receive financial aid, and they are more likely to work while they are in college (Castro, 1988).

Because they are poorer than the general population, it is also important for Hispanics to be able to live at home and attend low-tuition community colleges. Hispanic students are more likely than others to put aside academic plans to earn money for their families. Once they reach sixteen years of age, many Hispanic youngsters, particularly males, are expected to contribute to the financial support of their households. Families need the extra income that children can bring in because of the low salaries of the parents. Hispanic families tend to have more children than their white counterparts, placing an additional burden on the older siblings, who may be relied on to contribute monetarily, physically, and emotionally to raising their younger brothers and sisters. Hispanics are brought up to do things for the good of the family, and it is difficult for some to put themselves first (Fiske, 1988b).

Because finances are such an important factor for Hispanics, SCDEs must give this area serious consideration in attracting them into teacher education. Colleges must ensure not only that financial aid packages are available but also that this availability is known to the students and their families. Furthermore, applications for financial aid must be comprehensible, help must be available to those who need it, and deadlines must be clear.

In recruiting Hispanics into teacher education programs, SCDEs must work with parents and families of potential students. In addition to giving more consideration to economics and proximity in selecting a college than do students in general, Hispanics are more apt to be influenced by parental opinions. Parents of Hispanics are more likely than other parents to determine where their children will go to school ("Hispanic students continue . . . ," 1988). For financial reasons and also because of their close family ties, Hispanics are more likely than any other group to attend college close to home. A survey of student teachers conducted by AACTE (1990) found that most Hispanics attend school less than twenty miles from home.

The task of attracting Hispanics into teacher preparation programs is just a first step. Without a restructuring of SCDEs to provide a more responsive climate for the Hispanic student, education programs can become just another broken promise in their career paths. Hispanic college students, like their high school counterparts, are seriously at risk of dropping out. This risk is not necessarily academic in nature but is a complex phenomenon involving family, finances, and cultural and linguistic considerations.

In relation to Hispanic students, the traditional methods used by colleges to retain students do not seem to be effective. These traditional techniques have been to provide tutoring, academic and personal counseling, and financial aid. In creating a more responsive climate for Hispanics, SCDEs must consider issues of family, culture and language, and curriculum and also provide responsive support services to these students.

Just as the Hispanic family plays a crucial role in the selection of an institution, it can be equally important in the retention or attrition of the Hispanic college student. In research conducted on the Hispanic student population at Kean College of New Jersey, Sanchez and others (1989) found that the dropout and success rates of Hispanics in college were directly related to family issues. Students who withdrew from the institution cited family pressures (such as the belief of some family members that Hispanic women do not "belong" in college) as the reason for withdrawal, whereas students who persisted cited family support as the primary reason for their success. Sanchez and others (1989) also found that when Hispanic students withdrew from college, they were much more likely to consult the family than a faculty member or academic adviser.

Hispanic students in the Kean College study did not drop out for academic reasons; this was particularly the case with married students, who had the highest mean grade point average at the time of attrition (Sanchez and others, 1989). Students who persisted were more apt to be single and live at home with their parents than were those who dropped out. Successful students were also more apt to be full-time students and unemployed, or, when employed, they worked shorter hours than did those who dropped out. One finding was that the parents of persisters were less likely to have graduated from high school (Sanchez and others, 1989). This is surprising because persisters usually come from middle- or upper-income families.

Close family relationships exert profound influence on the experience of Hispanic college students. Some students feel great anxiety that staying in school will break close family ties ("Hispanic students continue . . . ," 1988). If Hispanic students are to be retained, SCDEs must encourage involvement of the entire family, whether it is the mother, the father, or, in the case of married students (who seem to be more at risk), spouse and children. Sanchez and others (1989) argue that family structure must be used as a retention tool. Family involvement in the education of Hispanics seems to be as crucial at the higher education level as it is in elementary and secondary education.

Many Hispanic students grow up in homes where English is not spoken. The AACTE/Metropolitan study (AACTE, 1990) of student teachers found that English is a second language for the majority of Hispanics surveyed. As previously stated, the study by Sanchez and others (1989) found that Hispanic students cited family support as the primary reason for their success in college. Availability of coursework in their native language was considered the second-most important factor in their retention.

The practice of teaching Hispanic students in their native language at the higher education level is highly controversial, although strongly supported by some educators. There are institutions such as Kean College and Hostos Community College (New York) that offer a bilingual approach. Historically black colleges and universities (HBCUs) are major providers of black teachers. There is no Hispanic counterpart to HBCUs, with the possible exception of Boricua College in New York City, a two-year institution established to serve the Hispanic community. According to Fiske (1988a), the absence of Hispanic counterparts to HBCUs has slowed the progress of Hispanics in higher education. Fiske quotes Michael Olivas, who believes that HBCUs "are committed to educating kids who on paper do not seem to be college material" and have "turned out a high percentage of black leadership" (p. 28).

For the Hispanic college student, cultural differences can be as much a barrier to success as is language. Fiske (1988b) points to loneliness and tensions felt by Hispanics as they try to find their way in an institution built around an alien culture. Hispanic college students often experience more stress than do their Anglo counterparts, and these differences in stress may account for the higher attrition rates of this population (Munoz, 1986). Nieves-Squires (1991) points out that the major cause of stress for many Hispanic women is cultural conflict. Many attitudes and values of the university culture are at odds with the character of Hispanic interpersonal relationships, forms of communication, and sex-role expectations (Melendez and Petrovich, 1989).

Hispanic students need to learn how to balance participation in two very different cultures. The values of their home culture can sometimes conflict with the values that lead to academic success. The way that they prefer to learn may not be how the institution prefers to teach. Hispanic students who have not yet become fully acculturated in the mainstream may prefer to learn in a setting that encourages group cooperation rather than individual competition. Although Hispanic students vary in their learning preferences, many, particularly those with a lesser degree of assimilation, tend to do better in courses where faculty emphasize practical applications and direct experiences over abstract theory. Anderson (1988) argues that one of the most critical problems encountered by students of color is that secondary school teachers and college faculty are not equipped to identify, interpret, and respond to the ways that some minority students learn. He states that a communication gap exists between the faculty teaching style and the students' indigenous learning styles. A symbolic, affective, reality-based approach to learning preferred by some students could be branded as deficient. Anderson (1988) cites the example of the writing styles of African Americans and Hispanic Americans, which are frequently viewed as "too flowery," too subjective, using too many metaphors, and so on.

The curricula in higher education rarely reflect the interests or contributions of Hispanics. If, as Fiske (1988b) argues, we validate cultures by studying them, Hispanic students typically do not see that their culture is acknowledged in their studies.

In most institutions of higher learning, there are few, if any, role models or support systems for Hispanics, and few individuals to act as mentors as students try to acclimate to the new environment without sacrificing family and personal values. SCDEs must consider that faculty teaching styles and practices, curricula, and institutional culture must change if we are to be successful in retaining and graduating Hispanic teacher education students.

Arturo Madrid, president of the Tomas Rivera Center in Claremont, California, believes that institutional efforts to increase the supply of Latino teachers are "limited in number, small in scale, uncoordinated, and, for the most part, unimaginative" (1989, p. 2). The Tomas Rivera Center has received funds from the Ford and Exxon Educational Foundations to study ways of increasing the number of Hispanic teachers. Madrid states that, ultimately, a remedy for the shortage of Hispanic teachers depends on the importance assigned to this issue by educational policymakers and on their willingness to seek a solution. The problem cannot be solved overnight or by one approach, program, or institution.

It is essential that we increase the number of Hispanics in the teaching force by strengthening our efforts in the recruitment and retention of these students in teacher preparation programs. Further, because in the immediate future most Hispanic children will be taught by those from different language and cultural backgrounds, it is just as crucial, if not more so, that we prepare all teachers to educate the growing numbers of Hispanics in the schools.

Preparing All Teachers to Educate Hispanic Students

How can SCDEs prepare future teachers to be effective instructors of Hispanic youngsters? Castro (1989) identifies three major problems in the preparation of teacher candidates for a culturally diverse student population: Most college faculty are not prepared to work with diverse students, most institutional efforts to sensitize students are sorely inadequate, and those students who could bring cultural understanding and sensitivities to the teaching profession are not completing the preparation process in significant numbers.

There is wide agreement that one cross-cultural or multicultural course is not enough to prepare teachers to work with Hispanic students. SCDEs must reform their teacher preparation curricula and, in doing so, must enlist the cooperation of the entire institutions. Preparation needed to meet the needs of Hispanic students must include study of Hispanic culture, history, and literature; the students' language or language variety; first-language acquisition, second-language learning, and the associations among language, culture, and identity; and the contributions of different cultural groups to American society.

In professional education courses, SCDEs must include

- Methodology and techniques for incorporating cultural elements into the teaching act, including nonverbal communication, values, learning styles, and communication patterns
- Methodology and techniques on how to teach English as a sec-

ond language, how to increase English language skills when
teaching content areas, and how to teach reading to children for
whom English is not a first and/or dominant language
- Field experiences in multicultural settings, starting at the freshman year[1]
- Techniques for working effectively with Hispanic teacher aides
and Hispanic parents
- Techniques for understanding and working with individual
and group differences
- Techniques for examining, adapting, and supplementing the
curriculum to reflect students' cultural backgrounds and experiences (Burstein and Cabello, 1989)
- Techniques for classroom management with a focus on strategies that consider cultural, socioeconomic, and linguistic factors
(Burstein and Cabello, 1989)

The task of preparing teachers of Hispanic students will require not only reformation of the general education and professional education curricula but also new assessment techniques that
reflect the competencies needed to teach children of diverse cultural
and linguistic backgrounds. In addition, the language used to refer
to ethnic minorities in the schools or in higher education must
reject such terms and concepts of the past as *remediation* and *language deficient*.

SCDEs must restructure curricula and field experiences so
that all teacher education students (majority and minority alike)
receive the preparation needed to serve the increasing number of
culturally and linguistically diverse Hispanic students in the public
schools. SCDEs must research what competencies are needed for
teachers to be effective with students from diverse settings and what
modifications must be made in the system to develop teachers who
possess these competencies.

What are the competencies that teachers of Hispanics must
have in order to be adequately prepared to teach these students?
Effective instructors of Hispanic students, whether or not they are
members of the same ethnic group as their pupils, display behaviors
similar to those of all successful teachers (Schuhmann, 1990).

Effective teachers of Hispanic students, like all effective

teachers, exhibit "active teaching" behaviors that correlate with increased student performance on academic tests of achievement in reading and mathematics. These teachers communicate clearly when giving directions, specifying tasks, presenting new information, and using appropriate strategies such as explaining, outlining, and demonstrating. They engage students in instructional tasks by maintaining task focus, pacing instruction appropriately, promoting involvement, and communicating their expectations for students' success in completing tasks. Further, they monitor students' progress and provide immediate feedback (Tikunoff, 1983). Effective teachers of Hispanic students, like effective teachers in general, communicate high expectations for student learning. Research on teacher and school effectiveness has established a correlation between teacher expectations and student achievement. As Brown (1986, p. 32) has observed, students "for whom low expectations for academic success are held are taught less effectively than those for whom teachers hold high expectations. In general, students who are not expected to make significant progress experience limited opportunities to engage actively in learning activities. Teachers are less likely to plan for or direct instruction toward this group. These students, most of whom are minorities, come under fewer demands for academic performance and increasingly greater demands for conformance in terms of behavior."

SCDEs must develop teachers who display proven characteristics of effective teaching. In addition to the features exhibited by successful instructors in general, there are additional behaviors needed by teachers of Hispanic children, practices that apply regardless of whether the teachers are members of the minority group. Effective teachers of Hispanics have a knowledge and appreciation of their pupils' culture and use this knowledge for instructional purposes. Tikunoff (1983) found that effective teachers use their understanding of their students' home cultures to promote engagement in educational tasks. Teachers use cultural information to (1) respond to or employ native language cultural referents to enhance instruction, (2) organize instructional activities to build on ways in which students naturally participate in discourse in their own home cultures, and (3) recognize and honor the values and norms of students' home cultures while teaching the values and norms of the majority culture.

Last, effective teachers of Hispanic students recognize the legitimacy of the language variety of the students and utilize the students' language or language variety in developing English or a standard variety of English. According to Brown (1986, p. 38),

> It is important for all of us, particularly those who have the responsibility for guiding the learning experiences of inner-city children, to recognize the legitimacy of the many dialects of American English and to utilize those dialects in establishing access routes to more effective communication. . . . Children whose basic speech patterns are comprised of dialectical variants are often reluctant to offer oral contributions to classroom activities. This is particularly true if they have good reason to believe that those contributions will be judged for their conformance with accepted language conventions rather than content. Reticence on the part of these students elicits teacher interactions that serve to exacerbate further an already dehumanizing experience. The students soon succumb to feelings of not belonging and withdraw completely from all learning activities. This may be thought of as the point of no return. Regardless of teacher efforts to get these children actively involved, the forces operating against meaningful interaction are too firmly entrenched. Predictably, the outcomes of these actions and reactions are the same. Another group of minority students continues to make only marginal progress over the course of the school year.

A large number of Hispanic students, but not all, enter school with little or no exposure to the English language. Nationwide, the need for teachers for limited English proficient (LEP) children is great. The U.S. Department of Education has indicated that a projected 72,500 additional teachers will be required to meet the needs of LEP students in this nation's schools.

AACTE (1990) found that the least desirable setting for a first-year teaching assignment, according to the student teachers surveyed, was work with non–English speaking children. Two-thirds of those surveyed indicated that they would not like to work with LEP students. There is a great need for SCDEs to prepare teachers capable of meeting the needs of Hispanic children who speak little or no English.

What additional competencies do instructors need to educate Hispanic students, if those students are LEP? In the Bilingual Instructional Features study, Tikunoff (1983) found that successful teachers of LEP students mediate effective instruction by using both L1 (native language) and L2 (second language, in this instance, English) effectively for instruction, alternating between the two languages whenever necessary to ensure clarity of instruction.

Successful teachers of LEP students mediate effective instruction in a second way by integrating English language development with academic skills development, focusing on LEP students' acquisition of English terms for concepts and lesson content even when L1 is used for a portion of the instruction. There is widespread agreement in the field of bilingual education that a teacher of LEP students should possess a thorough knowledge of both languages of instruction, and the ability to teach in both languages. The need for bilingual competence for teachers of LEP students is supported by a number of investigations. Rodriguez (1980) studied twenty elementary bilingual teachers to determine the competencies needed for effective bilingual teaching. She found that one of the characteristics of effective bilingual teaching was knowledge of the students' language. It was determined that effective bilingual teachers teach subject matter in the students' first language, while giving this language and English equal status. In addition, effective bilingual teachers encourage their students to use their native tongue.

A teacher of LEP students has the dual task of communicating information through one or two languages and, at the same time, developing the students' skills in a new language. Wong-Fillmore (1983) states that the language used for instructional purposes in bilingual classrooms must serve both as linguistic input for language learning purposes and, equally important, as a means to communicate information and skills associated with the subject matter being taught. Macias (1989) argues that teacher training for LEP students involves a paradigm shift that permeates the instructional process. Teachers must believe that language-minority students can and will learn, and that the use of non-English languages is not un-American.

Conclusion

The Hispanic population in the United States will continue to grow faster than the general population due to both natural increase and immigration (McKay, 1988). Hispanics will also become a larger segment of the work force. It is mandatory, then, that we address the current serious problem of Hispanic undereducation. Strong leadership and positive changes must occur at all levels of education, government, and industry to reverse the serious Hispanic high school dropout rate. SCDEs must work with elementary and secondary schools on improving the quality of education for Hispanics and on implementing early awareness and early intervention programs to ensure that all students complete high school.

Hispanics are seriously underrepresented in the teaching force. SCDEs must strengthen efforts to recruit, retain, and graduate Hispanics from teacher education programs. In order to achieve these goals, SCDEs must provide significant financial aid and incentives to prospective teacher education students, establish linkages with junior high schools, high schools, and two-year colleges, involve the family in the educational process, improve campus climate, reform higher education curricula to reflect the language and culture of the Hispanic student, provide mentors and role models, and create alternative assessment measures to determine aptitude and success in teacher preparation programs.

SCDEs must encourage students from all language and cultural backgrounds to pursue careers in teaching. Furthermore, the demographic changes and the critical need for schools that are effective in educating this country's students require that all teachers be better prepared to educate all students. Teacher education reform must advance the preparation of teachers for work with diverse student populations from the level of today's single course in multicultural education to the level of an organized and integrated component of the overall teacher training curriculum (Dash, 1988). To achieve the objective of preparing teachers to educate Hispanic students, SCDEs must have the cooperation of their entire universities. The general education and professional components of teacher preparation programs must be revised to ensure that all teachers possess the linguistic, cultural, and pedagogical competencies necessary to be effective instructors of Hispanic students.

Note

1. Mentoring by a Hispanic teacher or teacher aide, community aide, or parent should be considered for the student teaching experience. Castro (1989) believes that institutions should recognize the importance of field or classroom experiences in Latino communities. Goodwin (1990) argues that a primary objective of SCDEs ought to be an infusing of the entire education program with multicultural practices. Goodwin suggests that field experiences take the form of interviews, interactions with a wide variety of individuals, volunteer work, participation in community events, tutoring, intercultural mentoring, role playing, school visitations, ethnographic research, and so on. Goodwin further recommends carefully conceived and grounded field experiences to enhance the preparation of a culturally responsive teaching force.

References

American Association of Colleges for Teacher Education. (1989). *Recruiting minority teachers: A practice guide*. Washington, DC: American Association of Colleges for Teacher Education.

American Association of Colleges for Teacher Education. (1990). *AACTE/Metropolitan Life survey of teacher education students*. Washington, DC: American Association of Colleges for Teacher Education.

Anderson, J. A. (1988). Cognitive styles and multicultural populations. *Journal of Teacher Education, 39*(1), 2–9.

Anrig, G. R. (1986). Teacher education and teacher testing: The rush to mandate. In S. Packard (ed.), *The leading edge.* Washington, DC: American Association of Colleges for Teacher Education.

Applebome, P. (1987). Educators alarmed by growing rate of dropouts among Hispanic youth. *New York Times,* Mar. 15, p. 2.

Baratz, J. C. (1986). Black participation in the teacher pool. Unpublished manuscript, prepared for the Carnegie Forum Task Force on Teaching as a Profession.

Brown, T. J. (1986). *Teaching minorities more effectively.* Lanham, MD: University Press of America.

Burstein, N. D., and Cabello, B. (1989). Preparing teachers to work with culturally diverse students: A teacher education model. *Journal of Teacher Education, 40*(5), 9-16.

Castro, R. (1989). *Improving access of Latinos to the teaching profession.* Claremont, CA: Tomas Rivera Center.

Chapa, J. (1991). Special focus: Hispanic demographic and educational trends. In D. J. Carter and R. Wilson (eds.), *Ninth annual status report on minorities in higher education.* Washington, DC: American Council on Education.

Cooper, C. C. (1986). Strategies to assure certification and retention of black teachers. *Journal of Negro Education, 55*(1), 46-55.

Dash, R. (1988). *Roundtable: The challenge—Preparing teachers for diverse populations.* Northridge, CA: Far West Laboratory.

Fernandez, R. R., and Velez, W. (1989). *Who stays? Who leaves? Findings from the Aspira five cities dropout study.* Washington, DC: Institute for Policy Research, Aspira Associates.

Fiske, E. B. (1988a). Economic realities spur colleges on recruiting Hispanic students. *New York Times,* Mar. 20, pp. A28-A29.

Fiske, E. B. (1988b). The undergraduate Hispanic experience. *Change,* May-June, pp. 29-33.

Galambos, E. C. (1986). Testing teachers for certification and recertification. In T. J. Lasley (ed.), *Issues in teacher education,* Vol. 2: *Background papers from the National Commission for Excellence in Teacher Education.* Washington, DC: American Association of Colleges for Teacher Education.

Garcia, P. A. (1985). *A study on teacher competency testing and test validity with implications for minorities and the results and implications of the use of the Pre-Professional Skills Test (PPST) as a screening device for entrance into teacher education pro-*

grams in Texas. Washington, DC: National Institute of Education.

Garibaldi, A. M. (1987). *Quality and diversity in schools: The case for an expanded pool of minority teachers.* Racine, WI: American Association of Colleges for Teacher Education.

Garibaldi, A. M. (1989). The impact of school and college reforms on the recruitment of more minority teachers. In A. M. Garibaldi (ed.), *Teacher recruitment and retention.* Washington, DC: National Education Association.

Goodwin, A. L. (1990). Fostering diversity in the teaching profession through multicultural field experiences. Paper presented at the Next Level Symposium, American Association of Colleges for Teacher Education, Tampa, FL.

Hispanic students continue to be distinctive. (1988). *Change,* May-June, pp. 43-47.

Macias, R. F. (1989). *The national need for bilingual teachers.* Claremont, CA: Tomas Rivera Center.

McKay, E. G. (1988). *Changing Hispanic demographics.* Washington, DC: Policy Analysis Center, National Council of La Raza.

Madrid, A. (1989). The TRC educational agenda: Latinos and the teaching profession. *Tomas Rivera Center Report, 2*(2), 2.

Melendez, S. E., and Petrovich, J. (1989). Hispanic women students in higher education: Meeting the challenge of diversity. In C. S. Pearson, D. Shavlik, and J. Touchton (eds.), *Educating the majority: Women challenge tradition in higher education.* Washington, DC: American Council on Education/Macmillan.

Middleton, E. J., Mason, E. J., Stilwell, W. E., and Parker, W. C. (1988). A model for recruitment and retention of minority students in teacher preparation programs. *Journal of Teacher Education, 39*(1), 14-18.

Munoz, D. (1986). Identifying areas of stress for Chicano undergraduates. In M. Olivas (ed.), *Latino college students.* New York: Teachers College Press.

Nieves-Squires, S. (1991). *Hispanic women. Project on the status and education of women.* Washington, DC: Association of American Colleges.

Quality Education for Minorities Project. (1990). *Education that works: An action plan for the education of minorities.* Cambridge, MA: Quality Education for Minorities Project, Massachusetts Institute of Technology.

Rodman, B. (1985). Teaching's "endangered species." *Education Week, 3*(1), 11–13.

Rodriguez, A. M. (1980). Empirically defining competencies for effective bilingual teachers: A preliminary study. In R. V. Padilla (ed.), *Theory in bilingual education.* Ypsilanti: Department of Foreign Languages and Bilingual Studies, Eastern Michigan University.

Sanchez, J., and others. (1989). *Patterns of Hispanic attrition and persistence at Kean College.* Union, NJ: Division of Academic Services and Office of Institutional Research, Kean College.

Schuhmann, A. M. (1990). Improving the quality of teachers for minority students. In J. G. Bair and J. L. Herman (eds.), *Making schools work for underachieving minority students.* Westport, CT: Greenwood Press.

Smith, G. P. (1984). Minority teaching force dwindles with states' use of standard tests. *AACTE Briefs, 5*(9), 12–14.

Smith, G. P., Chang Miller, M., and Joy, J. (1988). A case study of the impact of performance-based testing on the supply of minority teachers. *Journal of Teacher Education, 39*(4), 45–53.

Tikunoff, W. J. (1983). Effective instruction for limited English proficient students. Paper presented at the 12th annual conference of the National Association for Bilingual Education, Washington, DC.

Webb, M. B. (1986). *Increasing minority participation in the teaching profession.* ERIC/CUE Digest, no. 31. New York: ERIC Clearinghouse on Urban Education.

Witty, E. P. (1982). *Prospects for black teachers: Preparation, certification, employment.* Washington, DC: ERIC Clearinghouse on Teacher Education.

Wong-Fillmore, L. (1983). Effective instruction of LEP students. Paper presented at the 12th annual conference of the National Association for Bilingual Education, Washington, DC.

7

Recruiting and Retaining Asian/Pacific American Teachers

Philip C. Chinn
Gay Yuen Wong

The recruitment and retention of ethnic minorities into teacher education was one of the major concerns of teacher education programs in the 1980s and will undoubtedly continue to be a concern through the 1990s. While the literature (for example, Zapata, 1988; Chinn, 1988; Winkler, 1985) addresses the problems related to declining numbers of African Americans and Hispanics in teacher education programs, Asians and Pacific Americans (APA's) are seldom mentioned. Any literature search will reveal that little has been written about this group's involvement in teacher education programs. It is likely that in many areas of the United States, Asians are such a small minority group that they often go unnoticed.

Demographic Profile

In areas such as New York City, Seattle, the San Francisco Bay area, Southern California, and the state of Hawaii, it would be almost impossible for APAs to go unnoticed. In 1988, the largest Buddhist temple-monastery in the Western hemisphere was built in Hacienda Heights, California, a Los Angeles suburb. Chinese characters on street and business signs in Monterey Park and Alhambra, Califor-

nia, and notations on Los Angeles area maps indicating Little To-
kyo, Koreatown, and Chinatown provide evidence of a significant
APA presence and cultural influence in many communities.

According to U.S. Census data, approximately 3.5 million
APAs were living in the United States in 1980. By 1985 that figure
grew to over 5 million. Measured in percentage growth, the APA
population is the fastest growing minority group in the United
States. Between 1970 and 1980, the APA population grew by 142
percent as compared to the 61 percent growth of Hispanics, 17.3
percent growth of blacks, and the overall population growth of 10.8
percent (Sing, 1989).

U.S. Census Bureau projections for the year 2000 set the APA
figure at 10 million or 4 percent of the total U.S. population. By
the year 2050, the U.S. Census Bureau projects an APA population
of 18 million, or 6.4 percent of the U.S. population. This is the same
percentage of the population that Hispanics held in the 1980 census
(Sing, 1989).

Who are the APAs in the United States, why have their
numbers increased so rapidly, and what characterizes these groups?
Table 7.1 lists the various Asian groups and their relative populations according to the 1990 Census. Table 7.2 lists the various Pacific groups according to the 1990 Census. The seven largest ethnic
groups among the APAs are Chinese (22.6 percent), Filipino (19.3
percent), Japanese (11.7 percent), Asian Indian (11.2 percent), Korean (11.0 percent), Vietnamese (8.4 percent), and Hawaiian (2.9
percent). Together they make up over 87.1 percent of the total APA
population.

The categorization of such diverse ethnic groups as Hmong
and Fijians under one main population category of APAs appears
to defy logic. Hispanics are bound by a common language, blacks
are bound by race. APAs are bound by neither.

The diversity of the APA groups creates difficulties in reports
of statistical data and in descriptions of group characteristics. Many
reports on Asians include only Asians, and any report of these findings as APA data would be incorrect. Consequently, in the remainder of this chapter, references to APAs denote both Asians and
Pacific Americans, and references to Asians denote Asians only (see

**Table 7.1. Asian Americans in the
1990 U.S. Census.**

Group	Number
Chinese	1,645,472
Filipino	1,406,770
Japanese	847,562
Asian Indian	815,447
Korean	798,849
Vietnamese	614,547
Laotian	149,014
Thai	91,275
Cambodian	147,411
Pakistani	81,371
Indonesian	29,252
Hmong	90,082
All others[a]	148,111
Total	6,865,163

[a]Includes groups such as Nepali and Bhutanese.

**Table 7.2. Pacific Americans in the
1990 Census.**

Group	Number
Polynesians	
Hawaiians	211,014
Samoans	62,964
Tongans	17,606
Tahitians	944
Micronesians	
Guamanians	49,345
Melanesians	
Fijians	7,036
Other Pacific Islanders	16,115
Total	365,024

Table 7.1). At times, when descriptions of Asians include only certain groups of Asians, these groups are identified.

Since the birthrate for Asian women is lower than the birthrates of whites, Hispanics, and African Americans, the growth in the APA population is primarily the result of Asian immigration into the United States. For example, 95 percent of the record 413 percent increase of Koreans during the decade of 1970 to 1980 can be traced directly to immigration from Korea. According to the 1980 Census data, over 60 percent of all Asian Americans are foreign born as compared to 6 percent of the total U.S. population (Johnson, Levin, and Paisano, 1988).

Although Asians, like African Americans and other minority groups, have a history of oppression in the United States, their increasing affluence and educational attainments belie the image of the typical oppressed subgroup. Their perceived successful efforts to assimilate, achieved with minimal discomfort to the dominant group, has earned them the dubious distinction of being labeled a "model minority." Their perceived diligence, frugality, and willingness to sacrifice has accelerated their upward mobility and the willingness of the dominant group to accept them—perhaps with some reservation (Kim, 1973; Crystal, 1989). Winnick (1990) even suggests that "model minority" is yesteryear's coinage, that Asians have been elevated to the more exalted station of "America's trophy population."

Crystal (1989) suggests that the discrepancy between the "model minority" myth and the reality of serious social and economic problems is related to both the internal dynamics of the Asian American community and the political needs of the dominant society. The need to "maintain face" is a powerful driving force behind much of the Asian behavior. Crystal (1989, p. 407) states that "considerable energy is expended in maintaining a dignified and decorous image no matter what the reality of the situation may be." The need to maintain appearances is ingrained in the culture of many Asians. Some Asians may deliberately perpetuate the model minority image, feeling that it enhances their standing in society and facilitates their acceptance by the dominant group.

The dominant culture's need to showcase a successful minority supports the belief that democracy works. The racism that the other groups complain about, it is argued, is in reality the result of their own shortcomings. Crystal (1989) suggests that this argument justifies the continuation of present programs that favor the privileged and provides scapegoats to absorb the dissatisfactions of the majority groups.

There are serious repercussions of the model minority label. Educators, social services providers, and policymakers may view Asians as a group without serious needs or problems. Consequently, Asians may in some instances not have adequate funds appropriated or designated to meet their social welfare, education, and other needs. Other minority groups may be baited with, "If the Asians can do it, why can't you?"—fueling the inevitable resentment toward Asians.

From the perspective of family income, it would seem that statistics point to an area of Asian success. In analyzing 1980 Census data, Suzuki (1989) found that the four largest Asian groups—Chinese, Filipino, Japanese, and Asian Indian—have higher reported median family and individual incomes than their white counterparts. However, he cites the work of several researchers (for example, Nee and Sanders, 1985; Cabezas, Shinagawa, and Kawaguchi, 1986–1986; Jiobu, 1988) who have utilized sophisticated statistical techniques to assess the income-related effects of education, years' work experience, wage earners per household, region of residence, age, ability to speak English, weeks worked, occupational status, and so on. Adjusting for the above factors, Suzuki concluded that, with the exception of the Japanese, none of the Asian groups has attained income parity with whites, and that whites gain a substantially higher return on their education (that is, more earning power for the same education). Suzuki further suggests that many Asians encounter a "glass ceiling," which inhibits upward mobility in business and industry.

Suzuki (1989) also points out that many Asian Americans live below the federal poverty level. With the exception of Japanese and Filipinos, a larger proportion of Asian families live below the government's poverty level than do comparable white families. The poverty rate is particularly high for Chinese living in the Chinatowns of New York, San Francisco, and Los Angeles. Hsia and Hirano-Nakanishi (1989) report that, in 1980, when 9.6 percent of

U.S. families lived below the poverty line, disproportionately large numbers of Southeast Asians were living in poverty: 33.5 percent of the Vietnamese, 48.7 percent of the Cambodians, 62.8 percent of the Hmong, and 65.9 percent of the Laotians.

The four metropolitan areas with the largest centers of the APA population—Honolulu, Los Angeles, San Francisco-Oakland, and New York—are among the cities with the highest cost of living. Most of the communities rounding out the top ten Asian population centers (for example, San Jose, San Diego, and Washington, D.C.) are also high-cost-of-living cities. Consequently, while most Asians may technically be living above the government's arbitrary poverty level, many in reality have lower standards of living than are implied by the statistics.

Statistics on education also seem to point to the academic successes of APAs. The U.S. Bureau of the Census (1989) reports that while, nationally, 66 percent of those who are twenty-five years of age and over are high school graduates, the figure for APAs is 75 percent. Thirty-three percent of APAs are college graduates, compared to 16 percent of the total U.S. population. The high school and college graduation rates for Pacific Islanders are lower than those of the Asian and Pacific groups, with Hawaiians the highest group at 10 percent completing higher education degrees. The percentages of APAs graduating from high school and college surpass those of non-Hispanic whites. Admission rates to prestigious schools such as Massachusetts Institute of Technology, Harvard, Brown, Stanford, University of California at Berkeley, University of California at Los Angeles, and California Institute of Technology are disproportionately high for Asians.

Combined statistics for all APA groups often obscure the data for individual or specific APA ethnic groups. Even within a given ethnic group, statistics can often be misleading. The statistics on the first wave of Vietnamese refugees in 1975 are likely to vary considerably from those of the second wave of 1978 with regard to wealth, income, and educational attainment. The overall statistics on income and educational achievement tend to support the model minority thesis for APAs. APAs are perceived by many as highly motivated, highly educated, economically successful, and valuable contributors to society. While some APAs do indeed match these stereotypes, there are many others who do not. While the majority of APAs are high school graduates, significant numbers are not, and over two-thirds are not college graduates. Many APAs, perhaps even the majority, live comfortably in the United States. Still, as previously stated, there are many poor APAs struggling to survive on their limited incomes.

Confucian Values

In order to understand the variables that affect career choices for Asians, it is helpful to understand their values. The task of identifying values or characteristics that hold across all Asian groups is difficult, if not impossible, since Asians constitute a heterogeneous mixture of ethnic groups. Indeed, because of the diversity of Asians living in the United States, the discussion here is necessarily limited to the four Asian groups most closely identified with Confucian values: the Chinese, Japanese, Koreans, and Vietnamese. These four groups comprise approximately two-thirds of the APA population. However, it should be noted that two large groups, the Filipinos and Asian Indians, are not included in this discussion. This limitation of the discussion should not be construed as negating the importance of the remaining groups, but rather as reflecting the impossibility of providing general statements that characterize all groups.

The Chinese, Japanese, Koreans, and Vietnamese share Confucian values, which have a philosophical rather than a religious base. Consequently, the values may transcend all Asian ethnic groups regardless of religious identification, socioeconomic status, or generation since initial immigration. Many Asians who are second-, third-, or even fourth-generation Americans maintain some of these values without even realizing their Confucian origins. Typically, they are values that are maintained in the home, passed on to successive generations, and accepted as appropriate and expected behavior. While all members of these four ethnic groups do not maintain identical values, the general values presented here may, in part, help to clarify the cultural underpinnings of Asian career choices and decisions.

Parental View of Their Children

Traditional Asians tend to perceive their children as "gifts from the Gods," and the center of the universe. They believe that their children are born predisposed toward goodness, but that they must be properly trained and taught in order to develop their "innate" positive characteristics (Chan, 1986).

Asian parents often make significant sacrifices to provide for their children's education and material comforts. Private tutors, travel, music lessons, and specialty camps (for example, summer computer camps) are often provided to children even when such activities place heavy financial burdens on family resources.

Parental Involvement in Educational Matters

With the value placed on education, Asian parents often take an active role in their children's educations. The attendance rates of English-speaking Asian parents at school meetings tend to be high. They often check their children's homework, and some are known to add work beyond the assignments of the teachers. A study by Stanford University sociologist Sanford Dornbusch found that Asian American students spent an average of eleven hours a week doing their homework, compared to seven hours by others (Brand, 1987). As a group, Suzuki (1989) indicates that Asians prepare themselves well to enter college. On average, they earn more credits in college preparatory subjects than do other ethnic groups. They earn more units in foreign languages, mathematics, and natural sciences than do other students (Snyder, 1989). In 1985, 70 percent of all Asian eighteen-year-olds took the Scholastic Aptitude Test, compared to 27 percent of the total population of eighteen-year-olds (Brand, 1987).

Asian parents typically monitor their children's grades as well as their courses of study and their choice of electives. This monitoring is often done with specific long-term career goals in mind.

Family Roles and Responsibilities

While traditional Asian parents may give generously of themselves to their children, specific behaviors are expected from the children in return. Roles in the family are clearly defined, as are the corresponding sets of behaviors for each family member.

Parents are responsible for the welfare and security of the family as a whole. They readily sacrifice their personal needs in serving the interests of their children. The primary family unit tends to be strong and exerts considerable control over its members (Sue and Sue, 1973). The parents' role is to define the law (rules and practices), and the children's role is to listen and obey. Parental authority may be extended to grandparents, aunts and uncles, and other family "elders." Deference to elders is essential, particularly to those in the family (Chan, 1986).

In Confucian philosophy, harmony is the keynote of existence. Chan (1986) states that the maintenance of harmony entails the maintenance of social order, which requires conformity to the rules of propriety. Each member of a family must know his or her place and act in accordance to prescribed roles. Chan further indicates that family and social behaviors are governed by esteem for hierarchical roles and relationships and the virtue of filial piety. Filial piety consists of unquestioning loyalty and obedience to one's parents and a concern and understanding of their wishes (Tseng, 1973). While traditional Asians tend to give much to their children, they expect much in return. Children must not bring shame or loss of face to their parents. Misbehavior and disobedience in the home and especially in the school or community brings shame to the entire family and reflects on the parents' ability to provide proper guidance. Sue and Sue (1973) suggest that Asian parents tend to use guilt-arousing techniques to control their children. Comments such as "How can you do this to us after all we have done for you" are typical from Asian parents. The child's responsibility is to bring honor to the family, and this can be achieved by excelling in school, gaining admission to a good or prestigious college or university, and entering a high-prestige or honorable profession upon graduation. Thus, a child bears the weight of the entire family's prestige and honor on his or her shoulders. Failure is more than personal embarrassment or humiliation. It is shame on the entire family, even ancestors who have long since passed on. Success is a primary motivating force. Failure, however, has the potential for severe emotional consequences.

It is not uncommon for parents to select a child's college or university or field of study; they may even select or influence choice of courses. The fields of study selected are characteristically those with high extrinsic rewards coupled with high prestige, such as medicine, dentistry, natural sciences, engineering, architecture, economics, accounting, and computer science.

Career Goals and Choices

Minatoya and Sedlacek (1981) studied Asian American undergraduates and, in their sample of two hundred eastern U.S. Asians, found that 54 percent chose career majors in life sciences, agriculture, mathematics, physical sciences, engineering, or allied health sciences; whereas 39 percent chose majors in behavioral or social sciences, arts, humanities, education, and other social and community service fields. Lujan (1989) reports the findings of the University of Washington Office of Minority Affairs, which collected data on the major fields of study of 577 Asian students in fall 1987: 19.1 percent chose social sciences, 17.5 percent engineering, 17 percent sciences, 17 percent arts and the performing arts, 9.2 percent humanities, 5.2 percent allied health services, 3.6 percent business, 2.6 percent fisheries and forestry, 1 percent architecture, and 7.8 percent "other" (including, apparently, education).

The Southeast Asian Refugee Youth study, conducted in San Diego high schools by Rumbaut and Ima (1987) for the Office of Refugee Resettlement, found that the career choices among the Vietnamese, Chinese-Vietnamese, Hmong, Khmer (Cambodian), and Laotian students fell into distinct groups on the bases of family and social backgrounds and gender. While the Vietnamese, Chinese-Vietnamese, and Hmong displayed characteristics and selected career goals that were very similar to the Chinese, Japanese, and Koreans, the Laotian and Khmer students were similar to the East Indian groups. Thirty-five percent of the males in the study selected science, engineering, and math-based careers, and 20 percent selected blue-collar work. The female students made different choices from the males. Twenty-one percent selected careers in health care, while 9 percent chose teaching, social work, and fine arts.

Vetter and Babco (1984), using data collected by the U.S.

Department of Education, found that the most popular college major for Asians was business and management. About 20 percent of Asians (and other students) pursued this area of study. Engineering was the second most popular field, attracting over 16 percent of the Asian students (compared to 8 percent of students in general). Social sciences attracted 8.8 percent of the Asian students (compared to 10.8 percent of other students), with biological sciences and health professions as the next two most popular fields of study for Asians in that research sample. A higher proportion of Asians pursued studies in the biological sciences, computer and information sciences, and mathematics, and a lower proportion in letters and education, than did students from other ethnic groups.

Asians in Teacher Education Programs

Suzuki (1989) suggests that given their strong emphasis on education, it is paradoxical that Asians are so underrepresented in the teaching profession. The problem of underrepresentation of ethnic minorities in teacher education programs has been a concern of educators throughout the 1980s (for example, Winkler, 1985; American Association of Colleges for Teacher Education [AACTE], 1987; Chinn, 1988). California State University, Los Angeles, with one of the largest teacher education programs in the United States, has one of the most ethnically diverse student populations in the country. Approximately two-thirds of the overall student population in 1990 were from ethnic minority backgrounds. Yet, only about one-third of the teacher education candidates are African American, Hispanic, or Asian. The most underrepresented minority group in teacher education are the Asians.

Vetter and Babco (1984) indicated that while nearly 12 percent of all college students pursue careers in education, less than 4 percent of Asian students select teacher education programs. Only 2 percent of Asian men and 5 percent of Asian women were found to be majoring in education in a national sample (Peng, 1985).

AACTE conducted a survey of teacher education students in fall 1988 (see AACTE, 1990). The sample included 472 students from thirty AACTE member institutions. There were eighteen Asians in the sample. Results related specifically to Asians indicate that more Asian teacher education students had C averages than did either white or Hispanic students. English was a second language for 61.1 percent of the Asians, compared to 51 percent of the Hispanics. Significantly fewer Asians reported A averages in high school that did students from other ethnic groups. More Asians reported receiving teacher education financial aid than did students from the other groups. The sample of Asians was extremely small and cannot be presumed to represent all Asians in teacher education programs. Also, there is no exact breakdown of the ethnic groups represented in the sample. This particular sample of Asian students suggests that at least some of the Asians in teacher education may not be academically high achievers. If this is true, perhaps a greater emphasis needs to be placed on the recruitment of academically strong Asian students into the field of education.

Teacher education is not one of the more commonly chosen fields of Asians. The reasons are numerous, and some are obvious. The perceived low level of extrinsic rewards is a major deterrent to Asians considering a career in education. While Asians generally have a high regard for teachers and scholars, the apparent low prestige level serves as a deterrent. Because of news media coverage, Asian parents are likely to be aware of teacher strikes, teacher complaints of low wages, and poor working conditions. Asian parents may seek out other professions that they perceive as higher in status.

In recent years, many Asian parents have come to see the American Dream, which is enhanced by education, as applicable to their daughters as well as their sons. Thus, Asian women are also making career choices in fields such as medicine and engineering. In other Asian families, however, career choices for daughters may be perceived differently from those of sons. Since they may view their daughters as future wives and mothers, they may be less prone to encourage or force the longer educational programs required for medicine and other professions onto their daughters. Instead, some may view their daughters' employment as supplements to the husbands' incomes. For some of these parents, career choices in education may be acceptable, particularly if they view their daughters as future mothers who will have their summers off to be with their children.

Since teaching is less likely than some other fields to receive parental approval, particularly for males, it may not be viewed as a viable option by many college-bound Asian students. To become a teacher, Asian males and females may have to consciously disappoint their parents. Although the price extracted by such defiant behavior varies across families, it is often sufficient to inhibit consideration of this field. Only 1 percent of the nation's 3,722,120 teachers are Asian. Of that number, 11,494 are males and 27,238 are women (Johnson, Levin, and Paisano, 1988). The trend of not choosing teaching as a profession may be an accurate forecast of the situation in the years to come unless universities and school districts actively revise their recruitment, training, and hiring and retention plans.

Competence Testing

In recent years, various states have introduced competence testing at the preservice level as a partial requirement for admission into or completion of teacher education programs. California introduced the California Basic Educational Skills Test (CBEST) in 1983. Texas followed with the Pre-Professional Skills Test in 1984. Proponents of preservice testing believe that it eliminates weak students and enhances quality and excellence in teacher education programs. Critics are concerned, however, that these tests are culture-bound and hence inherently biased against ethnic minorities whose language backgrounds and cognitive styles are different from the mainstream majority culture. The purpose of this section is not to discuss the appropriateness of these tests but rather to consider how they may inhibit minority students in general, and APAs in particular, from entering teacher education programs.

In California, the CBEST passing rate for whites was considerably higher than that of non whites. As reported in Majetic (1989), whites had passing rates of 80 to 82 percent between 1985 and 1989. African Americans had passing rates of 34 to 41 percent during those same years, Mexican Americans were at 50 to 59 percent, other Hispanics were 48 to 62 percent, and Asians were 61 to 62 percent (figures reported as Asian but may be APA). While the Asian passing rates were somewhat higher than those of other minority students, they were still significantly lower than those of their white peers (see Table 7.3).

What is clear is that nearly 40 percent of the Asians attempting the CBEST fail on their first tries. In some traditional Asian families, a failure of this nature is seen to bring shame to the family. Some Asians, aware of the high failure rate for their ethnic group, may be reluctant to risk embarrassment to themselves and their families and may avoid subjecting themselves to a testing procedure that they view as either discriminatory or likely to result in failure.

While overall, Asians tend to perform comparably to whites on the Scholastic Aptitude Test and the American College Test, they score lower on verbal ability and higher on quantitative ability than do their white counterparts. Ramist and Arbeiter (1984) indicate that these differences held even for Asian students who felt that English was their best language.

Clearly, the English verbal-linguistic skills of many Asians are lacking. In addition to contributing to lower test scores on college admissions tests and on competence tests for admission into teacher education programs, these problems in English proficiency are evident as well in the writing skills of Asians. Both in high school and in college, their writing skills are less proficient than those of their white classmates (Suzuki, 1989; Hsia, 1988).

Hsia (1988) indicates that in order to optimize their chances for financial aid and admissions, Asian high school students concentrate on advance-level courses in science and math and take fewer courses than do their non-Asian schoolmates in English and social

Table 7.3. Asian Passing Rates for First-Time Examinees on the California Basic Educational Skills Test.

School Year	Number Tested	Percentage Passing
1985–86	1125	62
1986–87	1257	61
1987–88	1012	62
1988–89	1133	62

Source: Majetic, 1989.

studies. This trend is particularly understandable among the immigrants who arrive in the United States with strong backgrounds in math and science but with limited English skills. Gravitating to their areas of strength, many concentrate on the fields and subjects that require limited classroom participation and written assignments. Some may also opt for careers in science and math because they feel that they will be judged more objectively in those fields. Hsia (1988) states that the contrast between Asian Americans' achievement in quantitative fields and their avoidance of and difficulties in fields that demand well-developed verbal skills is stark among recent immigrants and is still noticeable, even after several generations, among the native born.

Another variable that may inhibit Asians from considering teaching as a profession is a perceived lack of social skills. Some Asians have not sought or have not achieved a level of acculturation that would enable them to function comfortably in the social realms of the dominant culture. While these individuals are both comfortable and competent socially in their own cultural groups, they may feel uncomfortable or inept functioning in an environment that demands Western social skills. While some of these individuals may actually have adequate verbal and social skills to function as teachers, their own perceived lack of skills may inhibit serious consideration of a career in teaching.

Need for Asian and Pacific American Educators

APA educators are needed in our schools to serve a number of functions. As with other ethnic minority teachers, APA teachers serve as role models for APA children, as well as for children of other ethnic groups. The absence of APA teachers distorts social reality and is detrimental to both students and teachers of all ethnic groups (Chinn, 1988). The entire educational system suffers from the underrepresentation of teachers from APA and other ethnic groups. Minority teachers enrich their classrooms by contributing unique cultural characteristics.

For APA immigrant students, learning in school is complicated by their language differences. Asian bilingual teachers provide the primary- and secondary-language support necessary to facilitate

English language acquisition and academic learning for limited English proficient students. APA teachers can serve as mediators to assist their non-APA colleagues in identifying and implementing instructional strategies that are effective in working with Asian students and their parents. The educational system is likely to survive without APA educators, but with them the system will be more effective in serving the growing number of APA students in the United States.

The call for more APA teachers in the United States is based on the social, cultural, and linguistic needs that this group is equipped to address. In searching for ways to increase the number of APA teachers, we must look to the areas of recruitment and retention. As discussed earlier, APA students and their parents are less likely to select teaching as a career choice because of the low returns (salaries) for the amount of initial investment, insecurities related to oral and written language proficiency, and a general lack of information about the teaching profession. The following are recommendations to addressing the recruitment, training, and retention of APA teachers.

Early Identification and Recruitment

It is important to outreach potential teacher candidates at an early age. Information about a career in teaching should be available to students in junior high and high schools. School teachers and counselors play significant and influential roles in the lives of Asian American students, who view them as figures of authority, and therefore respect. With proper counseling, encouragement, and information, junior high and high school students may decide early on to pursue careers in education. School districts, state educational agencies, and universities should cooperate to establish and support "Future Teacher Clubs" at the junior and high school sites. Club activities could include tutoring of students in lower grades, pairing of students with teacher mentors who would serve as counselors or confidants, participation in Future Teacher Institutes during spring and summer breaks, and paid or unpaid internships to assist teachers in actual classrooms, which would also earn graduation credits.

In communities with Asian language newspapers, this medium may be an excellent source for reaching out to APAs. Many immigrants are college graduates and potential candidates for teacher education programs. California State University, Los Angeles, had a successful response to an effort to reach the Asian community. Reporters from Asian language newspapers were contacted and asked to run feature articles on teaching opportunities. A Saturday morning meeting was scheduled at the university and publicized in the articles. The meeting included a description of credential programs, admissions requirements, and employment opportunities. Several staff members from the admissions office were present, and transcripts were either evaluated that day or appointments were scheduled for a later date. The response to this recruitment effort was overwhelming. Similar efforts have the potential for deepening the pool of Asian teacher education candidates.

Provide Strong Academic Support at the Universities

Once identified and recruited, Asian teacher education candidates should be provided with support throughout their years in the university undergraduate and teacher education programs. A network of support that includes counseling, advisement, and tutoring needs to be available for each of the candidates, beginning with their freshman years at the universities. Students need to be carefully monitored for academic progress, and early intervention must be available for those who may be at risk.

Non-native English speaking students should be provided with extra help in the development of English speaking and literacy skills. English basic skills exams have been mandated by legislation in a number of states. Opportunities to practice and improve test taking with diagnostic feedback would help foreign-born Asian students pass the exams required for completion of teaching credentials or certificates.

Asian students who were born and raised in the United States may also need assistance to better develop their oral communication skills. Universities need to provide workshops and classes that assess areas of weakness and prescribe intervention strategies for each student.

Asian students should be paired with university faculty mentors who can provide guidance and advisement throughout the university years. Mentors would guide the students in taking the right courses in the right sequence and in submitting paperwork on time, and they would monitor for academic success or failure. Mentors working closely with students would be able to identify problems during the early stages and cooperatively find solutions.

Just as it is important to have positive teacher role models in the K-12 school system, it is equally important to have positive Asian faculty models at the universities. Universities and colleges need to hire faculty and administrators who share the cultural, social, and linguistic backgrounds of the target Asian teacher education students.

Asian students need to have an organization of peers for mutual support and sharing of ideas, frustrations, and successes. Student teacher clubs at the university level provide this kind of social network. The presence of a caring "family" of peers for mutual support could make the difference between success and failure.

Provide Incentives and Financial Support to Encourage Entry into the Teaching Profession

State and federal legislation must be enacted to provide low-interest and forgiveness loans as incentives for Asian American and other minority students to enter the teaching field. Students would be eligible for the loans after deciding on teaching as the objective of their university studies. The students would be allowed to apply for loans in their senior years in high school, to ensure that financial support would be available from the beginning of their freshman years at the universities. Students who successfully complete a teacher education program and become teachers in a public school system would be allowed to have a percentage of their loans reduced or forgiven for every year that they are employed as a teacher. An additional incentive for the recruitment of Asian and other minority teachers is to have state and federal governments reward colleges

and universities that make concerted efforts to increase the number
of minority graduates from their teacher education programs.

Give Credit for Teacher Education Coursework and Teaching Experience Overseas

Universities should recognize and accept coursework completed in
teacher education programs at colleges and universities overseas.
Many older, foreign-born Asian teacher education students were
previously teachers in their countries of origin. These foreign-born
bilingual teachers often are their native countries' best and brightest. Yet, many do not continue in the field of education in this
country because of the difficulties faced in trying to earn teaching
credentials. Owing to differences in how universities are structured
in other countries, many of the Asian teachers were certified at
"normal" or teacher training colleges rather than at four-year institutions. Their transcripts, when available, often indicate that
they have not earned a bachelor's degree or its equivalent. To enter
teacher education programs, especially in states that require an additional year beyond a bachelor's degree, Asian teachers are often
asked to first complete a bachelor's degree before concentrating on
a teacher education program. These candidates are often the sole
sources of financial support for their families and are unable to
devote two to five additional years to a bachelor's degree program.
Given the need and shortage of Asian bilingual-bicultural teachers
in the United States, this large pool of experienced teachers is not
being effectively tapped.

   Another source of potential bilingual-bicultural teachers is
the pool of Asian paraprofessionals who are already working in the
schools. Many of these individuals have teaching responsibilities in
the classrooms and are providing bilingual instruction to limited
English proficient students. There needs to be a career-ladder program with financial incentives to encourage this group of paraprofessionals to enter university teacher education programs.

Develop More Effective Programs to Enhance Social and Communication Skills

Schools that are content with overall high achievement and Scholastic Aptitude Test scores tend to overlook the relatively weak ver-

bal skills of Asian students. This attitude is unfortunate since early development of these skills can enhance social interaction with non-Asian peers and reduce the avoidance of courses out of the quantitative areas. The development of verbal skills, coupled with the acquisition of social skills, can enhance the likelihood of Asians branching out from their traditional areas of study and thus help in their recruitment into teacher education programs.

Unless schools help Asians to develop appropriate communicative and social skills, their education cannot be considered adequate. Even highly educated Asians with advanced degrees seldom advance beyond midmanagement positions in business and industry, and few Asians in higher education are appointed to administrative positions. While many charge that racial discrimination explains the lack of advancements, critics of Asians suggest that their limited verbal skills and social sophistication inhibit their upward mobility. If Asian American students develop these skills, the critics will either have to promote Asians or find other reasons or excuses for not doing so.

Conclusion

The problems related to the recruitment and retention of Asians into teacher education programs are complex and multifaceted. Clearly, Asians are a growing and significant segment of the nation's population, a trend that will continue in the decades to come. Educators can continue to complain about the declining enrollments of minorities in teacher education and can continue to do little to reverse the problem. Or they can develop and carry out proactive plans to address the problem. The leadership must come from education deans, state and district superintendents, and school board members. Unfortunately, most will choose to do nothing, and the ultimate losers will be our nation's children.

References

American Association of Colleges for Teacher Education. (1987). *Equity and teacher education.* Unpublished manuscript, Washington, DC.

American Association of Colleges for Teacher Education. (1990). *AACTE/Metropolitan Life survey of teacher education students.* Washington, DC: AACTE.

Brand, D. (1987). The whiz kids. *Time, 130*(9), 42–51.

Cabezas, A., Shinagawa, L., and Kawaguchi, G. (1986–1987). New inquiries into the socioeconomic status of Filipino Americans in California in 1980. *Amerasia Journal, 13*, 1–21.

Chan, S. Q. (1986). Parents of exceptional Asian children. In M. K. Kitano and P. C. Chinn (eds.), *Exceptional Asian children and youth.* Reston, VA: Council for Exceptional Children.

Chinn, P. C. (1988). The ethnic minority educator: Near extinction? *Teacher Education and Practice, 4*(2), 15–17.

Crystal, D. (1989). Asian Americans and the myth of the model minority. *Social Casework, 70*, 405–413.

Hsia, J. (1988). *Asian Americans in higher education and at work.* Hillsdale, NJ: Erlbaum.

Hsia, J., and Hirano-Nakanishi, M. (1989). The demographics of diversity: Asian Americans and higher education. *Change,* Nov.-Dec., 20–27.

Jiobu, R. M. (1988). *Ethnicity and assimilation.* Albany: State University of New York Press.

Johnson, D. L., Levin, M. J., and Paisano, E. L. (1988). *We the Asian and the Pacific Islander Americans.* U.S. Department of Commerce, Bureau of the Census. Washington, DC: Government Printing Office.

Kim, B.L.C. (1973). Asian Americans: No model minority. *Social Work, 18*, 44–53.

Lujan, H. D. (1989). Asian Americans and the quality of education: A policy view. In G. M. Nomura, R. Endo, S. H. Sumida, and R. C. Long (eds), *Frontiers of Asian American studies.* Pullman: Washington State University Press.

Majetic, R. M. (1989). *California basic educational skills test: Annual report of examination results.* Sacramento: State of California Commission on Teacher Credentialing.

Minatoya, L. Y., and Sedlacek, W. E. (1981). Another look at the melting pot: Perceptions of Asian American undergraduates. *Journal of College Student Personnel, 22*(4), 328–336.

Nee, V., and Sanders, J. (1985). The road to parity: Determinants of the socioeconomic achievement of Asian Americans. *Ethnic and Racial Studies, 28,* 281–306.

Peng, S. S. (1985). *Enrollment patterns of Asian American students in postsecondary education.* Paper presented at the annual meeting of the American Educational Research Association, Chicago.

Ramist, L., and Arbeiter, S. (1984). *Profiles: College-bound seniors, 1982.* New York: College Entrance Examination Board.

Rumbaut, R. G., and Ima, K. (1987). *The adaptation of southeast Asian refugee youth: A comparative study.* Final Report to the Office of Refugee Resettlement. San Diego, CA: San Diego State University.

Sing, B. (ed.). (1989). *Asian Pacific Americans.* Los Angeles: National Conference of Christians and Jews.

Snyder, T. D. (1989). *Digest of education statistics, 1987.* Washington, DC: Center for Education Statistics.

Sue, S., and Sue, D. W. (1973). Chinese-American personality and mental health. In S. Sue and N. N. Wagner (eds.), *Asian-Americans, psychological perspectives.* Palo Alto, CA: Science and Behavior Books.

Suzuki, B. H. (1989). *Asian Americans in higher education: A research agenda for the 1990s and beyond.* Paper presented at the conference Educating One-Third of a Nation: What Works, American Council on Education, San Francisco.

Tseng, W. (1973). The concept of personality in Confucian thought. *Psychiatry, 50,* 76–86.

U.S. Bureau of the Census. Information provided by J. Wong, Los Angeles office, during telephone interview, November 14, 1989.

Vetter, B. M., and Babco, E. L. (1984). *Professional women and minorities: A manpower data resource service.* (5th ed.) Washington, DC: Scientific Manpower Commission.

Winkler, K. J. (1985). Rigor is urged in preparation of new teachers. *Chronicle of Higher Education,* Mar. 6, pp. 13–21.

Winnick, L. (1990). America's model minority. *Commentary, 90,* 22–29.

Zapata, J. T. (1988). Impact of testing on Hispanic teacher candidates. *Teacher Education and Practice, 4*(2), 19–23.

8

Accommodating the Minority Teacher Candidate: Non-Black Students in Predominantly Black Colleges

Johnnie Ruth Mills
Cozetta W. Buckley

Why is the cultural diversity issue important to effective educational reform? Why must predominantly black schools, colleges, and departments of education provide for non-black minority students in restructuring their teacher education programs? Burstein and Cabello (1989, p. 9) have offered what might be considered a bottom-line response to these questions: "With the increasing population of culturally diverse students, particularly in urban areas, and given our failure to provide successful school experiences for those students, there is a critical need for teacher education programs to equip teachers with knowledge and skill to work with the culturally diverse."

The restructuring of programs to educate and better prepare teachers for the vast diversity of students in today's schools is no longer a frill. It is a must for all schools, colleges, and departments of education (Anderson, 1988; Backus, 1984; Fleming, 1981; Mungo, 1989; and Scollon, 1981). Implicit in this challenge is the need for these programs (1) to know how to successfully confront the diversity that the teacher candidates themselves bring to the university culture and (2) to seize the opportunities that diverse student populations present to model cultural pluralism in the education process.

This chapter examines the restructuring that must take place within predominantly black schools, colleges, and departments of education to accommodate non-black—in particular, white—teacher candidates, who represent a steadily growing minority on these campuses. To limit the restructuring of teacher education units on black campuses solely to the altruistic purpose of accommodating white minorities, however, would be to circumvent altogether the true goal of current reform efforts. The ultimate purpose of this chapter is to further encourage the delivery of quality education in our nation's schools by all teachers for all youth.

A major assumption of this chapter is that the restructuring of teacher education programs in schools, colleges, and departments of education, especially those at predominantly black institutions, must reflect a sensitivity to cross-cultural understanding, cultural pluralism in the treatment of white minorities, and the preparation of white teachers for a multicultural society. In order to achieve this sensitivity, white candidates must be taught to learn in culturally different environments as preprofessionals and to teach in culturally diverse classrooms as professionals—issues seldom addressed by educators. Ideas for how these two objectives might be accomplished are provided throughout this chapter. Although the ideas are appropriate for candidates of all racial and ethnic backgrounds, they are considered fundamental in the acculturation and training of whites who, prior to enrolling in predominantly black institutions, have had limited contact with blacks.

There is no desire here to minimize in any way the importance of continuing to recruit and train black and other minority teachers. Rather, the intent is to acknowledge reality. Black teachers in particular are fast disappearing from the profession, causing an imbalance in the ratio of black teachers to black public school students. At the same time, it is generally recognized that a growing population of white students is going into teaching from both predominantly white and black teacher education programs (Mungo, 1989; Burstein and Cabello, 1989). To offset the adverse impact of this situation on non-white students (Anderson, 1988), every effort must be made to ensure that all teachers understand the role of diverse cultures in the teaching-learning process and the role of self as a cultural being and navigator of culture. Predominantly black institutions, because of their growing participation in the education of white teachers, have an opportunity to utilize their experience and resources to help teacher candidates become proficient in both cross-cultural understanding and navigation of the culture of the black children whom they will be entrusted to educate.

The presence of whites on black campuses represents reverse desegregation. Just as efforts continue to be made by white institutions to accommodate the cultural differences of the blacks who desegregate their campuses, so too must the same be done for the white minority by black institutions. Effective accommodation will in large measure depend on how well the cultural lifeways of these white teacher candidates are understood and given consideration during their education.

An existing myth is that white lifeways, because of the group's dominance historically, need not be analyzed. The common misperception is that everyone knows about "them." Nothing could be further from the truth. Moreover, the lack of cross-cultural knowledge and the presence of ethnocentric attitudes, which leads to acts of prejudice and racism when left unchallenged, can sabotage the academic accomplishments of all ethnic groups, including blacks. According to Pate (1981), knowledge alone does not reduce prejudice; knowledge is a prerequisite of prejudice reduction, not the sole means. Strategies that address these deficits beg attention.

It is instructive to note that the phenomenon of white minorities on black campuses induces a type of culture shock for both the whites and the blacks involved (Bellamy, 1982). The minority whites are thrust into new roles that require an understanding of not only the "white self" in a new environment but also the "black other" and the unfamiliar institutional culture. Often, at least initially, the shock experienced by white teacher candidates on black campuses is exacerbated by less than positive, daily interactions with black students and faculty. The consequence of these interactions for whites is that they either stop growing academically or leave the institutions (Standley, 1978). It is not unthinkable that the negative feelings of the uninformed will later find their way into classroom interactions with students.

White Minorities on Black Campuses:
Retrospective and Current Context

The enrollment of most whites at predominantly black institutions has resulted from federal mandates that link eligibility for federal funds to desegregation of the institutions. A few studies from the late 1970s and early 1980s documented the effects of the mandates on predominantly black campuses as well as the attitudes and perceptions of whites who enrolled in black institutions during those early years. These reports support the information presented in this chapter. Reviews of selected seminal studies, findings from two recent investigations, our experience, and expert opinion are provided as background to the recommendations in the conclusion of this chapter.

Bellamy (1982) explored several questions in his study of reverse desegregation at Fort Valley State College in Georgia. Among them were, Why have white students elected to enroll at traditionally black institutions? What was Fort Valley's response to reverse desegregation? As Bellamy reported, a majority of the white students at Fort Valley said that they enrolled primarily because of convenience. They also cited such reasons as curriculum, scholarships, and affordable costs. Bellamy ultimately concluded that a definite relationship existed between the undergraduate white enrollment and financial aid awards. Foremost among Fort Valley's strategies to attract white students were the addition of new curriculum offerings, changes in the racial mix of the faculty, improvements in the physical plant, and provision of financial aid.

Standley (1978) surveyed white students at twenty predominantly black colleges and universities to ascertain their perceptions of and attitudes toward their own educational experiences and their impact on the institutions and to provide useful data for university decision makers. Despite positive feelings about their instructors, their own personal growth in understanding cultural diversity, and their overall educational experiences, a majority felt that administrators did not exert leadership in recruiting non-black students. Moreover, all of the students expressed feelings of ambiguity about their sense of belonging and their interpersonal relations on the black campuses. A majority of the students did not consider race a deterrent to learning.

Smith (1973) studied eighteen preprofessional white students enrolled in the Cross-Cultural Experience Program sponsored by the Carnegie Foundation. The program was held on the campus of Florida A&M University, in cooperation with the University of Florida, and was designed to integrate southern white students into a predominantly black university. Smith's study explored the changes in attitudes of white participants resulting from their exposure to a variety of planned interactions with black students and faculty. The investigation confirmed the merit of the contact theory for changing racial attitudes. "Pre- and post-test data validated that the students' attitudes toward Blacks became more positive over time" (Smith, 1973, p. 629). Smith concluded that the program helped the white students to prepare for their roles as minorities and to work "sensitively and responsibly" in a black majority situation.

Brown and Stein (1972) surveyed 23 percent of white students enrolled at the five predominantly black colleges of North Carolina to determine their expectations and experiences as minorities on black campuses and to assess whether special orientation programs were needed to facilitate their adjustment. From the data collected, Brown constructed general profiles of white male and female students, which he considered representative of white students on any black campus. Among his findings were that (1) males aspired for degrees beyond the bachelor's degree more frequently than did females, (2) a larger percentage of females chose teaching as a career than did males, (3) 81 percent of the respondents did not enroll in a black college immediately after graduation from high school, (4) the impressions of males regarding black colleges and universities were more positive than were those of females, (5) males expressed greater satisfaction than did females with the quality of instruction, their professors, and levels of social acceptance, (6) a large percentage of both males and females agreed that they would be more comfortable reciting in class if they were black and resented being asked to enroll in black studies courses, and (7) both male and females preferred to approach individually professors, academic advisers, and friends about academic and social problems and opposed an initial formal orientation program for white students.

Recently, we pursued two investigations designed to build on the knowledge base pioneered by these earlier studies. Our work provides a contemporary glimpse of the white minority problem on black campuses. The following are detailed summaries of these two studies.

Alpha Study

Alpha Study, initiated in 1989, is the first part of an ongoing, two-part investigation into the minority problems confronting predominantly black schools, colleges, and departments of education. The study seeks to determine the extent to which the nontraditional minority (that is, the white minority) problem exists today and to field-test the survey instrument and procedures to be used in the second and more comprehensive part of the investigation. Preliminary findings from this pilot study appear to confirm earlier reports of increasing numbers of white students in teacher education programs on black campuses and yield information that could advance the institutional restructuring needed to better educate them.

Unlike past studies that surveyed student expectations, opinions, and perceptions of their experiences, Alpha Study surveyed deans and directors of selected historically black schools, colleges, and departments of education to ascertain their perceptions relative to the current status of nontraditional minority students on their respective campuses. The sample was limited to the members of the Black Collegian Research Consortium, consisting of deans and directors of teacher education programs in historically black colleges and universities located primarily in the southeast United States. The thirteen institutions represented in the survey constitute 15 percent of the eighty-nine historically black colleges and universities nationwide that train teachers. The exploratory nature of the study and the small number of respondents compared to the total number of predominantly black colleges and universities limited sophisticated data analysis and the generalizability of findings. Nonetheless, the data collected were sufficient to warrant further investigation in this area of inquiry.

Specifically, Alpha Study sought information from predominantly black schools, colleges, and departments of education in the following categories: institutional characteristics, characteristics of teacher training, factors contributing to white enrollment, white enrollment trends, white students' programs, and special support services for white students. Findings in each of these categories are briefly reported below.

The enrollments of participating institutions ranged from less than 1,500 to over 6,000 students, with a majority exceeding 3,000. Enrollments in undergraduate teacher education programs were between 150 to over 450 students, while enrollments for graduate programs were generally less than 450 students. Although white students represented the largest minority population on the campuses surveyed, they represented less than 15 percent of the total enrollment at a majority of the institutions. Degrees in education were offered by all thirteen of the institutions, but graduate programs beyond the master's level were offered on only two campuses.

One aspect of the Alpha Study concentrated on motivational factors influencing white student enrollment at historically black institutions. We found that the most critical factors affecting nontraditional minority student enrollment were special incentives, focused recruitment strategies, quality of graduates, cost, and location.

Enrollments of whites varied across the sample campuses, with no significant trend or pattern apparent. While several respondents reported increases in enrollments at both the undergraduate and graduate levels, one reported a decrease in white student enrollment and others noted that enrollments were stabilizing.

The enrollments of other minorities (Hispanics, American Indians, and Asians) were minimal on all campuses. Hispanics outnumbered American Indians and Asians, but the trends for both undergraduate and graduate programs were decreasing Hispanic enrollments and more or less stabilized enrollments for American Indians and Asians.

Twelve sociocultural problems grounded in feelings and attitudes and known to occasion the desegregation of monocultural environments (Mills, 1986) were presented to the respondents. They were instructed to select the problems that they perceived as operant on their campuses. These problems included isolation, perceived discrimination, communication and language barriers, presence (how teachers present themselves to students, for example, through dress, mannerisms), student aggression, instructional grievances, conflicting value differences, student-faculty conflict, student-student conflict, disrespect for blacks, failure to follow traditional norms, and powerlessness.

Of the twelve problems identified, four were not perceived to exist on any of the campuses surveyed: presence, student aggression, student-faculty conflict, and student-student conflict. The problems perceived to exist most frequently were disrespect for blacks, failure to follow traditional norms, perceived discrimination, and conflicting value differences.

The provision of special and academic support services has been a critical element in the recruitment of nontraditional minority students to predominantly black institutions. To assess the current importance of this factor, the respondents were asked to select from a menu of eight academic support services usually provided to accommodate minority students. Among those services claimed most frequently were counseling services and multicultural course content.

In summary, the enrollment of white students on black campuses appeared to result from such motivational factors as special incentives, focused recruitment, quality of graduates, cost, and location. A majority of the respondents agreed that white enrollments on black campuses were increasing, Hispanic enrollments were on the decline, and enrollments among other minorities were stable. The greatest perceived problem on the campuses was the lack of respect that whites had for blacks. Finally, the respondents identified counseling services and the integration of multicultural course content as the special and academic support services most frequently provided for minority students.

Beta Study

The earlier work of Mills (1986) on cross-cultural conflict in higher education is important to present restructuring challenges and serves as another major source of data on nontraditional minority students. We refer to this work as Beta Study to distinguish it from the author's most recent work on nontraditional minorities. Beta

Study focused on the explicit and implicit culture-bound behaviors and perceptions of instructors and students and delimited the issues of cultural conflict in higher education. Participants from seventy-three public and private institutions, representing thirty-five states selected on the basis of size, geographical location, and governance structure, responded to the survey. A total of 516 problem descriptions were collected from 314 students representing various ethnic and racial groups, and 307 descriptions were collected from 103 culturally diverse instructors.

Generally, this study found that both students and educators considered personality differences to be the leading cause of cross-cultural conflict in higher education. The respondents suggested as well that in higher education conflict occurs a majority of the time in regular classroom situations with people who significantly differ, first, in racial background; second, in gender; and, third, in age. Beta Study also revealed the following:

1. Cross-cultural conflict results from differences in the values attached to moral rules, proper dress, equality of opportunity and treatment, personal integrity, fairness, individual flexibility, and tolerance.
2. Culturally diverse students tend to distrust the motives, attitudes, and behaviors of educators in cross-cultural learning situations.
3. The most significant communication problems between culturally diverse students and educators include age differences, accents, speaking styles, nonverbal messages, and dialects.
4. The specifics of who educates and who learns in terms of age, handicaps, and social distance affect not only the level of perceived cross-cultural conflict but also the learning behavior and academic progress of students.
5. Cross-cultural conflicts appear to occur most frequently between and within black and white subcultural groups.

Toward Restructuring to Accommodate Cultural Diversity

Austin (1986) suggested that teachers are culturally illiterate and blind. She noted that when faced with cross-cultural situations, teachers often experience fear, confusion, anger, and despair. The possible ill effects of these negative feelings on the education process renders them appropriate targets of cultural literacy training. The need is for teachers to understand their students and themselves as well. They must understand how their backgrounds affect their instructional behaviors and relations with students (Mills, 1986).

Some of the cultural dimensions of teachers are personality, values, social backgrounds, self-concepts, motivations, fears, courage, comfort, personal deficits, loneliness, and feelings of power or powerlessness (Anderson, 1988). These implicit dimensions, together with explicit factors such as age, sex, class, race, and physical handicaps, typify the cultural baggage that educators, as well as students, bring to learning situations. Essentially, culture is the ultimate source of the rules by which teachers consciously and unconsciously operate as they design and deliver instruction, set role expectations for themselves and students, assign value to students' contributions, and interpret the behavior of students.

Culture also influences teachers in other, less transparent ways. Manifestations of this influence are observable in the respect given, rewards and punishments handed out, and status assigned to students, as well as in the power shared with them (Mills, 1986). From the perspective of students, culture is also the filter through which they process educators, instruction, and subject matter.

The literature supports the notion that while students must learn to adjust to the culture and subcultures of academic environments, so too must such environments be restructured to accommodate students, in this case, white minority teacher candidates. Additionally, although many institutions of higher learning recruit minority students, they continue to operate traditional programs. Research findings indicate that adjustment to culturally diverse students is difficult for most educators as well as for most institutional administrators (Fleming, 1981; Tippeconnic, 1983; Scollon, 1981; Jenkins, 1983; Anderson, 1988). Our guess is that these findings also represent conditions at predominantly black institutions that are faced with educating white teacher candidates.

Restructuring Considerations and Recommendations

Teacher education programs are shaped by a number of factors both within and outside of schools, colleges, and departments of education. Institutional norms and processes, curriculum, learning environment, and the nature of instruction by general education and professional education faculty are among the most critical building blocks. Findings from our Alpha and Beta studies, the research literature, and our own experiences confirm that a restructuring to accommodate white students must take these building blocks into consideration. Given the difficulty that historically black institutions may encounter in the restructuring process to accommodate white teacher candidates, recommendations that address the "how to" issues of restructuring are offered in the remainder of this chapter.

Institutional Norms and Processes

The accommodation of white teacher candidates is not just the problem of schools, colleges, and departments of education. Rather, like teacher education, it is an institutional responsibility. Under normal conditions, these nontraditional education majors will interact with the entire campus, including people, processes, resources, and facilities. Institutional norms and processes tend to shape programs, student life, and academic outcomes campuswide. It seems safe to conclude, then, that they also can determine the success or failure of any restructuring efforts within individual units of the institution.

To accommodate whites in predominantly black teacher education units, restructuring should begin at the institutional level and permeate every aspect of the campus environment. It should involve the adjustment of an institution's mission and goals, with concomitant changes in the goals and objectives of all academic and support units, and guide the establishment and maintenance of policies and accountability measures that reflect commitment to a culturally pluralistic campus climate, campuswide academic support systems to promote sensitivity to the special needs of minority students, and internal monitoring and evaluation systems of all such restructuring efforts and outcomes.

Whatever the restructuring attempted, careful management of change in the institution is crucial. Change of this magnitude requires credible leadership that is both structured and systematic. Ideally, this leadership should be assigned to one or more individuals who are held accountable for achieving a set of specified goals and objectives: (1) ensuring cooperation and collaboration among all units at the institution, (2) serving as an advisory body to campus units and central administration, and (3) facilitating cross-cultural understanding among faculty, staff, and students. The dynamics of change for cross-cultural purposes suggest that a culturally diverse team provides the most effective leadership for accomplishing these objectives.

Mission and Goals

There is likely a lack of emphasis on providing for white students in the mission statements of most predominantly black institutions. The special historical and monocultural purposes for which they were first established might preclude such comprehensiveness.

Thus, once the responsibility for leadership is assigned, attention should be given to adjusting the institution's mission and goals. Subsequent and more definitive objectives will derive from this guiding philosophical base. Additionally, these guides are fundamental to clarifying the purpose of restructuring and related activities. While it is impossible here to recommend specific mission and goal statements, examples of necessary components include preparation of all students for living and working in a culturally diverse society, recognition of changing demographics and protection of the rights of the cultural and ethnic minorities who represent these changes, cultural pluralism as demonstrated through an instructional philosophy that capitalizes on the backgrounds of students and responsive pedagogy in promoting cognitive development, and provision of equal opportunities to all students to experience education in a pluralistic society and cross-cultural learning environment (American Association of Colleges for Teacher Education, 1991).

The new mission and philosophy should be well articulated, and activities to advance their acceptance and institutionalization campuswide must be implemented as soon as possible. Systematic orientation of all appropriate role groups on campus (administrators, faculty, and support unit staff), followed by translation of the new mission statement into specific unit goals and objectives, seem to hold the greatest promise for generating acceptance of white minorities and action to affirm this acceptance. Orientation should (1) be more than a one-time affair and should occur as often as needed, (2) be for informational purposes rather than skill building, (3) provide for input by participants as well as output by session leaders, (4) set the stage for subsequent staff and program development, and (5) be responsive to the variability of academic, support, and administrative circumstances of institutional units.

Policy and Accountability

One of the most salient supporting roles that the central administration of predominantly black institutions can provide teacher education units is to back their efforts to accommodate white teaching majors through the passage of appropriate institutional policies. Discrimination, shared power, access, extracurricular activities, plans for addressing cultural diversity and infusing multicultural education into the curriculum are among the most crucial areas for policy development. Each has a well-defined set of issues that are popularly associated with minorities in majority situations. Further, it is predictable that, without adequate policies, there will be those who seek to influence change negatively as it pertains to accommodating white minorities in these areas.

The intent of institutional administrators should be to hold all units accountable for the "letter and the spirit of whatever policies that evolve" (Elmore and McLaughlin, 1982, p. 173). When policies fail, they do so either because people have not done what the policy prescribed or because people have done what the policy requires and the expected results have not followed (Elmore and McLaughlin, 1982). Preventive strategies for these two outcomes necessarily include putting into place special accountability measures campuswide. Since these measures are most effective when tailored to the unique new policies of individual institutions, we cannot explore this matter in detail here.

Implementation of cross-cultural institutional policies and enforcement of compliance with the policies are formidable accountability tasks that require support at the institutional level in three areas. First, administrators must ensure that all representative groups have participated in the policy development process. This democratic approach exacts a degree of ownership from those who have implementation and monitoring responsibilities. Second, each policy should have a set of related guidelines and regulations that spells out procedures, offers accurate interpretations for practical application, and is able to withstand legal scrutiny. Third, efforts must be made to provide all campus units with the resources needed to comply with the new policies. Simply put, additional financial and technical assistance will be needed.

Academic Support Systems

Regardless of the setting, when one assumes minority membership (traditional or nontraditional), that person's level of power is diminished. Most often, the person will be outnumbered and confounded by a majority of dissimilar cultural backgrounds, communication systems, and behavioral norms. In fact, minorities can anticipate exposure to ambiguous expectations, racial stereotypes, racist treatment, and general nonacceptance by others. It should occasion no surprise, therefore, that exposure of this nature is likely to have a grave impact on the academic performance of white students and the black institution's capacity to retain them in its programs.

Our Alpha and Beta studies found that special academic support systems are definitely needed for all students in minority situations, although what the exact nature of this support should be was not entirely clear. Expert opinion, coupled with logic and deductive reasoning, suggests that white minorities on black campuses can benefit most from academic support systems that provide increased understanding of the black culture, regularly scheduled cross-cultural counseling sessions, cross-cultural peer and faculty mentoring programs, and easy access to cross-cultural information and curriculum materials.

Earlier studies indicated that the white student on the predominantly black campus typically is older than the black students, usually married, lives off campus, and tends to be academically competent (Standley, 1978; Baptiste, Baptiste, and Gollnick, 1980; Grant, Sahol, and Sleeter, 1980). If this profile is valid, the design of the academic support systems described above should reflect, among other things, consideration of the nonacademic responsibilities of students, the convenience of times that support services are offered, and the cultural sophistication of faculty and peer student counselors. Additionally, special efforts should be made to help students develop successful cross-cultural relationships in both academic and social activities.

The white minority recruiter, an existing position on many black campuses, can do a great deal to advance recommended support systems. Not only are these recruiters usually the first to come in contact (during recruitment) with the white students who will enroll in black institutions, but also they can use the racial bonds that they share to increase the comfort levels of these students. Well-seasoned recruiters may also serve as resource persons for counselors, mentors, and the students themselves. For example, they may assist in placing white students with counselors and mentors, monitor the students' progress, and lead special orientation sessions, workshops, and seminars. In the double role of recruiter and resource person, they become much-needed bridges between cultures.

Curriculum

Educators agree that multicultural education should be integrated into the content and methods courses and into the clinical experiences of teaching majors (Banks, 1977; Gay, 1977; Kohut, 1980; Burstein and Cabello, 1989; Mills, 1983, 1984). The National Council for Accreditation of Teacher Education (NCATE) and the American Association of Colleges for Teacher Education are among the major professional organizations that also endorse this integration as a standard for program design. NCATE, in particular, currently requires that multicultural education be addressed in courses, seminars, and clinical experiences. For present purposes, multicultural education means a philosophy and process by which schools, colleges, and departments of education demonstrate acceptance and respect for human diversity. It means that the program is sensitive to more than the skin colors, backgrounds, and religious beliefs of people. Rather, the curriculum must educate teachers in a manner that supports the elimination of classism, racism, sexism, ageism, and handicappism.

According to Galluzzo and Arends (1989), the typical curriculum for training elementary teachers consists of the following: fifty-eight credits in general studies, forty-two credits in professional preparation, twenty credits in an academic concentration or minor, and twelve credits in student teaching. Secondary teaching majors, on the other hand, complete approximately fifty-four credits in general studies, thirty-nine credits in an academic major, twenty credits in a minor, seven credits in methods courses, nine credits in foundations courses, and twelve credits in student teaching. Galluzzo and Arends also found that early clinical requirements, measured in clock hours, included 166 hours for special education majors, 140 hours for early childhood and elementary education majors, and 90 hours for secondary teaching majors.

Despite the need to infuse multicultural content throughout the teacher education curriculum, three special areas stand out as ripe for initial restructuring efforts (see Mills, 1983, 1984):

General Studies or Academic Foundation Courses. These courses should (1) offer in-depth historical, sociological, and psychological information about various ethnic and cultural groups, (2) utilize comparative content and modes of instruction, (3) employ at least one cultural universal model so that students have a standard framework from which to study various groups, and (4) include (without exception) comparative information about whites, blacks, Hispanics, Asian Americans, and American Indians or other major groups in the immediate community.

Professional Preparation Courses. The curriculum area in which students are instructed in the methodologies of teaching should have as a major focus the design, development, and delivery of instruction for diverse learner populations. In addition, it should (1) analyze the effects of ethnicity and culture on the social interactive behaviors of teachers and pupils in educational settings, (2) utilize comparative content and modes of instruction, (3) include comparative information and teacher training activities that focus on major ethnic minorities and cultural groups, (4) show evidence of planned, hands-on activities other than the tasting of ethnic foods and visits to ethnic ghettos, and (5) provide a coherent and philosophical methodological framework for organizing multicultural education curricula.

Field-Based Experiences. Kohut (1980) found that preservice teachers who experienced instruction and interaction with culturally different learners became less prejudiced than did those who received only instruction. In fact, the latter group was found to be more prejudiced following instruction. The work of both Kohut (1980) and Smith (1973) substantiate the merits of cultural contact in helping people to gain respect for cultural diversity. Early, supervised clinical experiences and student teaching are the best vehicles for incorporating cultural contact into the professional curriculum for teachers. These experiences should at least include both a knowledge component and a skills development component, as recommended in the literature. Both components should stress development of the preservice teacher's talent in assessment, curriculum development, instruction, and evaluation of culturally diverse students (Burstein and Cabello, 1989). During field experiences, students should be required to demonstrate their competence in these areas as they work with students.

Activities that generally support academic growth were identified by Kohut (1980) for preservice teachers, but they are also applicable to the specialized training needs of nontraditional minorities. Included among Kohut's suggested activities are practice at day-care centers and schools, volunteer work with children in hospitals, counseling and tutoring in juvenile detention centers, and involvement in community-sponsored youth projects. Additional field-based experiences may include voluntary teaching in Sunday schools, peer tutoring, assisting with special projects that involve the training of parents, and interning with business organizations that have employee training programs. Of course, emphasis should be on placement in environments with large, culturally diverse populations. For nontraditional minorities such as whites, special efforts should be made to ensure continuous, intensive interactions with blacks.

As with areas previously discussed, there are recommended guidelines for implementing field-based training for nontraditional minorities. First, this aspect of the training should be supervised by persons who respect cultural diversity and can demonstrate this respect in the classroom. Second, provisions should be made to have students reflect on each field experience as soon as possible after its occurrence in a guided discussion led by qualified faculty members. Discussions should be designed to help the students understand their observations and feelings, the linkage between theory and practice, and the role that culture played in the experience. Third, the students should be provided opportunities for multiple field-based experiences throughout the training program in a variety of settings.

To facilitate infusion of multicultural education into field-based experiences, the revision of selected courses may be necessary. Course revision should include expansion of course objectives to embrace multicultural concepts and methods for teaching culturally diverse populations, incorporation of course activities that require students to apply relevant concepts and skills in teaching and problem solving, design of parallel observation and participation activities in the schools for reflection and discussion, and adjustment of course examinations to cover related concept formation and application skills.

Learning Environment

The responsibility that historically black schools, colleges, and departments of education have to white students extends beyond admission to an institution (Mills, 1986). Commitment to and demonstration of respect for cultural diversity should exist throughout the total learning environment. Very often, institutional operations appear grounded in rigidity and universalism. One merely has to look at the nationwide standardization of curriculum models, schedules, credit-hour structures, program degree designs, instructional models, and symbolic communication patterns.

The restructuring of learning environments for white minorities should ensure that these students see themselves as being accepted, participating, deciding on their own needs, and being informed. In essence, they must not perceive themselves as isolated. Effective restructuring activities include anticipating students' unrestrained curiosity about cultural diversity by building a climate of trust that allows them to comfortably explore explicit and implicit differences and similarities among people; fostering several two-way channels of communication between educators and students, or between blacks and whites, so that if one channel becomes clogged, other conduits for feedback are available; facilitating a free-flowing exchange of information as a preventive approach to cross-cultural conflict; and allowing individuals to negotiate a mutual culture of learning with each newly formed academic work group or for each new situation.

Instruction

Because educators are cultural beings through whom curriculum concepts are sifted and communicated during instruction, it is conceivable that instruction is largely culture-bound behavior reflecting the beliefs and attitudes of the educators who design and implement it. Understandably, then, some white students and black educators find the instructional process a direct source of cross-cultural conflict (Mills, 1986).

Both research and experience point to several sensitive areas for personal reflection and exploration by educators who must accommodate the cultural diversity of blacks and whites during instruction. Mills (1986, pp. 38–39) composed a list of these areas:

1. The teacher's expectations and standards for
   a. Teacher-student interactions
   b. Dress, cleanliness, and beauty
   c. How students should think
   d. Appropriate learning behavior
   e. Self-expression
   f. Minority and majority students in class
   g. What students should do in their free time
2. The teacher's personal definition of
   a. Intellectual brightness
   b. Effort
   c. Respect for authority
   d. Academic honesty and dishonesty
   e. Successful learning

     f.   Maturity
     g.   Beauty, ugliness (physical features)
     h.   Egalitarianism
3. The teacher's way of
     a.   Handling fear, frustration, and conflict
     b.   Communicating acceptance and rejection
     c.   Using and handling humor
     d.   Manipulating people
     e.   Showing power and authority
     f.   Doing more for students than what the job calls for
     g.   Dealing with emotions (happiness, sadness, disappointment, and so on) of others and self
4. The teacher's feelings about
     a.   Who or what is responsible for the academic unpreparedness of some students
     b.   The type of student who is worthy of the teacher's high esteem
5. The teacher's preference for
     a.   Treating students the same or treating them differently
     b.   Assigning group or individual learning activities
     c.   Being a minority or being poor
     d.   Teaching aggressive or docile students
     e.   Dark or bright colors

Most instruction today derives from monocultural models designed for monocultural groups of students. These models are no longer relevant for what is proposed in this chapter; they are naturally challenged by the culturally diverse backgrounds of students and educators. Alternative models of instruction are needed.

Staff Development

Alpha Study suggested that few predominantly black schools, colleges, and departments of education offer development programs for faculty and university staff who work with white minorities. Yet, there is support for these programs as a fundamental step toward ensuring positive academic and social outcomes for these students (Baker, 1983). The ultimate goal, however, should be to help faculty and staff develop the expertise needed to provide multicultural education to all students in teacher education.

Since culture comprises the complex social systems of people and their lifeways, staff development in this area is a delicate intervention. Values, norms, language, ethnicity, sex, age, and beliefs are all areas known to frequently evoke such consequences as pain, defensiveness, anger, rejection, and failure. At a minimum, staff development should be designed around experiences that enhance the development of teachers in the three domains identified by Mills (1986, p. 45): "Affective Domain-Experiences which cultivate the attitudes of acceptance and respect for worth, dignity, and integrity of various groups and individuals. Cognitive Domain Experiences which expand knowledge and understanding of various ethnic groups and culturally diverse individuals, including the explicit and implicit characteristics of their lifeways. Interpersonal Interactions-Experiences which develop skill in communication and behaving appropriately with the culturally diverse."

To omit an exploration of white culture in staff development sessions for university personnel and in the teacher preparation curriculum is to engage in programmatic sabotage. Despite the fact that America continues to be controlled by the white cultural majority, opportunities for members and nonmembers to gain a clearer understanding of this culture are necessary. The assumption that the longevity or pervasiveness of white culture breeds understanding of it is naive. Members and nonmembers of the white majority need to recognize that, like other cultural groups, white culture too is a composite of many subcultures, each with its own distinguishing ethics, lifeways, and artifacts. One has only to ask people who consider themselves members to compare stories of their childhoods. The cultural patterns reflected in these stories will be very different in most instances. Thus, when the term *culturally different* is used, reference is to differences between two or more patterned lifeways, not to skin color or race. It is important that staff developers distinguish the characteristics of those varying lifeways within the majority culture.

Indications are that another fundamental challenge for education faculty and students involves learning how to demonstrate their acceptance of individual differences in appropriate ways. Concrete ideas with immediate application and results may be necessary to help them see the need for adjusting their instructional behaviors.

The following techniques for accommodating cultural differences during instruction are recommended (Mills, 1986):

1. Initiate each new classroom situation by negotiating with students a subculture of learning to fit the needs of that particular group. Be sure that everyone's expectations are made public. The negotiating process should include these elements of a culture: value system, worldview, social organization, academic technology, form of governance, language, and key components of the educational process for the new subculture.

2. Implement a system of checks and balances by frequently conducting, with the assistance of students, short-term action research on students' perceptions of verbal and nonverbal putdowns, sarcasm, and inappropriate use of humor. Students may tally or list instances of each behavior that occur during instructor-student interactions over a specified period of time. A reporting system that allows discussion and clarification of misperceptions should be made available to students.

3. Distinguish publicly personal opinions from facts and give students the option to agree or disagree. Teachers' and students' opinions are closely tied to their cultural backgrounds and lifeways. To deny students options is to force them to assume another's culture without having an experiential point of reference.

4. Strive to see oneself as actually seen by students, not as one desires to be seen. Attempt to determine the reasons for students' perceptions by asking them. Educators must also be ready to hear students' responses and help them to clarify abstract words and broad generalizations. Students should always be required to speak with a high degree of specificity, giving times and places and using specific verbs and adjectives.

5. For personal evaluation only, faculty should periodically audiotape their lectures, conversations, and conferences. After playback of the tapes, ask, "Did I talk too fast or too much? Did

I pronounce words clearly? Did I use words known to be unfamiliar to students?"

Conclusion

In the years following the 1964 Civil Rights legislation, the phenomenon of white students on black campuses has been too easily
overlooked. This benign neglect has led to missed opportunities in
promoting cross-cultural understanding, not only on campuses and
in classrooms but also in society as a whole. It leads us now to
confront painfully our underpreparation for the threat of an almost
totally white teaching force by the year 2000, teachers who in all
probability lack adequate knowledge and skills for teaching in culturally diverse classrooms.

There is no way to undo the neglect of the past. However,
there is still a way to ensure that all teachers have the tools that they
need to improve instruction, thereby improving both the quality of
education and cross-cultural understanding: Schools, colleges, and
departments of education must make comprehensive changes in
their programs in order to accommodate human diversity. For reasons cited earlier, predominantly black schools, colleges, and departments of education have a moral mandate to assume a position
of leadership in this thrust. It is incumbent on each of them to
demonstrate a level of commitment and expertise that will ensure
positive contributions to the education of all children in America.

Throughout this chapter, we have made recommendations
about what changes to make in teacher preparation and how to
make them. Although the advice is simple to state, implementation
may be quite enigmatic. We acknowledge that predominantly black
schools, colleges, and departments of education are besieged with
competing demands and competing priorities that must be evaluated and dealt with from the perspective of their individual and
unique vantage points. Further, we realize that these units are under
critical appraisal from diverse forces. Unfortunately, many of the
units are not held in high esteem, even on their own campuses,
which makes it difficult to gain the support necessary to do the job
at hand. But, ultimately, they must move beyond the competing
variables and wavering support. They must make a commitment to

excellence in the preparation of all persons who seek to teach. The future of children in America depends on this commitment.

References

American Association of Colleges for Teacher Education. (1991). *Minority teacher supply and demand: The next level.* Washington, DC: American Association of Colleges for Teacher Education.

Anderson, J. A. (1988). Cognitive styles and multicultural populations. *Journal of Teacher Education, 39*(1), 2–9.

Austin, J. S. (1976). Cultural dynamics of the elementary school classroom: An ethnographic approach. Unpublished doctoral dissertation, Department of Childhood Education, Florida State University.

Backus, J. M. (1984). Adult student needs and university instructional practices. *Journal of Teacher Education, 35*(3), 11–15.

Baker, G. C. (1983). Development of the multicultural program. In F. H. Klassen and D. M. Gollnick (eds.), *Pluralism and the American teacher: Issues and case studies* Washington, DC: Ethnic Heritage Center for Teacher Education, American Association of Colleges for Teacher Education.

Banks, J. A. (1977). The implications of multicultural education for teacher education. In F. H. Klassen and D. M. Gollnick (eds.), *Pluralism and the American teacher: Issues and case studies.* Washington, DC: Ethnic Heritage Center for Teacher Education, American Association of Colleges for Teacher Education.

Baptiste, H. T., Baptiste, M. L., and Gollnick, D. M. (eds.). (1980). *Multicultural teacher education: Preparing educators to provide educational equity.* Vol. 1. Washington, DC: Commission on Multicultural Education, American Association of Colleges for Teacher Education.

Bellamy, D. D. (1982). White students—historically black Fort Valley State College: A study of reverse desegregation in Georgia. *Negro Educational Review, 33*(3–4), 112–134.

Brown, C. I., and Stein, P. R. (1972). The white student in five predominantly black universities. *Negro Educational Review, 23*(4), 148–169.

Burstein, N. D., and Cabello, B. (1989). Preparing teachers to work with culturally diverse students: A teacher education model. *Journal of Teacher Education, 40*(5), 9–16.

Elmore, R. F., and McLaughlin, M. W. (1982). Strategic choice in federal education policy: The compliance-assistance trade-off. In A. F. Lieberman and M. W. McLaughlin (eds.), *Policy making in education: Eighty-first yearbook of the National Society for the Study of Education.* Chicago: University of Chicago Press.

Fleming, J. (1981). Special needs of blacks and other minorities. In A. Chickering and Associates (eds.), *The modern American college: Responding to the new realities of diverse students and a changing society.* San Francisco: Jossey-Bass.

Galluzzo, G. R., and Arends, R. I. (1989). The RATE project: A profile of teacher education institutions. *Journal of Teacher Education, 40*(4), 56–58.

Gay, C. (1977). Changing conceptions of multicultural education. *Educational Perspectives, 16*(4), 4–9.

Grant, C. A. (1989). Urban teachers: Their new colleagues and curriculum. *Phi Delta Kappan, 70,* 764–770.

Grant, C. S., Sahol, C., and Sleeter, C. (1980). Recruitment, admissions, retention, and placement for educational equity: An analysis of the process. In H. T. Baptiste, M. L. Baptiste, and D. M. Gollnick (eds.), *Multicultural teacher education: Preparing educators to provide educational equity.* Vol. 1. Washington, DC: Commission on Multicultural Education, American Association of Colleges for Teacher Education.

Jenkins, M. (1983). *Removing bias: Guidelines for student faculty communication.* Annandale, VA: Speech Communication Association.

Kohut, S., Jr. (1980). Field experiences in preservice professional studies. In H. T. Baptiste, M. L. Baptiste, and D. M. Gollnick (eds.), *Multicultural teacher education: Preparing educators to provide educational equity.* Vol. 1. Washington, DC: Commission on Multicultural Education, American Association of Colleges for Teacher Education.

Mills, J. R. (1983). Multicultural education: Where do we go from here? *Journal of Social and Behavioral Sciences, 29,* 43–52.

Mills, J. R. (1984). Addressing the separate-but-equal predicament in teacher preparation: A case study. *Journal of Teacher Education, 35*(6), 18–23.

Mills, J. R. (1986). *Cross-cultural conflict in higher education.* Boone, NC: National Association for Developmental Education.

Mungo, S. (1989). Today's teachers, tomorrow's students: A cross-cultural confrontation. *Black Issues in Higher Education, 3*(6), 21.

Pate, G. S. (1981). Research on prejudice reduction. *Educational Leadership, 4*(38), 288–291.

Scollon, S. (1981). Professional development seminars: A model for making higher education more culturally sensitive. Paper presented at the conference of the National Association for Asian and Pacific American Education, Honolulu, HI.

Smith, B. S. (1973). A cross-cultural program for attitude modification of white students on a black university campus. *Phi Delta Kappan, 54,* 629–630.

Standley, N. V. (1978). *White students enrolled in black colleges and universities: Their attitudes and perspectives.* Atlanta, GA: Southern Regional Education Board.

Tippeconnic, J. W. III. (1983). Training teachers of American Indian students. *Peabody Journal of Education, 61,* 6–15.

9

Tapping Nontraditional Sources of Minority Teaching Talent

Richard I. Arends
Shelley Clemson
James Henkelman

Between 1983 and 1990, over a thousand reform reports were written about the shortcomings of education in the United States. Some educational historians remind us that the current reform effort carries many agenda from earlier eras (Cuban, 1989; Brown, this volume). However, one top agenda item is new: recruitment of a teaching force in the United States that reflects the nation's cultural diversity and preparation of candidates so that they are instructionally effective and culturally aware.

This problem of recruiting and preparing a multicultural teaching force, like so many other important problems in education, is complex and not amenable to simple or single-approach solutions. It grows out of deeply rooted societal and institutional traditions and arrangements and requires planned and sustained initiatives for change. In this chapter, we suggest that one way to approach the problem is to tap nontraditional pools of minorities for teaching and to create new forms of cooperation between local schools and universities for the purpose of delivering redesigned teacher education programs. After providing our perspective about the problem, we describe a program in the state of Maryland that holds promise as a model for others.

Reaching Beyond Traditional Students
to Achieve Cultural Diversity

Minority recruitment goals are easier to set than to achieve. In the past decade, several recruitment strategies have been developed to entice more minorities into teaching. These include forgiveness loans or scholarships, mentoring programs, training in test taking, mass media advertising, and peer and professional contact with minority students while they are still in K–12 schools. All of these investments have yielded few returns according to those who have closely observed these strategies (Haberman, 1989). Although the overall number of people preparing to teach is rising, the number of minority students who choose teaching as a career is decreasing. Recent figures from a national survey of teacher education institutions (Rodman, 1988) show, for example, that in fall 1986 only 4.3 percent of teacher education candidates in the United States were black, 1.5 percent were Hispanic, and 1.4 percent were Asian or Pacific Islanders, and these figures represented a decrease from 4.6 percent black, 2.8 percent Hispanic, and 1.5 percent Asian or Pacific Islanders from the previous year. This general trend has been confirmed elsewhere (American Association of Colleges for Teacher Education [AACTE], 1988).

In the state of Maryland, scholarships for minorities preparing to teach have been provided, and the state Department of Education and many colleges and universities have employed additional personnel to recruit and assist minority teacher education students in campus-based teacher preparation programs. Yet, this effort so far has not produced the desired results. In fact, the percentage of minority graduates of teacher education programs in the state has declined steadily from 11.7 percent in 1987, to 7.8 percent in 1988, to 5.7 percent in 1989 (Maryland State Department of Education, 1989). These figures reflect all graduates of the twenty colleges in Maryland that prepare teachers, including Maryland's historically black colleges.

As a response to the traditional pool of college-age minority candidates for teaching, prominent educators such as Haberman (1989) have advocated the pursuit of nontraditional minority populations as recruitment sources: the community college student, the adult with a bachelor's degree, and paraprofessionals working in school systems. According to this line of thinking, with which we agree, powerful cultural, sociological, and psychological factors are discouraging college-age minority students from majoring in teaching, and those forces will take many years to counteract. Instead of gearing recruitment strategies to the traditional minority college student, therefore, it is wise to seek out the older candidates, those who are seeking career changes or have graduated with college degrees in the arts, sciences, business, or communications only to discover that jobs are not as plentiful or salaries as high as they had anticipated. We have learned, in fact, that many of these nontraditional recruits had considered teaching as a career at one time but were discouraged by well-meaning friends and family.

Recruitment of a more diverse teaching force is only a first step. Restructuring of teacher education to develop more instructionally effective and culturally aware teachers is another. This problem, like recruitment, is also complex and multifaceted.

Restructured Teacher Education for
Instructional Effectiveness and Cultural Awareness

Teacher education as practiced today is simply not working. Reformers (Carnegie Forum on Education and the Economy, 1986; Holmes Group, 1986), the public critics from within the institution, and students think and write in negative terms about the whole enterprise. Several states (New Jersey, Virginia, Texas, and California) have taken steps to establish alternative routes to certification or to severely limit college-based programs. Although, as teacher educators, we do not necessarily agree with many of these initiatives, they nonetheless represent the larger society's perception of a problem that exists independently of the issues of cultural diversity and awareness.

The crux of the problem, from our perspective, is that teacher education programs, as currently conceived, are not powerful enough interventions in the lives of teacher candidates to help them to become effective and reflective practitioners. As educational historian William Johnson (1989, p. 238) has observed, in teacher education, unlike other fields such as law, medicine, and architecture wherein the university-based professional schools revolutionized training and practice, the professional schools have failed to find "a training paradigm that has transformed the education of teachers" or their practices. Teacher education is simply too weak either to produce a paradigm shift for teacher candidates or to provide them with a sufficient repertoire to make serious departures from what they think they already know and can do well.

Time is still a factor. For well over a decade, calls have gone out from both inside and outside the teacher education community for extended training programs. However, the length of programs remains (except in a few places) essentially unchanged. During the past five years, a team of researchers, working under the auspices of the AACTE, has been studying teacher education programs and students in over seven hundred institutions that make up the association's membership. Known as the Research About Teacher Education (RATE) Project, researchers annually survey a random sample of ninety institutions stratified by types (small liberal arts colleges, medium-size regional colleges, and large research universities). This work has produced information on thousands of teacher candidates and their teacher education programs (AACTE, 1987, 1988).

Information collected in the RATE studies reveals that the average secondary teacher candidate's program consists of twenty-six semester hours of work—two methods courses, three courses in educational foundations, one early field experience, and student teaching. The course of study for elementary teachers is pretty much the same except that they are required to take six or seven methods courses, making their total program about fifty semester hours. This training, in well over 90 percent of the institutions, is spread over three years. This format makes the amount of attention focused on professional training at any particular time, except during student teaching and the methods semester for elementary students, a very small portion in relation to other studies and activities that consume the lives of undergraduate college students. These findings are consistent with the data of other researchers who have counted the amount of time that teacher candidates spend in preparation (Conant, 1963; AACTE, 1976; Kerr, 1983), and this time commitment has remained remarkably constant since 1920. If anything, it has decreased slightly (about 2 percent), according to Kerr (1983), in the fifty-year period between 1929 and 1979. This decrease contrasts sharply with the extension of professional training in every other field during the same fifty-year period (Kerr, 1983).

The need for a restructuring of teacher education is further highlighted as new and important data come to light about the characteristics of those enrolled in teacher education programs. Zimpher and Ashburn (this volume) provide a portrait of the persons preparing to teach. Essentially, they describe the group as culturally insulated. The large majority of teacher candidates in the RATE studies reported that they had selected their teacher training institution for its proximity to home and because it was accessible and affordable. Most reported that they planned to stay close to their institutions or to their hometowns—and certainly within the particular state—to teach. They preferred to teach "normal" students and middle-income students and had little interest in working in culturally diverse schools. Teacher candidates were slightly above average in ability, filled with idealism, and eager to enter the profession for the purpose of helping children grow and learn, a goal similar to the one described by Lortie (1975) over two decades ago. They were predominantly white, and less than one-third reported fluency in a second language.

Equally informing is the work of Weinstein (1988, 1989) who has been studying the beliefs of teacher candidates and their expectations about their abilities. In two different studies, she asked teacher candidates to rate their future teaching performance compared to peers in their respective teacher education programs and to provide information about their views of the ideal teacher. Weinstein found that teacher candidates, even as early as their sophomore years, were extremely optimistic about their abilities to be good teachers. On a 7-point scale (with 1 meaning well below average and 7 much above average), the mean rating of 131 teacher candidates surveyed in one study was 5.4. In fact, nearly 85 percent of the candidates believed that their future teaching performance would be above average or better. Only 1 subject out of the 131 gave a self-rating of slightly below average. Weinstein reports that this optimism also extended to areas documented for years as troublesome for beginners. They were confident in their abilities to teach students from different cultures and backgrounds, to maintain discipline, to establish and enforce class rules and procedures, and to deal with individual differences.

The RATE studies uncovered a similar phenomenon among teacher candidates. Candidates were asked to rate their readiness to teach on twelve facets of teaching: planning instruction, using proper teaching methods, evaluating student learning, working with other teachers, using materials properly, responding to student differences, managing classrooms, developing materials, diagnosing learner needs, dealing with misbehavior, developing curricula, and using computers. For all of the facets, except using computers, over two-thirds of the students in their junior years reported that they already had "high-level" readiness to teach (AACTE, 1988).

This phenomenon, labeled "unrealistic optimism" by Weinstein (1989), describes a situation where students enter teacher education with a high level of confidence and the conviction that they possess the attributes and skills needed for teaching. Although confidence may be a good thing, Weinstein (1989, p. 59) warns that teacher candidates "who hold unrealistic optimism about their own success may devalue the need for professional preparation."

The RATE data, coupled with Weinstein's findings, present a portrait of teacher candidates that is both promising and challenging. On the one hand, it is good to know that average to above-average people are choosing teaching and that they are confident of their abilities. The teaching profession of the next century will not be filled with the illiterates that some predict. The challenge, however, is to work effectively with the cultural insularity of prospective teachers and their unrealistic conceptions about themselves and teaching while striving to recruit and prepare a more culturally diverse teaching force.

Observers for over three decades (Conant, 1963; Joyce and others, 1977; Kerr, 1983; Goodlad, 1984) have repeatedly reported that teacher education consists of a number of college courses taught in rather traditional and individualistic ways, without thematic structures or interrelated experiences. What is most striking is that observer after observer reports that programs across all kinds of institutions are essentially alike and contain the same inadequacies. This situation must change as we move toward recruitment of a more diverse teaching force and as we strive to replace cultural insularity with instructional effectiveness and cultural awareness. Programs must become much more demanding and provide the kind of knowledge and experiences that can change prior conceptions of teaching held by candidates; the programs must become watershed experiences wherein one set of ideas is destroyed and other sets of ideas are introduced in compelling fashion to replace the earlier held conceptions. The kind of program that we envision is less traumatic than army bootcamp in terms of the way that people are treated, but every bit as intensive and demanding. Programs must strive to get candidates to think and talk teaching, just as training programs for other professionals get prospective practitioners to think and talk in specified ways.

A powerful teacher education program must be organized around a set of themes or principles aimed at providing consistency across courses and experiences and targeted specifically at altering and busting the prior conceptions of teacher candidates, while at the same time helping them develop well-organized schemata about teaching and learning. The processes and pedagogy of the program would be modeled consistently by those responsible for the program. Most important, a powerful program must give teacher candidates ample opportunities for group work and other experiences aimed at providing an experiential basis for understanding and building norms of collegiality in teaching.

Skeptics might argue that because there is not an agreed-upon paradigm for teaching and teacher education, it is impossible to build a program around such themes. Although there is some merit in this argument, it is dated. In our opinion, the research on teaching and learning has been sufficiently developed over the past thirty years to form the basis for a knowledge-based teacher education curriculum. Today, programs can be designed to reflect the knowledge base on teaching and learning in such a way as to ensure that graduates from the program have powerful conceptions about the goals of teaching, how students learn, and, most important, how to match pedagogical approaches to both. All of this can be done with a culturally diverse group of students.

A Redesigned Teacher Education Program

The particular program that we describe here grew out of the mutual concern of three organizations in the State of Maryland regarding three specific needs: shortages of minority teachers, lack of alternative teacher training programs that are attractive to special populations of students, and lack of preparation programs sufficiently demanding to ensure instructionally effective and culturally aware teachers.

Initial discussions between the University of Maryland College Park (UMCP) and the Montgomery County Public Schools (MCPS) began in summer 1986. At that time, UMCP had established an affirmative action goal to increase the number of minority students admitted to teacher education programs to 10 percent by 1990. At the same time, MCPS was actively recruiting minority teachers in order to provide classroom models for its increasingly culturally diverse student population. Their efforts, which included international recruitment, had met with limited success, even though teachers' salaries in this system were among the highest in the country. The lack of sufficient numbers of minority students enrolled in teacher education programs across the country made recruitment of new minority teachers very difficult. Although enticement of experienced teachers from other school systems helped solve the local problem, this strategy did nothing to solve the larger national shortage. Thus, MCPS was as interested as UMCP in developing an alternative teacher education program to address this issue.

The two agencies found support from the Maryland State Department of Education (MSDE), which also had been actively trying to increase the pool of eligible minority teachers in the state. Over a two-year period, a committee consisting of members from UMCP, MCPS, and MSDE planned a cooperative program to recruit and prepare a special population of elementary teachers. The final design of this program featured the following:

- Recruitment of a cohort of twelve persons who already had bachelor's degrees for participation in a two-year teacher education program leading to a master's degree and a teaching certif-

icate. Candidates would be selected from among instructional
assistants already employed by MCPS.

- Selected candidates would represent cultural diversity with at
  least three-fourths of the students from minority groups (black,
  Hispanic, and Asian).
- Candidates and faculty would form a learning community representing the diversity of the multicultural population involved.
- MCPS would employ the teacher candidates as instructional
  assistants and give candidates released time to attend classes held
  in Montgomery County.
- Faculty from UMCP and staff development personnel from
  MCPS would teach the on-site classes and provide for overall
  supervision of the candidates.
- MSDE and the Higher Education Commission would contribute human resources by providing technical assistance and instructional support, and financial support by providing
  scholarships to the teacher candidates.
- The training program would extend over two years (two
  summers and four academic semesters) and would be built
  around a redesigned, thematic set of courses and experiences.
- Successful graduates from the program would be granted certification and guaranteed teaching positions with MCPS if they
  promised to remain in the county and teach for a minimum of
  two years.

Features of Recruitment and Selection

A cohort of twelve persons who already had bachelor's degrees were
recruited to the program during summer 1988. Working within very
short timelines, the planners announced the program through a
letter to the 277 instructional assistants in Montgomery County who
had bachelor's degrees, 157 of whom had been identified as minorities. In total, 80 instructional assistants attended an orientation
meeting where the program and application procedures were described; 38 completed the applications, and 12 were admitted to the
first cohort. All of those admitted were women: 7 were from minority backgrounds and 5 were not.

Candidates for the program were selected by a committee

consisting of UMCP faculty who had agreed to teach in the program, staff from the MCPS Personnel Office, and Montgomery County Staff Development personnel. The existing standards for admission to graduate school (3.0 grade point average in undergraduate work, 40th percentile on the Miller Analogy Test) were used as a starting point for recommendations made to the graduate school at UMCP for admission and to the MCPS Personnel Office for employment. All candidates' transcripts were reviewed for appropriate arts and sciences undergraduate coursework. In reality, the admission standards were applied flexibly since a number of the candidates had nontraditional backgrounds; several candidates were finally admitted with provisional status. All provisionally admitted students completed the program successfully.

Features of the Training Program

The teacher education program extends over two years, during which candidates complete over fifty semester hours of work. The curriculum is theme based, aims at the building of a repertoire and the acquisition of knowledge, and reflects our image of what is needed to help teachers become culturally aware and effective teachers.

As described previously, we believe that teacher education, regardless of the population that it is designed to serve, is more effective if built on a thematic structure. Although several ideas could be good candidates for themes, we chose research, repertoire, reflection, and relationships.

Research. This theme is an attempt to get teacher candidates to understand and to value the knowledge base that informs teaching and learning. The theme is based on two propositions: (1) there is a set of teaching practices that produces (more or less) better results than do other sets and (2) the traditional view of many teacher candidates that "it all depends" or that a strategy must be consistent with one's own personality or idiosyncratic view of teaching and learning is simply not sufficient. This strong stance is taken, however, with full recognition that context makes a difference and that approaches to teaching and learning are filtered through the conceptual lenses of teachers and learners.

Repertoire. This theme aims at getting teacher candidates to accept that there is no single "best" method of teaching. Different teaching strategies have been developed and tested over the years to achieve a variety of important educational goals. The effective teacher has (and can use appropriately) a variety of best practices in his or her repertoire. The task of building a repertoire is a life-long process for teachers, just as it is for musicians or others who start practice with a small number of techniques or approaches and master more as they mature professionally.

Reflection. A repertoire based on research and the wisdom of practice is important. However, teaching is simply too complex to reduce to a set of recipes that can be used over and over. Effective practitioners are those who can analyze and reflect on their teaching methods and on particular teaching situations. They can match methods appropriately to particular groups of students at particular times in particular settings for particular learning goals.

Relationships. Like many other professional activities in our society, effectiveness is determined not only by the quality of the practice but also by the quality of the relationships built between the professional and those being helped. The primary relationships for teachers are with their students, although relationships with colleagues and supervisors are also critical. In today's world of cultural heterogeneity, these relationships must be built within a multicultural context that respects and enhances appreciation for the rich social diversity of the contemporary classroom.

Structures and Processes of the Program

Associated skills, attitudes, and practices are promoted through carefully integrated coursework held on site, an extended internship, weekly professional seminars, coaching teams, and a number of additional support mechanisms. An overview of the various features of the program is provided in Exhibit 9.1.

Exhibit 9.1. UMCP-MCPS Alternative Teacher Education Program Experiences and Support Mechanisms.

- Coaching teams meet throughout program
- Internships each semester (twelve semester hours credit)
- Proseminar (with weekly meetings) each semester (four semester hours credit)
- Coursework (thirty-six semester hours credit)

Fall 1988	Contemporary Social Issues in Education
	Mainstreaming
Spring 1989	Models and Processes of Teaching
	Cognitive Basis for Instruction
Summer 1989	Teaching Reading and Writing
	Objectives and Criterion-Referenced Instruments
	Classroom Management
	First Seminar Paper (review of research on teaching)
	Mathematics Content Course I (Some students satisfy this requirement by testing.)
Fall 1989	Educational Research/Measurement
	Mathematics Content Course II (Some students satisfy this requirement by testing.)
Spring 1990	Study of Research on Teaching
	Mathematics in the Elementary School
Summer 1990	Elementary Instruction in Content Areas
	Second Seminar Paper (action research project)
First Year of Teaching: Ethnic Minorities	

Many of the competencies for teaching are being developed outside the course structure. These include such diverse areas as word processing, computer competence, general education, and preparation for the NTE (a national teachers examination). Students work with their coaching teams to determine individual learning goals and the ways to meet them. For competencies needed by all of the students in the program, the proseminar is utilized. The internship is available continuously as a clinical setting to develop competencies.

The professional core of the teacher education curriculum has been organized around an integrated set of experiences that focus on the development of the four R's of the teacher education curriculum: research, repertoire, reflection, and relationships. The curriculum of this alternative program is based on research and current knowledge from primarily six fields of inquiry: research on teaching based on naturalistic studies about what effective teachers do, research from cognitive psychology, theory-driven studies of teaching, research from effective schooling, research on learning to teach, and research on minority teacher education. Students review an aspect of the research on teaching for their first seminar paper and conduct an action research project for their second seminar paper.

Students develop a repertoire of teaching skills and strategies through a series of laboratory and clinical experiences that utilize a model of training involving careful presentation of teaching principles followed by demonstration, practice with coaching, feedback, and additional practice. Microteaching and videotape analysis are employed consistently and systematically in a number of courses. In addition, various field trips to classrooms implementing special programs and to centers that provide resource support and technical assistance to teachers are a part of the program.

The program is designed to help students become skilled and reflective practitioners. The faculty strive to develop in students the attitude that learning to teach is developmental, a life-long process, and that teachers can discover their own best practice through reflection and critical inquiry. Procedures and strategies to promote reflective teaching and decision making include a weekly proseminar, self-help laboratories, maintenance of individual journals, coaching, and special seminar papers.

Finally, the establishment and maintenance of effective relationships with students, colleagues, supervisors, parents, and others in the larger multicultural community is a major theme in the program. In particular, attention is given to the teacher's role as a member of the school team and the teaching profession. Various aspects of membership and participation in the multicultural community are emphasized.

Planned internships are a part of the program experience throughout the two years. Candidates are assigned as interns in an elementary school. The internship differs from usual student teaching experiences in two important ways. First, the internship is much longer in duration since interns work in classrooms throughout the two years of the program. Second, the program is fully experiential from the beginning unlike most student teaching experiences, which serve as a culmination of a training program. For most instructional assistants, four hours per day is spent primarily working to enhance the educational program for students in the elementary school, and two hours per day is spent primarily developing teacher skills through specific activities.

Weekly meetings of faculty and participants in the program, called the proseminar, provide a setting for linking practice to theory and back to practice again. Many of the competencies in the program are developed outside the course structure, and these are coordinated through the proseminar. The proseminar is also used as a key mechanism in the support system. One of the proposed techniques is a self-help laboratory where participants meet during part of the seminar to share experiences and problems and then work out their own solutions.

Coaching teams provide the focus for the creative tension between challenge and support in a personalized and professional manner. Coaching teams are based in the elementary school in which an intern is placed. These teams include the principal, a coaching teacher, an intern, and one member of the faculty team from UMCP or MCPS. The primary responsibility of the coaching teams is to help the interns assess themselves and to plan learning experiences. The work of the interns is designed to meet both the needs of the school and the learning needs of the interns. The coaching teams are responsible for continuous assessment of the progress of the interns in fulfilling their learning goals and for helping them set new goals.

The cohort of students and the team of faculty form a mutual learning community. The mutual learning community reflects the need for both equity and excellence in education.

Demanding programs require adequate support mechanisms. In addition to those already described, a number of other experiences and activities are offered to provide a support system for program participants.

- *Cohort Approach.* As mentioned earlier, the cohort of students and the team of faculty constitute a mutual learning community. The cohort of students provides support through the development of a climate of trust amidst risk. They assist one another in projects, assignments, and other tasks related to the program. Cooperative learning permeates all aspects of the program.

- *Multicultural Learning Community.* One of the ways that the program meets the standards of equity and excellence is through the role modeling of teaching education candidates. One of the responsibilities of the teacher education candidates is to develop projects with minority students in the schools in which they are working. This project is guided by the coaching team in the school. The role modeling provided by all of the interns, but particularly by the minority interns, is important to the development of both students and interns. There is also an expectation that this aspect of the project will be a catalyst for wider efforts to raise the self-esteem of minority students.

- *Support in Mathematics.* In order to address the issue of inadequate preparation in mathematics by students applying for this program, two special courses in mathematics are offered. Candidates who have had no difficulty in mathematics are given an opportunity to take a test on the content of these two courses. Successful completion of the test indicates appropriate preparation. Faculty are committed to facilitating the success of all students in this area.

- *Support in Taking Standardized Tests.* The issue of the high failure rate of minority students and teachers who take standardized tests is addressed in several ways in the program. The main feature has been special preparation sessions for the NTE (a national teachers examination), which is required by MSDE for teacher certification.

- *Support During Induction.* Another source of support involves the extension of aspects of the program into the teacher candidate's first two years of teaching in the MCPS system. Specifically, two aspects of the program are continued: the coaching teams and the proseminars. The continuation of the coaching teams further encourages the growth of the beginning teachers. The continuation of the proseminar enables the mutual learning community to maintain its work as a support mechanism.

- *Developing Multicultural Awareness.* The development of multicultural awareness is essential to the fulfillment of the relationship theme. This awareness is developed through modeling at all levels of the program. The teaching staff of the program represents a multicultural mix; the teacher candidates represent blacks, Asians, Hispanics, and whites; and multicultural issues are addressed in the curriculum and in each teaching activity. However, the most powerful way in which this awareness is developed is through the life of the community. Individuals are asked to examine their behavior in relation to others in the group. Although a course in understanding ethnic minorities is included in the program, the probing of individual attitudes within the community promotes deeper awareness and sensitivity to the uniqueness of individuals from different cultural backgrounds.

Administration and Management

The program has an administrative structure that reflects its cooperative nature. A policy board reflects the collaboration of UMCP, MCPS, and MSDE. Representatives from UMCP include administrators and faculty; representatives from MCPS include central office personnel, staff development personnel, a principal, and a coaching teacher; and the sole representative from MSDE is a member of the Teacher Education and Certification Branch. Two students from the program also serve on the policy board. In addition, a member of the Maryland Higher Education Commission serves on the board. This board represents the multicultural diversity of the program.

The day-to-day management of the program is handled by a coordinator from UMCP and one from MCPS. These co-coordinators are the primary communication link for the program. They also serve as the faculty for the ongoing proseminar.

What We Have Learned and Prospects for the Future

As with any effort to change existing structures and processes in complex situations, there are anticipated and unanticipated effects. Based on four years of experience with and reflection about our redesigned teacher preparation program, we can now make tentative judgments about our efforts and report the program's strengths and weaknesses.

Strengths of the Program

Financial Aid. One obvious strength of the program has been its ability to attract minority candidates. In a very short period of time (less than one month), from the eighty persons who initially expressed interest in the program, thirty-eight completed applications were received and the twelve available slots were filled. We attribute this positive response primarily to the substantial salary and diminished workload offered to candidates during the training period. This success in recruitment substantiates one of our initial beliefs that a reason for the lack of minorities preparing to teach is economic. It also substantiates the belief that minorities who are more mature and hold bachelor's degrees are ready to consider teaching if training programs can be devised to match their unique needs and aspirations.

Personal and Professional Support. All of the support mechanisms that have been built into the program are effective in maintaining the cohort. The proseminars and the coaching teams have been particularly effective. Nine of the twelve original candidates in the program graduated in summer 1990. One of the original candidates was dropped from the program early when it was discovered that her bachelor's degree from another country was not the equivalent of a bachelor's degree taken in the United States. This candidate completed a bachelor's degree in another program and joined the cohort that began in 1990. A second candidate withdrew from the program during spring 1989 because she decided that teaching was not an appropriate career for her. She had applied for the program at the strong suggestion of family members who were educators, and she quickly made the decision to withdraw.

Cohort. Our judgment at this time is that the practice of bringing candidates along in a cohort group adds substantially to the program. It provides a means for building a learning community among the candidates and their professors, which in turn provides an important source of support for everyone. A cohort, in various and sometimes subtle ways, forces faculty to make deeper commitments to candidates and to more carefully integrate content and experiences across the curriculum. A cohort of culturally diverse persons also challenges everyone to examine attitudes and confront insular behaviors that are a product of our different cultural backgrounds.

Thematic Core. The thematic core, based on the four R's (research, repertoire, reflection, and relationships), has proved to be a powerful driving force of the program. The four R's were conceived initially in general and abstract terms. However, as the program has evolved, they have taken on a meaning that is deeper than anyone expected. Curriculum decisions as well as faculty and teacher candidates' expectations have been shaped by the four themes.

Internships. The extension of the internship over a two-year period of time has provided rich opportunities for the teacher candidates to develop as teachers. Unlike traditional student teaching, the candidates are in the classroom every day and have the opportunity to develop units of work, practice a variety of teaching strategies, and participate in their own action research. They do not, however, struggle with having to prove in a short period of time that they are, indeed, teachers.

Weaknesses of the Program

Lack of Male Teacher Candidates. Although this program is successful in recruiting minority teachers candidates, they have been predominantly women. Only one male candidate applied for the first cohort, and he was not accepted into the program. The second cohort, which began in 1990, included three males in a group of fifteen. Very few men are instructional assistants in elementary schools, and it is likely that other recruitment strategies and other populations will need to be tapped to achieve gender balance.

Tensions. Two areas of tension surfaced and continue throughout the program: (1) balancing demands of program and personal life and (2) balancing demands of being both an instructional assistant and an intern. All of the teacher candidates were full-time instructional assistants before entering the program, and most were members of families where both spouses worked. Obviously, the program made new demands on already crowded and busy personal lives. The teacher candidates experience constant tension between their jobs (instructional assistants) and their training (internship). Continuous effort goes into negotiating a balance and preserving quality time for the internship.

Reinforcing Traditional Practices. Our ability to recruit persons who serve as instructional assistants in schools (some for a number of years) and to keep them in schools and classrooms on a daily basis is a strength of the program. Conversely, it is also a weakness. The dual pressures of work and training are demanding from a time perspective. Equally important, daily work in classrooms has made the process of breaking down conventional ideas about teaching and replacing them with new ones difficult. It seems as though candidates are often too caught up in the day-to-day life of classrooms and schools to allow themselves to pull back for thoughtful analysis and reflection.

Program Evaluation

The current evaluation data about the program have been informative. Christensen (1990) conducted systematic data gathering for the first cohort of this program. The central findings of her study led to the conclusion that the program delivers what it claims. An extensive follow-up study, Graduate Teacher Education Evaluation Project, is now being conducted to determine the differences between the graduates of this alternative program and more traditional programs. These data will inform future decision making in formulating teacher education programs.

Conclusion

We are convinced that cooperative programs between universities and local schools, aimed at preparing minorities who have bachelor's degrees for teaching, do work. In fact, UMCP and MCPS have recruited and are training a second cohort of minority teachers that began in summer 1990.

There is value in exploring how well strategies that are tailor-made for one setting apply to other settings—for example, using community colleges, working with minority middle and high school students, providing financial aid and promises of jobs. The UMCP-MCPS program model should be explored elsewhere for several reasons. The financial support (instructional assistants' salaries) already exists in many school systems around the country. New resources do not need to be acquired. Most states have procedures for alternative or experimental programs that allow these new efforts to proceed with relative ease. Finally, the pool of nontraditional candidates seeking second careers in teaching is fairly large. Although MCPS is a large school system, we suspect that many other urban and suburban school systems have minority instructional assistants who are college graduates.

The scale of the enterprise must be mentioned in closing. Our first cohort had ten students, and our second has fifteen— obviously, small numbers. However, if this action were repeated in only one-half of the twelve hundred institutions nationwide that prepare teachers, it would almost double the number of minority teachers entering the teaching force yearly.

References

American Association of Colleges for Teacher Education. (1976). *Educating a profession.* Washington, DC: American Association of Colleges for Teacher Education.

American Association of Colleges for Teacher Education. (1987). *RATE I. Teaching teachers: Facts and figures.* Washington, DC: American Association of Colleges for Teacher Education.

American Association of Colleges for Teacher Education. (1988). *RATE II. Teaching teachers: Facts and figures.* Washington, DC: American Association of Colleges for Teacher Education.

Carnegie Forum on Education and the Economy. (1986). *A nation prepared: Teachers for the 21st century.* New York: Carnegie Forum on Education and the Economy.

Christensen, P. (1990, August). *University of Maryland at College Park and Montgomery County Public Schools Creative Initiative in Teacher Education (CITE) Program.* Paper presented at the summer conference of the ATE, Towson, MD.

Conant, J. B. (1963). *The education of American teachers.* New York: McGraw-Hill.

Cuban, L. (1989). The persistence of reform in schools. In D. Warren (ed.), *American teachers: Histories of a profession at work.* New York: Macmillan.

Goodlad, J. I. (1984). *A place called school.* New York: McGraw-Hill.

Haberman, M. (1989). More minority teachers. *Phi Delta Kappan, 18,* 771–776.

Holmes Group. (1986). *Tomorrow's teachers: A report of the Holmes Group.* East Lansing, MI: Holmes Group.

Johnson, W. R. (1989). Teachers and teacher training in the twentieth century. In D. Warren (ed.), *American teachers: Histories of a profession at work.* New York: Macmillan.

Joyce, B., and others. (1977). *Preservice teacher education.* Palo Alto, CA: Lewin & Associates.

Kerr, D. (1983). Teaching competence and teacher education in the United States. In L. S. Shulman and G. Sykes (eds.), *Handbook of teaching and policy.* White Plains, NY: Longman.

Lortie, D. C. (1975). *School teacher: A sociological study.* Chicago: University of Chicago Press.

Maryland State Department of Education. (1989). *Minority enrollment trends.* Baltimore: Maryland State Department of Education.

Rodman, B. (1988). Teacher-training enrollment surging upward, poll finds. *Education Week,* Mar. 2, pp. 1, 26.

Weinstein, C. S. (1988). Preservice teachers' expectations about the first year of teaching. *Teaching and Teacher Education, 4,* 31–40.

Weinstein, C. S. (1989). Teacher education students' preconceptions of teaching. *Journal of Teacher Education, 70,* 53–60.

10

Changing School Culture to Accommodate Student Diversity

Linda F. Winfield
JoAnn B. Manning

In this chapter, we focus the discussion of the restructuring of schools on needed changes in the culture of schools in order to accommodate diverse student populations. First, a definition of diversity within the urban context is presented, along with a review of past attempts at accommodating student diversity through federal aid to schools and districts. Second, the resulting impact on school culture is considered in terms of students' access to knowledge and their opportunities to learn. Quality of teaching and inequities in the curriculum are discussed as two of the factors that impact access of diverse student groups. Third, programs that focus on specific aspects of school culture and are designed to accommodate diverse student populations are discussed.

Demographic shifts in the school-age population indicate increases in the numbers of students from low socioeconomic backgrounds and racial and ethnic minorities attending public schools. Many of these students experience a greater degree of academic failure than do students from higher socioeconomic backgrounds. Restructuring of schools to provide for a multicultural teaching force and student population will require changes in the school culture to accommodate diversity. The notion of school culture or climate,

an intangible construct, refers to the core assumptions, understandings, and implicit rules of behavior that characterize the school organization (Corcoran, 1985). Participants (in this case, principals
and teachers) are likely to view cultural patterns as just the way
things are done in their workplaces (Hawley, 1988; Metz, 1988).
Others contend that culture is a product of an organization's system
of beliefs (mission, values, norms) and its structure (Peters and Waterman, 1982). They suggest that it is easier to change organizational culture than to change individual personalities of employees.
The culture or social organization of schools has effects on teachers'
efficacy and job satisfaction (Lee, Dedrick, and Smith, 1991). In
order to change school culture to accommodate diverse student populations, it is critical for teacher educators to understand the issue
of diversity as well as the norms and structures that contribute to
the culture of a school.

One of the unique features of urban schools is the diversity
of students who attend. Students differ in terms of socioeconomic
levels, racial and ethnic groups, and native language groups, as well
as in developmental stages, home academic support, "giftedness,"
religion, and handicaps. In addition to intergroup differences,
within each particular student grouping there are also individual
differences in learning rates, attitudes, interests, and motivation levels—resulting in different achievement outcomes—that schools and
teachers must accommodate (Epstein, 1988).

The current emphasis on diversity initially developed out of
a concern for students from various racial and ethnic groups and
lower socioeconomic backgrounds. As Gordon (1982, p. 1975) notes,

> In earlier work, great attention was given to the char-
> acteristics of these populations and the ways in which
> they differed from the so-called majority population.
> As that work progressed, we have come to realize that
> it was in error . . . by implying they represented a rel-
> atively homogeneous group. They do not. . . . They
> have poverty and low status and certain kinds of neg-
> lect and maltreatment as common characteristics, but
> in terms of their other characteristics they vary as
> much within this group as they do between the lower-

and higher-status groups. . . . Ethnic and class status
is important for political purposes but relatively
unimportant for pedagogical purposes.

During the last decade, evidence from exemplary urban
schools that are successful in facilitating achievement among "disadvantaged" students confirms the importance of within-school
conditions (Purkey and Smith, 1983, 1985). A critical component
identified in effective schools is a strong culture in which norms are
imposed on participants in order to facilitate greater academic and
behavioral demands on students (Purkey and Smith, 1983, 1985;
Corcoran, 1985).

Restructuring of schools to accommodate student diversity in
learning raises questions about whether differences in learning outcomes should be reduced, maintained, or increased (Epstein, 1988).
Differences between groups can be reduced or eliminated by restrict-
ing the advancement of capable students or by increasing the advancement of slower students (Epstein, 1988). Methods such as whole
class instruction, mastery learning, remedial instruction, and emphasis on minimum competence testing are designed to minimize
diversity; whereas individualized instruction, homogeneous grouping, gifted and talented programs, and advanced placement courses
are designed to increase diversity among students (Epstein, 1988). In
general, whether to promote or reduce diversity of outcomes is not
a "cut-and-dried" management decision. School community values
as well as the philosophy of the district may be considered. Schools
may choose to minimize differences in achievement in some subjects
(for example, basic skills in reading) and to increase diversity in
others (for example, advanced level mathematics). With the advent
of many district- and state-level assessment programs, decisions regarding which subject areas are sufficiently important for all students to master have been partially predetermined.

A pressing national concern is to change what occurs in
schools to prevent the high proportions of failure among students
from diverse racial, ethnic, and socioeconomic backgrounds. Educators acknowledge the ideals of cultural pluralism, but, traditionally, schools and classrooms have not adapted pedagogy to reflect
the needs of students from diverse cultures, socioeconomic back-

grounds, and racial and ethnic groups (Barton and Wilder, 1964; Winfield, 1991b). Additionally, schools have made little progress in incorporating information in the curricula concerning the achievements of traditionally underrepresented groups. A Euro-centric bias has dominated the American educational system (Hare, 1989). Changing schools to better serve students from diverse backgrounds, particularly African American students, is a goal that the American public school system has been reluctant to accept (Maeroff, 1988). A pluralistic approach requires fundamental changes in a school's self-image, philosophy, curriculum, and approach to its multiethnic student population (Hare, 1989).

Reforms based on a cultural infusion model have focused on changes in curriculum content to make it more appropriate for diverse student populations, or to correct perceived deficiencies of African American children (Shujaa, 1991). The curriculum infusion model is necessary, but not sufficient, to reduce, and even eradicate, the disproportionately large numbers of African American and Hispanic students who fail in school. The problems identified in this chapter—inequity in access to knowledge and opportunity to learn—require total restructuring of the system in order to optimize the "fit" and connections between schools' instructional resources and students' needs.

One of the challenges facing teacher educators is to prepare future teachers who are capable of maximizing the fit between instruction and students' learning, regardless of racial or ethnic group or socioeconomic background. Identification of patterns of diversity among students means that decisions must be made regarding the allocation of time, the assignment of personnel to classrooms, and the assignment of students to instructional groups (Jones, 1989). These decisions regarding resources partially determine the culture of the school and affect students' access to knowledge and opportunity to learn. Traditional solutions that "blame the victim" and attempt to change the student have generally failed. The alternative is to adapt schools and classrooms to student needs (Epstein, 1988).

Remnants of Past Attempts at Dealing with Diversity

Individuals preparing future teachers have been primarily concerned with content and methods of instruction in classrooms and

typically have failed to consider the impact of the larger school organization on teacher beliefs and practices. Two federal mandates
that recognized the issue of diverse student needs based on inequitable learning outcomes have had a major impact on school organization and on teacher beliefs and practices. The Elementary and
Secondary Education Act (ESEA) of 1965 (reauthorized as Chapter
1 of the Education Consolidation and Improvement Act of 1981)
and Public Law 94-142, the Education for All Handicapped Children Act of 1975, were designed to target resources to schools based
on student needs. In the case of ESEA Title I, the criteria were based
on educational and economic needs, whereas for Public Law 94-142
the criteria were based on the needs of exceptional or special children. These two federal programs provided substantial fiscal and
legal incentives for school districts to offer additional instructional
services for children, many of whom were from diverse backgrounds
and had experienced difficulties in the regular curriculum (Allington and McGill-Franzen, 1989; Turnbull, 1986). The implementation of these programs at the school level influenced the quality of
instruction received by diverse student groups.

Implementation Problems

With the increased funding to schools and districts came government regulations for compliance, so schools and districts established separate administrative structures to oversee the federal
categorical programs. At the district level, a director of federal programs is typically in charge of hiring staff and overseeing curriculum and instruction for eligible students under Chapter 1. The
director typically has little or no interaction with other directors or
curriculum supervisors within the district who may be responsible
for curriculum and instruction. Most districts have separate administrative structures for Chapter 1 and special education (Allington
and McGill-Franzen, 1989). In general, the process of identifying
eligible students is separate from instructional planning; group-
administered standardized achievement tests are used to determine
eligibility, and no identified curriculum for the reading instruction
is provided in supplementary programs (Allington and McGill-
Franzen, 1989).

At the school level, federal regulations require that the allocation of resources be restricted to poor or low-scoring students. Teachers funded by Chapter 1 can provide additional instructional services to eligible students only. Because Chapter 1 is a supplemental program, students should also receive instruction in the regular school program. The "supplement not supplant" rule is often misinterpreted to mean that instruction in Chapter 1 has to be totally different from the regular classroom instruction, resulting in a lack of consistency across the curriculum (Johnston, Allington, and Afflerbach, 1985; Allington and Johnston, 1989; McGill-Franzen and Allington, 1991). The implementation of these regulations result in a "profession-oriented" delivery of instructional services (Venezky and Winfield, 1979). This type of service delivery occurs when each program retains its own independence, emphasizes its own special instruction and materials, and establishes territorial claims to certain groups of students.

Past attempts at managing diversity have resulted in a proliferation of separate categorical and special programs, labeling, and dramatic increases in the numbers of students placed in special education (Walberg and Wang, 1987). The rigidity that developed in operating this system made it virtually impossible to serve students adequately (Carter, 1984; Winfield, 1986a). Often, the culture of many of these schools reflected a maintenance of the status quo and low expectations for students' academic progress. The teaching staff, and often the principals, failed to assume the responsibility for ensuring the success of the lowest-achieving students (Winfield, 1986b). Moreover, the school experiences of students enrolled in these programs were typically fragmented and involved lower quantity and quality of instruction (Allington, 1987; Allington and Johnston, 1989; Johnston, Allington, and Afflerbach, 1985; McGill-Franzen and Allington, 1991).

A major problem with past attempts to meet the diversity of student needs was the underlying assumption that schools did not have to change (Kaestle and Smith, 1982). The focus was on changing various subpopulations. Those few exemplary school programs in urban areas that were successful in increasing the levels of student achievement derived systems for coordinating service delivery to students based on student needs (Venezky and Winfield, 1979). In several schools, the principals were key people in facilitating the establishment of collaborative, coordinated environments; in others, district officials were critical (Allington and McGill-Franzen, 1989; Venezky and Winfield, 1979). Where this effort did not occur, students' access to knowledge and opportunity to learn was severely limited (Winfield, 1986b).

Problems of Access to Knowledge

The categorical programs, as implemented, produced conditions that limited student access to knowledge and produced inequities in the quality of teaching and the curriculum. The quality of the available and future teaching force can be considered in terms of personal characteristics and structural constraints (for example, the working conditions). It is beyond the scope of this chapter to provide a comprehensive review of the factors that influence teacher quality, but two factors that affect student access to knowledge are pertinent here. The first, teacher beliefs, is related to the notion of personal responsibility for students' learning. At issue are individuals' belief systems, but also teacher preparation and knowledge of effective strategies for instructing students of various achievement levels. The second factor, personnel assignment, reflects a management decision regarding the allocation of resources.

Teacher Beliefs

Knowledge of the content of teacher beliefs is basic to identification of variables within the school culture that mediate the thinking and practice of teachers (Bunting, 1984). Beliefs about teaching and learning influence expectations and judgments made about student abilities, effort, and progress within a particular classroom. In case studies of urban schools, Winfield (1986b) found that teacher beliefs about low-achievement students could be categorized on two dimensions: (1) whether teachers believed some type of instructional assistance was needed to improve the performance of low-achievement students or whether they ignored the students' low levels of performance and (2) whether teachers assumed the responsibility for improving instruction or shifted the responsibility to others. A cross-classification analysis revealed different types of belief-behavior patterns within this framework. These patterns are depicted in Figure 10.1

Teachers in the first cell were labeled "tutors" because they indicated that it was their responsibility to provide the instruction necessary to improve the reading achievement of the bottom reading group. An example of teachers' responses in the first cell is, "I work with the low group about twenty minutes a day to reinforce skills."

Teachers' responses in the second cell indicated that they thought remedial instruction was needed, but it was not necessarily their responsibility. A frequent response from teachers listed in this category was, "I send my bottom group to the Title I [now Chapter 1] aide." Another response was, "We have a district-funded supplementary remedial program for the low achievers." These teachers were called "general contractors" because students were distributed to other individuals who were responsible for improving achievement.

Teachers' responses in the third cell reflected the belief that there was little or nothing that could be done to improve the performance of academically at-risk students. An example of a response in this category is, "A few will be on grade level, the other students will just get passed on." Another frequent claim was, "These kids need some high-interest, low-level reading materials." Teachers in this cell were labeled "custodians" because their primary concern was maintenance of low levels of achievement.

Teachers' responses in the fourth cell reflected an attitude similar to that of "custodians"; however, the responsibility for maintenance was shifted to others. Unlike "general contractors," teachers in this fourth cell felt that at-risk students were generally incapable of learning in a classroom situation or in supplementary programs. These teachers were labeled "referral agents" because they commonly referred students for psychological testing or special education.

Teachers' beliefs derive from their sense of control over classroom learning, and their knowledge (or lack thereof) of appropriate strategies and interventions in urban settings. The larger school context also influences teachers' beliefs. The proportion of teachers' responses categorized as maintenance-oriented (cells 3 and 4) were substantially higher in urban schools with multiple instructional

Figure 10.1. Behaviors Toward Academically At-Risk Students.

Beliefs About Academically At-Risk Students	Assume Responsibility	Shift Responsibility
Improvement	1. Tutors	2. General Contractors
Maintenance	3. Custodians	4. Referral Agents

Source: Winfield, 1986b, p. 257. Used by permission.

programs utilizing a profession-oriented service delivery model. It is within the context of these models that the responsibility becomes diffused for students who are having difficulty. Teachers must use information from a variety of sources in making pedagogical decisions. Teachers construct simplified models of reality that influence their behavior (Shavelson and Stern, 1981). In their model of teacher decision making, Shavelson and Stern (1981) suggested that institutional constraints also influence teacher judgments and decisions.

In many urban schools, the number of discrete and uncoordinated federally and district-funded supplementary instructional programs may function as institutional constraints that influence teachers' judgments and discretionary behaviors. Some teachers become "general contractors" and relegate the responsibility for student learning to special programs available in the school buildings. These programs in effect become an institutional license that allows regular classroom teachers to avoid teaching less academically able students. In order to increase teacher responsibility and sense of control in the classroom, teacher education programs must include research-based strategies that are effective with students of differing abilities.

Assignment of Personnel

In addition to teacher belief systems, the assignment of teachers to classrooms affects school culture through the quality of teaching available to diverse student groups. Underqualified teachers are disproportionately found in predominantly African American, Hispanic, and Native American schools and classrooms (Oakes and Keating, 1988). Teacher shortages are greater and higher numbers of underqualified entrants to teaching are found in inner-city schools where most poor and racial and ethnic minority students reside (Watson and Traylor, 1988).

In general, administrators have little discretion over teachers assigned to their schools, and district personnel policies and union contractual agreements impose limits on personnel assigned to schools. Overall, two factors contribute to the inequality in personnel assignments. First, school incentive structures make less difficult assignments the only reward for seniority and skill. As a result, beginning teachers typically teach the most challenging students in the tougher schools and then transfer out to schools where there are better working conditions and students that are easier to teach (Darling-Hammond, 1990). Second, and related to the first factor, there is the tracking of teachers within a school building. Teacher assignment to classes reflects a decision regarding the allocation of instructional resources. Several studies have found that lower-level classes are often taught by poorer teachers (Coleman and others, 1966; Spady, 1973). This may be due in part to the preference of more able teachers to work with higher-level classes, to seniority, or to a school-level assignment policy that favors the brighter students (Darling-Hammond, 1990; Hargreaves, 1967; National Education Association, 1968; Rosenbaum, 1976; Finley, 1984).

In one urban elementary school investigated by Winfield (1982), the principal acknowledged that the group of second-grade teachers in his school were "weak," that is, inexperienced and lacking skill in teaching reading. All of the classrooms were organized heterogeneously. The task of managing a heterogeneous classroom requires training that few teachers receive and skills that relatively few of them acquire (Darling-Hammond, 1990). For the prior two to three years, students' performance in second grade had been far below the standardized test performance of the other grades. The principal's solution was to assign all of the weak second-grade teachers to teach third grade, rather than to mobilize available resources to assist and strengthen the teachers' skills in teaching reading or to assign well-prepared, highly skilled teachers to the second graders. In his view, the immediate problem at second grade was solved. However, for that cohort of students who would have the weak teachers again in third grade, the problem was exacerbated.

Other urban elementary schools establish what is known as an *X-roster* class, which consists of all of the students identified by teachers as having academic and behavior problems. The new, inexperienced teacher, long-term substitute, or "forced transfer" teacher is usually assigned to this class. At the other extreme, the most skilled teachers offer rich, challenging curricula to select groups of students identified as "gifted" (Darling-Hammond, 1990).

At the secondary school level, teacher assignments reflect compromises and tacit agreements regarding the allocation of desirable and undesirable classes. The school culture is shaped by the various activities used to increase teachers' individual rewards (Finley, 1984). Although teachers indicate their formal preferences, an informal process occurs among department members. Electives and advanced courses are considered the property of teachers who currently teach them. However, creation of a selective course in the elective program or a new course targeted toward higher-ability students reduces the number of allotted classes and minimizes the likelihood of teaching remedial students. Teachers influence class composition by encouraging certain students who may be having problems to transfer out in the first weeks of school. Other teachers may gain a reputation for being tough by failing many remedial students, so the least motivated students select other teachers of the same course. The diminished social status attributed to lower tracks (for example, vocational versus academic tracks) also accrues to teachers. These activities shape the tracking system by creating above-average, below-average, middle, and advanced classes partially related to teaching expertise (Darling-Hammond, 1990). Teacher tracks add to the institutionalized tracking that occurs in secondary schools and create more curricular inequities for the many students from diverse backgrounds who are overrepresented in the lower tracks.

Inequity in Curriculum

As a result of belief systems and ability grouping and tracking, there is inequity in the curriculum for many racial and ethnic minority students (Oakes and Lipton, 1990). Students in the lower-ability groups or tracks do not have equal access to knowledge and opportunity to learn. Numerous studies have found minimal effects on achievement for most forms of ability grouping (Slavin, 1988) and tracking (Gamoran and Berends, 1987); however, the rationale typically provided by schools and teachers is to increase the fit between school programs and students of different abilities. Schools are limited in their efforts to match instructional programs and classes with student capabilities by the distribution of student ability, class size, the physical arrangement of classrooms, the availability of teachers and other instructional resources, externally imposed curriculum requirements, and the norms governing access of students to educational resources (Hallinan and Sorensen, 1983). Despite these structural and organizational constraints, grouping in various forms has been the primary method for accommodating student diversity.

In general, racial and ethnic minorities and students from lower socioeconomic backgrounds are overrepresented in the lower or non-college-bound groups and are underrepresented in programs for the gifted (Darling-Hammond, 1985; Braddock, 1989). Oakes (1985) suggests that teachers' assumptions are made about what different kinds of students are able to learn. These assumptions extend not only to what skills they are able to master but also to what ideas and concepts they are able to comprehend. Several studies of lower-tracked classes at the secondary level have found that instruction is conceptually simplified and proceeds more slowly than in higher-tracked classes (Gamoran and Berends, 1987). In lower-tracked classrooms, teachers lower academic standards, tend to emphasize basic skills and factual knowledge, and resort more frequently to structured activities and drill (Hargreaves, 1967; Heathers, 1969; Leacock, 1969; Keddie, 1971; Rosenbaum, 1976, 1980; Metz, 1978; Schwartz, 1981; Evertson, 1982; Oakes, 1985). Teachers may omit topics from their lessons altogether (Oakes, 1985). Oakes (1985) found that the content taught in lower-tracked classes locked students into that track level, not so much as a result of the topics that were included for instruction but rather as a result of the topics omitted.

At the elementary school level, inequity in the curriculum is reflected in opportunity to learn, which is substantially limited for students in the lower-ability groups. The pace of instruction is slower (Barr and Dreeben, 1983; Rowan and Miracle, 1983), and differential pacing reinforces initial achievement differentials (Rowan and Miracle, 1983). For example, in first-grade classrooms in lower groups, Eder (1981) found that students paid attention only about 60 percent of the listening time, whereas their counterparts in the higher groups were attending nearly 80 percent of the time. There were twice as many management acts and reading-turn disruptions in lower as in higher groups. For students in remedial reading, such as Chapter 1, both the quantity and quality of instruction is less (Allington, 1987; Allington and Johnston, 1989).

The task of preparing future teachers to work with diverse student groups requires that we impart not only knowledge of content and strategies but also an understanding of how personal belief systems and practices affect students' access to knowledge. Special programs for at-risk students are unlikely to succeed "if they do not attend to the structural conditions of schools that place these children at risk, not only from their home or community circumstances but from their school experiences as well" (Darling-Hammond, 1990, p. 249). In order to change the school culture to accommodate student diversity, changes must also occur in the roles of teachers and the norms affecting teacher behavior. Variables such as cooperation, consistent policy enforcement, shared decision making, sense of control over work, and high discretionary effort have been identified as important in creating a professional teaching culture (Corcoran, 1985). In the next section, we discuss these variables and describe strategies that have been used by schools and districts to accommodate student diversity.

Changing the School Culture

The most effective schools provide learning environments that are responsive to a wide range of student needs. These schools incorporate a social organization of remediation that addresses not only instruction in academic skills but also the social support systems needed by students to achieve schooling success (Epstein, 1988). Changes in schools to accommodate student diversity depend on closer consideration of individual students, conducted in a manner different from approaches of the past. Empirical evidence obtained over the last decade suggests that it is more effective to change the organizational culture to improve student outcomes than to change personalities of individuals (Purkey and Smith, 1983; Corcoran, 1985). Restructuring efforts to change the culture of schools will vary in the manipulation of specific structures and must be developed on a case-by-case basis because each school differs considerably in terms of its particular constituency, students, and support needs of staff in constructing new experiences for students.

The most persuasive research suggests that student academic performance is strongly affected by school culture (Brookover and others, 1979). As dynamic social systems, school cultures vary in terms of the composition of the staff and student body and the environment in which the school exists, giving each school a unique climate (Brookover and others, 1979; Purkey and Smith, 1985). Change is brought about when the focus is on systemic, organizational reform that involves staff participation in all phases of school planning.

The aspects of school culture discussed in the literature on organization have been categorized on the basis of dimensions that have operational meaning for policy and practice in schools (Corcoran, 1985). We consider here five dimensions pertinent to restructuring school culture for diverse student populations.

Shared Decision Making

The primary aim of shared decision making is to establish a school management and instructional team that makes decisions in accordance with the goals and resources of a particular school. Staff participation is integral to the process of creating a positive school culture (Purkey and Smith, 1985). Numerous researchers have identified the participation of teachers in decisions and their influence over policy as central to school effectiveness. Decision making is an alterable feature of the school authority structure that can be adapted to a team approach. The inclusion of teachers in school leadership, decision making, and problem solving directly engages their expertise and provides an incentive for them to use their initiative. Research indicates that shared decision making by teachers and principals, based on collaborative planning, collegial problem solving, and intellectual sharing, produces greater job satisfaction, retention, decision quality, commitment, productivity, and student achievement (Purkey and Smith, 1985; Guthrie, 1986; Darling-Hammond, 1988, 1990).

Consistent Policy Enforcement

Schools have loosely linked mechanisms that coordinate the range of activities basic to their operation. These include the enforcement of school policy, expectations, rewards, and punishments. The culture of a school is affected by the consistent or inconsistent enforcement of the school procedures, rules, and beliefs that guide the daily functioning of the staff and students.

A growing literature suggests that the principal has an important management responsibility to create coherence between the school's policy and its culture. For example, many urban schools that have diverse student populations have a core or standardized curriculum. In order for teachers to meet the instructional needs of individual students, refinement of the curriculum is necessary. Principals who send inconsistent and unclear policy enforcement messages can hinder student success and produce teacher tension and frustration, but principals who clearly and consistently enforce school policy and the administration of rewards and punishment can produce improved discipline and higher student achievement. Consistency in relations between teachers and administrators results in increased teacher productivity (Corcoran, 1985).

Cooperation and Coordination

Coordinated programming promotes closer relationships among teachers and increases learning alternatives. In urban schools in which accommodation of diversity, academic skills, social skills, and personal characteristics are organizational goals, cooperation and coordination among teachers and related resource personnel is vital (Wang and Vaughan, 1987). Attempts at change are more successful when teachers and administrators work together; cooperation breaks down barriers and encourages the kind of intellectual sharing that can lead to consensus, productivity, feelings of unity and commonality among staff, and student success (Little, 1981; Slavin, Braddock, Hall, and Petza, 1989; Corcoran, 1985).

Coordination of program efforts promotes closer relationships among teachers and increases the number of learning alternatives available to meet the needs of a diverse student population. The principal influences school restructuring by becoming a team leader. The literature on effective schools suggests that the principal is the key to implementing an integrated, cohesive instructional plan that serves a range of student needs. This leadership ensures cooperation and coordination by forging disparate members of the school staff into a working team (Blum, Butler, and Olsen, 1987; Manning, 1987).

Sense of Control over Work

The degree of teacher autonomy or control over daily work is related to the quality of teachers' professional lives. A primary task of schools is to find ways to encourage staff competence and effectiveness while imposing fewer organizational procedures and rules on what, when, and how students are to be taught. School organizations need to be modified to allow staff to maintain discretion and judgment in meeting the unique needs of their students. Under such conditions, teachers can work collegially to design programs, shape appropriate learning experiences, and develop shared standards of instructional practice. Effective schools encourage staff initiative and report higher teacher autonomy and professional accountability (Corcoran, 1985; Darling-Hammond, 1989). Other research has shown that teacher efficacy is an important dimension of teacher satisfaction and facilitation of higher student achievement (Lee, Dedrick, and Smith, 1991).

Discretionary Effort

Schools that have effective climates report that teachers work beyond what is required by contracts and give extra time to school-related activities such as tutoring, counseling, and extracurricular activities. They also put more time into lesson planning and grading (Corcoran and Wilson, 1986). The amount of discretionary effort that teachers and others give is related to their influence over decisions affecting their work, the amount of autonomy granted to complete tasks, and consensus on school goals (Yankelovich and Immerwahr, 1983). In successful schools where there is supportive leadership, substantial teacher participation in policy making, and opportunity for collegiality and recognition, teachers feel more positive about their work and more effective in their classrooms, have higher morale, and give extra effort.

These five components of school culture can accommodate diversity in the school setting and enhance multicultural understanding. In schools characterized by a high degree of shared decision making, there is a greater sense of community. Principals are more likely to communicate with staff and to be perceived as knowledgeable about problems faced by staff. The professional culture in these schools is one in which teachers feel a high degree of efficacy and control over student behavior and the instructional process. Teachers are also more likely to perceive their efforts as fruitful rather than as wastes of time. There is strong agreement among teachers concerning coordination, cooperation, and sharing, and teachers are more likely to make conscious efforts toward these ends (Winfield, 1990).

Programs That Build on Diversity

In this section, specific programs that use various aspects of the dimensions described above are briefly presented. Each program mixes and matches the dimensions to develop strategies that meet its unique needs. The programs have three themes in common: school organization, school-home-community linkage, and improved student learning. Many of these programs are recent developments, and there is limited empirical data available on their long-term effectiveness.

School Organization

Programs in this category are geared toward restructuring schools to create cultures and implementation support systems that allow teachers and other school personnel to use their instructional expertise and subject matter knowledge to enhance student learning. Four critical elements of these restructuring efforts are (1) a team approach to problem solving and decision making, and redeployment of school resources; (2) built-in flexibility in scheduling of staff and student time to more effectively meet the needs of all students; (3) roles and responsibilities determined by the expertise of the staff and the needs of students; and (4) data-based staff development programs designed to meet the training and technical assistance needs of individual staff members.

Restructuring efforts entail the application of these elements to systemic issues such as staff development, student achievement, site-based management, and high school graduation rates. Two programs with different emphases that utilize a school organization approach to improving teaching and learning are the Miami-Dade County school-based management model and the Schoolwide Projects model in the Philadelphia school system.

Miami-Dade County. The Miami-Dade County School District in Florida is implementing instructional programming and related services in a school-based management and shared decision-making project that empowers school staff to improve educational practice by sharing authority. The project incorporates organizational change, participatory decision making, and implementation of innovative programs. The decision-making process includes curriculum planning, collegial teamwork, and comprehensive planning to improve school-centered programs so that all students receive the best education possible.

Under the school-based management system, principals encourage teachers to develop and refine the curricula. The diversity of needs and abilities in urban schools warrants a corresponding diversity in intervention (Wehlage, Rutter, and Turnbaugh, 1987). District curricula are revised according to local needs, resulting in more usable instructional plans. Curricula are more individualized to respond to student differences, enriched to reflect specialized interests and knowledge of students and teachers (Glatthorn, 1987), and are more interdisciplinary.

Philadelphia Schoolwide Projects. The Philadelphia Schoolwide Projects model, implemented at sites in which at least 75 percent of the students are economically disadvantaged, is based on effective schools research and site-based management. A whole school approach is emphasized, remedial "pull outs" are minimized, staff and principals have control over Chapter 1 funds, and participatory decision making and collaborative teaching are emphasized. Staff development for schools undergoing change was intensive and focused simultaneously on changing school structures as well as teacher beliefs and norms regarding student learning. Preliminary assessment data indicate positive effects on student achievement (Winfield and Stringfield, 1991; Winfield, 1991a; Lytle and others, 1990; Davidoff and Pierson, 1991).

School-Home-Community Linkage

Programs in this category are based on the premise that because of the rapid changes in society today, schools, families, and communities must share the responsibility of mobilizing resources and expertise (see Nettles, 1991). School-home-community programs cite the following focal points in the effort to improve schools: (1) a wide variety of strategies to increase families' interest in and capacity to foster positive attitudes and readiness for school learning; (2) alternative delivery systems that engage families, community agencies, universities, and the private sector to support schools and student success; (3) coordination and linkage of the work of social and health service agencies and the community resources for students and families; and (4) programs to increase family involvement in school activities as volunteers, including participation in the planning and implementation of these programs.

Comer Process. In his approach to increasing school and community participation, James Comer (1986) emphasizes changes in the attitudes and working relationships of schools and families. A critical function of the school management team (composed of the principal, school psychologist, teachers, and parents) is to increase school and community involvement and to design and carry out a social activities calendar for the entire school year, with parents playing a primary role. When schools and families work together, children view learning as a value of the school and the family. School and family involvement activities include bringing parents and teachers together to support children's success in school, teaching families and school staff how to provide a home and school environment that encourages learning, providing parenting workshops, visiting homes and the school, giving parents and teachers strategies for helping the children at home, and asking parents and teachers to work together in the school.

Comprehensive Student Support Services (CSSS). In the Philadelphia School District, a program was initiated to develop school-based teams in which school staff, parents, organizations, and community agencies work collaboratively to deliver social services and community support. The school is considered to be the most stable institution in the community and an important social network that children and families need if they are to thrive. The school facilitates the communication of information regarding students' affective and social needs to outside community agencies as well as to teachers in the schools (Manning, 1987). CSSS is a process model designed to address attendance, counseling, special education, parental involvement, public service resources, and staff development needs at urban schools with large, diverse student populations.

Improved Student Learning

Programs in this category focus on adapting either the classroom organization or curriculum and instruction to meet the instructional needs of individual students. Programs that use this approach are based on the premise that every classroom contains students who have different interests, talents, and learning needs, and that they not only learn in different ways and at varying rates but also require varying curriculum design and instructional approaches. The most common approaches to the improvement of student learning include curriculum design and modification efforts that use one or more of the following features: (1) curriculum-based assessment approaches to assess students' current levels of performance and to provide teachers with instructionally relevant information for instructional planning and placement decisions; (2) frequent checkpoints for monitoring student progress, planning, and instruction and for providing feedback; (3) a focus on the mastery of both subject matter content and critical basic skills required for efficient information processing and successful performance; (4) provision within the curriculum for direct instruction, as well as opportunity for students to explore and solve problems independently; (5) a continuum of alternative paths and a variety of learning activities; (6) built-in flexibility in terms of pacing for individual students and the amount of time teachers spend on providing direct instruction to individual students when needed; (7) materials and an instructional management system that convey the expectation that students take responsibility for the management of their own learning progress and behaviors; and (8) built-in opportunity for students to work cooperatively in groups.

Cooperative Teaching Approaches. Throughout the country in integrated urban schools, teachers are participating in shared decision making to address the problems of minority students or students with special needs who are often disproportionately represented in lower-track programs. Instead of traditional high, middle, and low grades in elementary schools and advanced, general, and basic tracks in middle, junior, and high schools, many schools are developing alternatives to traditional ability-grouping practices. For example, some schools are using team-teaching approaches to teach major subjects and are regularly regrouping students according to the results of ongoing evaluations; in other schools, teachers are writing their own course outlines, experiments, and tests, and each activity is designed from easy to challenging to accommodate all levels of students. These schools provide in-depth staff development that includes topics such as classroom management, cooperative learning, learning styles, study skills, and motivational techniques. The Washington Elementary School in Salt Lake City, Utah; Harding Middle School in Cedar Rapids, Iowa; Maplewood Middle School in Maplewood, Minnesota; and Central Park East High School in New York City are a few of the schools implementing cooperative teaching approaches and alternatives to tracking and ability grouping (Slavin, Braddock, Hall, and Petza, 1989).

Mastery Learning Model. The Johnson City School District in New York operates a mastery model of staff development in which participating school staff are involved in a clear procedure that develops participants from learners and practitioners to coaches of other staff members. Staff development is integrally linked to school goals, to individual staff performance goals, and to the learning process. The procedure encourages collegiality and cooperation. It requires, first, that the participants master the facts about a particular innovation; second, that they apply the practice in controlled and predictable situations; third, that they apply the practice in additional areas; and, finally, that they design new components based on the innovative practice (Vickery, 1988).

Coalition of Essential Schools. The Coalition of Essential Schools Project, chaired by Theodore Sizer at Brown University in Providence, Rhode Island, is a group of schools in which the restructuring focuses on the relationships between teachers and students and on changes in the curriculum to reduce fragmentation, increase depth of coverage, and help students understand the relationship of school subjects to real-life demands (see Beckum, this volume). Sizer's philosophy of school change is based on principles such as the necessity of having students actively engaged in their own learning. Tracking is reduced or eliminated, regrouping of students occurs more frequently, and the student-teacher ratio is reduced. Critical thinking skills and subject matter are incorporated into the curriculum in a meaningful manner, not in isolation. Students in an essential coalition school in an urban area had better attendance and academic performance than did comparable students not in the program (Billups, 1991).

Exemplary Schools. The Exemplary Schools Project is a collaborative venture between the Philadelphia School District and Temple University, focused on the coordination of instructional programming and related service delivery to diverse student groups. Over a three-year period, the elementary, middle, and high schools involved in the project have implemented multi-age grouping, cooperating learning, flexible pacing, and team teaching in order to change existing organizational structures. Curriculum refinement efforts concentrate on developing a variety and range of options, such as enrichment programs and programs that address academic as well as social skills, in order to enhance the opportunities of teachers to meet the needs of individual students. Extensive collaboration with museums, corporations, and community businesses provide opportunities for mentoring, enrichment activities, and career exploration.

Comprehensive Restructuring: Success for All

Success for All is a comprehensive restructuring program that incorporates many of the research-based practices described here. This program is a collaborative effort of the Baltimore City Public Schools, the local Abell Foundation, and the Center for Research on Effective Schooling for Disadvantaged Students at Johns Hopkins University. The program restructures the elementary school with one commitment in mind: Do everything necessary to ensure that all students perform at grade level in the basic skills of reading, writing, and mathematics by the end of third grade. This objective is accomplished through the concentration of resources in prekindergarten through third grade and the use of instructional programs based on the best available research. Funding comes from a variety of sources. Chapter 1 provides the school with federal funds to improve education for disadvantaged children, Chapter 2 funds supplement the effort, the Abell Foundation provides funding for implementation and evaluation, the Office of Educational Research and Improvement funds the Center staff working with the school to carry out the project. The program's philosophy that all children can learn translates into a schoolwide commitment to provide the following resources.

Preschool and Kindergarten

A Success for All school provides a half-day preschool and a full-day kindergarten, both of which focus on balanced and developmentally appropriate learning experiences for young children. The curricula emphasize the development and use of language, balancing academic readiness and music, art, and movement activities. Readiness activities include use of Peabody Language Development Kits and the Story Telling and Retelling program in which students retell stories read to them by teachers. Prereading activities begin in the second semester of kindergarten.

Family Support Team

Two social workers and one parent liaison work full-time in the school. This team provides parenting education and works to involve parents in their children's success in school. The team provides family support assistance for children who are not receiving adequate sleep or nutrition, who need glasses, who are not attending school regularly, or who have serious behavior problems.

Reading Program

For ninety-minute reading periods each day, students in first grade through third grade are regrouped into classes of fifteen students who are all at the same reading level. Thus, a reading class might contain a mix of first, second, and third graders, but each child would be at the same reading level. This regrouping is a form of the Joplin Plan, which has been shown to increase reading achievement in the elementary grades (Slavin, 1988). Beginning in the middle of their kindergarten year and continuing until they reach reading level 2-1 (the first half of the second grade), the children learn auditory discrimination, sound recognition, and sound blending, using phonetic minibooks rather than basals. They often work together in pairs, reading to one another and working on "share sheets." They read high-interest trade books in school and at home. At reading level 2-1, children begin a form of the Cooperative Integrated Reading and Composition program. They work in small teams in which they read to one another; identify characters, settings, problems, and problem solutions in narratives; summarize stories; and write.

Reading Tutors

In each participating elementary school, six tutors are provided for the approximately three hundred students in grades K–3. Each tutor works one-on-one with a total of eleven students per day. First graders get priority for the tutoring, however, on the assumption that the primary function of the tutors is to help all students be successful in reading when they first begin—success that would negate the need for tutors in subsequent grades. The tutors are certified, experienced teachers. They work one-on-one with children who are having trouble keeping up in their regular reading groups. The tutoring is conducted in twenty-minute sessions, taken out of a hour-long social studies period, and addresses the objectives covered in the regular reading curriculum. During the daily ninety-minute reading periods, the tutors serve as additional regular reading teachers. They coordinate their tutoring activities with the activities of the regular reading teachers through specific information forms and scheduled meetings.

Individual Academic Plans

At least every eight weeks, based on assessment of progress by the reading teachers, individual academic plans are developed for each student to determine who is to receive tutoring, to suggest other adaptations in a child's program, and to identify children who may need special assistance, such as family intervention or screening for vision or hearing.

Program Facilitator

A program facilitator works at each school full-time to coordinate the operation of Success for All. The facilitator works with the principal to plan and schedule the program and visits classrooms and tutoring sessions frequently to help with individual problems.

The facilitator works with individual children when needed to find strategies for helping them, helps teachers and tutors deal with behavior problems, and coordinates the activities of the family support team with those of the instructional staff.

Teacher Training

The teachers and tutors are regular certified teachers. They received two days of in-service training at the beginning of the year and work from detailed teachers' manuals to carry out the Success for All program. Several brief in-service workshops are provided during the year on topics such as classroom management, instructional pace, and implementation of the reading curriculum.

Advisory Committee

An advisory committee meets weekly to review the progress of the program. The committee includes the school principal, the program facilitator, teacher representatives, a social worker, and the Johns Hopkins University research staff. Evaluations of the program over the last three years have found that from prekindergarten through third grade, Success for All students outscored students in a control school on multiple measures of reading readiness through reading comprehension (Madden and others, 1988; Slavin and others, 1990). In addition, for grades 1–3 in Success for All schools, retentions and special education referrals decreased after program implementation.

Conclusion

The strategies and programs implemented to accommodate student diversity vary in targets for change, in philosophies, and in degree of comprehensiveness. Despite the differences, there is a common underlying assumption: To improve schools as places for students and teachers to learn, a fundamental change is required in school culture. The existing norms and behaviors of teachers and students, belief systems, and supporting structures must be dramatically altered to accommodate the growing diversity in urban populations.

Many of these parameters of schooling have been and continue to be affected by federal, state, and district policies (for example, Chapter 1) as well as by specific practices at the local school level (for example, student and teacher tracking). For teacher educators, and for all of those preparing the next generation of teachers, preservice coursework should be revised to include an understanding of the larger policy contexts of schools and how policy affects school culture, teacher beliefs, and opportunity to learn. New entrants into teaching will encounter an increasingly diverse student population in their classrooms and will need to understand how school policies influence classroom decisions and practices. This knowledge is critical to teachers who will eventually assume more active responsibility for decision making and school governance.

Moreover, research on effective instructional strategies with diverse student populations, such as cooperative learning and collaborative teaching, should be encouraged among participants in preservice courses and incorporated routinely into other teacher education classes in order to prepare teachers for urban schools. Changes in school culture ultimately mean changes in the beliefs and behaviors of teachers and administrators. In order to assume the responsibility for improving student learning outcomes, research on effective strategies and practices must become a part of the tacit knowledge base of teaching.

Change in school culture can be brought about by providing the next generation of teachers with a better understanding of the ways in which specific behaviors and practices operate to create inequitable conditions for diverse groups. True accommodation of student diversity means the elimination of those inequities.

References

Allington, R. L. (1987). Shattered hopes: Why two federal reading programs have failed to correct reading failure. *Learning, 16*(1), 60–62.

Allington, R. L., and Johnston, P. (1989). Coordination, collaboration, and consistency: The redesign of compensatory and special education interventions. In R. Slavin, N. Madden, and N.

Karweit (eds.), *Preventing school failure: Effective programs for students at risk*. Needham Heights, MA: Allyn & Bacon.

Allington, R. L., and McGill-Franzen, A. (1989). School response to reading failure: Chapter 1 and special education students in grades 2, 4, and 8. *Elementary School Journal*.

Barr, R., and Dreeben, R. (1983). *How schools work*. Chicago: University of Chicago Press.

Barton, A. H., and Wilder, P. E. (1964). Research and practice in the teaching of reading: A progress report. In M. B. Miles (ed.), *Innovations in education*. New York: Teachers College Press.

Billups, S. (1991). The impact of the essential school versus traditional instructional methods on the academic performance and attendance rates of urban high school students. Paper presented at the annual meeting of the American Educational Research Association, Chicago.

Blum, R. E., Butler, J. A., and Olsen, N. L. (1987). Leadership for excellence: Research-based training for principals. *Educational Leadership, 45*, 25–29.

Braddock, J. H. (1989). *Tracking of black, Hispanic, Asian, Native American, and white students: National patterns and trends*. Baltimore, MD: Center for Research on Effective Schooling of Disadvantaged Students, Johns Hopkins University.

Brookover, W. B., and others. (1979). Elementary school social climate and school achievement. *American Educational Research Journal, 15*(2), 301–318.

Bunting, C. E. (1984). Dimensionality of teacher education beliefs: An exploratory study. *Journal of Experimental Education, 52*(4), 195–198.

Carter, L. F. (1984). The sustaining effects study of compensatory and elementary education. *Educational Researcher, 13*, 4–13.

Comer, J. P. (1980). *School power*. New York: Macmillan.

Comer, J. P. (1986). Academic and affective gains from the school development program: A model for school improvement. ERIC Document No. 274750.

Coleman, J. S., and others. (1966). *Equality of educational opportunity*. Washington, DC: Government Printing Office.

Corcoran, T. B. (1985). *Improving school climate: A brief review of school climate variables*. Philadelphia: Research for Better Schools.

Corcoran, T. B., and Wilson, B. (1986). *The search for successful secondary schools: The first three years of the secondary school recognition program*. Philadelphia: Research for Better Schools.

Darling-Hammond, L. (1985). *Equality and excellence: The educational status of black Americans*. New York: College Board.

Darling-Hammond, L. (1988). Accountability and teacher professionalism. *American Educator, 12*(4), 8–13.

Darling-Hammond, L. (1989). Teacher quality and educational equality. Paper presented at the conference Literacy Among Black Youth: Issues in Learning, Teaching, and Schooling, Literacy Research Center, Graduate School for Education, University of Pennsylvania.

Darling-Hammond, L. (1990). Teacher quality and equality. In J. I. Goodlad and P. Keating (eds.), *Access to knowledge*. New York: College Entrance Examination Board.

Davidoff, S. H., and Pierson, E. M. (1991). A continued look at the promise of schoolwide projects. Paper presented at the annual meeting of the American Educational Research Association, Chicago.

Eastman, G. (1988). *Family involvement in education*. Madison: Wisconsin Department of Public Instruction. (Bulletin No. 8926, ERIC Document No. 316802)

Eder, D. (1981). Ability grouping as a self-fulfilling prophecy: A micro-analysis of teacher-student interaction. *Sociology of Education, 54*, 151–162.

Epstein, J. L. (1988). Effective schools or effective students: Dealing with diversity. In R. Haskins and D. MacRae (eds.), *Policies for America's public schools*. Norwood, NJ: Ablex.

Evertson, C. M. (1982). Differences in instructional activities in higher- and lower-achieving junior high English and math classes. *Elementary School Journal, 82*, 329–350.

Finley, M. K. (1984). Teachers and tracking in a comprehensive high school. *Sociology of Education, 57*, 233–243.

Gamoran, A., and Berends, M. (1987). The effects of stratification in secondary schools: Synthesis of survey and ethnographic research. *Review of Educational Research, 57*, 415–435.

Glatthorn, A. A. (1987). *Curriculum renewal*. Alexandria, VA: Association for Supervision and Curriculum Development.

Gordon, E. (1982). Urban Education. In H. E. Mitzel (ed.), *Encyclopedia of educational research*. Vol. 4. (5th ed.) New York: Macmillan.

Guthrie, J. W. (1986). School-based management: The next needed education reform. *Phi Delta Kappan, 68*(4), 305–309.

Hallinan, M. T., and Sorensen, A. B. (1983). The formation and stability of instructional groups. *American Sociological Review, 48*, 838–851.

Hare, B. S. (1989). *State University of New York task force for the cultivation of pluralism*. Unpublished manuscript. State University of New York, Stony Brook.

Hargreaves, D. H. (1967). *Social relations in a secondary school*. New York: Routledge & Kegan Paul.

Hawley, W. (1988). Missing pieces of the educational reform agenda: Or why the first and second waves may miss the boat. *Educational Administration Quarterly, 24*(4), 416–437.

Heathers, G. (1969). Grouping. In R. L. Ebel (ed.), *Encyclopedia of educational research*. (4th ed.) New York: Macmillan.

Johnston, P. H., Allington, R. L., and Afflerbach, P. (1985). The congruence of classroom and remedial instruction. *Elementary School Journal, 85*, 465–478.

Jones, B. F. (1989). *Managing instruction for equity and excellence resource guide: Effective alternatives to tracking*. Alexandria, VA: Public Broadcasting Service and North Central Regional Educational Laboratory.

Kaestle, C. F., and Smith, M. S. (1982). The federal role in elementary and secondary education, 1940–1980. *Harvard Educational Review, 52*(4), 384–408.

Keddie, N. (1971). Classroom knowledge. In M.F.D. Young (ed.), *Knowledge and control*. London, England: Macmillan.

Leacock, E. (1969). *Teaching and learning in city schools*. New York: Basic Books.

Lee, V. E., Dedrick, R. B., and Smith, J. B. (1991). The effect of the social organization of schools on teacher satisfaction. *Sociology of Education, 64*, 190–208.

Little, J. W. (1981). School success and staff development in urban desegregated schools: A summary of recently completed research. Paper presented at the annual meeting of the American Educational Research Association, Los Angeles.

Lytle, J. H., and others. (1990). The promise of schoolwide projects. Paper presented at the annual meeting of the American Educational Research Association, Boston.

McGill-Franzen, A., and Allington, R. L. (1991). The gridlock of low reading achievement: Perspectives on practice and policy. *Remedial and Special Education, 12*(3), 20–30.

Madden, R. L., and others. (1988). *Success for all: Effects on student achievement, retentions, and special education referrals.* Baltimore, MD: Center for Research on Elementary and Middle Schools, Johns Hopkins University.

Maeroff, G. I. (1988). Withered hopes, stillborn dreams: The dismal panorama of urban schools. *Phi Delta Kappan,* May, 633–638.

Manning, J. B. (1987). Roles and activities of special education elementary support teams members; perceptions of Philadelphia school principals. Unpublished doctoral dissertation, College of Education, Temple University.

Metz, M. H. (1978). *Classrooms and corridors: The crisis of authority in desegregated secondary schools.* Berkeley and Los Angeles: University of California Press.

Metz, M. H. (1988). Some missing elements in the school reform movement. *Educational Administration Quarterly, 24*(4), 446–460.

National Education Association. (1968). *Ability grouping: Research summary.* Washington, DC: National Educational Association, Research Division.

Nettles, S. M. (1991). Community involvement and disadvantaged students: A review. *Review of Educational Research, 61*(3), 379–406.

Oakes, J. (1985). *Keeping track: How schools structure inequality.* New Haven, CT: Yale University Press.

Oakes, J., and Keating, P. (1988). Access to knowledge: Breaking down school barriers to learning. Unpublished manuscript, prepared for Education Commission of the States, Denver, and the College Board, New York.

Oakes, J., and Lipton, M. (1990). Tracking and ability grouping:

A structural barrier to access and achievement. In J. I. Goodlad and P. Keating (eds.), *Access to knowledge.* New York: College Entrance Examination Board.

Peters, T. J., and Waterman, R. H. (1982). *In search of excellence.* New York: Warner Books.

Purkey, S. C., and Smith, M. S. (1983). Effective schools: A review. *Elementary School Journal, 85,* 427–452.

Purkey, S. C., and Smith, M. S. (1985). School reform: The district policy implications of the effective schools literature. *Elementary School Journal, 85*(5), 353–389.

Rosenbaum, J. E. (1976). *Making inequality: The hidden curriculum of high school tracking.* New York: Wiley.

Rosenbaum, J. E. (1980). Social implications of educational grouping. In D. C. Berliner (ed.), *Review of research in education.* Vol. 8. Itasca, IL: Peacock.

Rowan, B., and Miracle, A. W., Jr. (1983). Systems of ability grouping and the stratification of achievement in elementary schools. *Sociology of Education, 56,* 133–144.

Schwartz, F. (1981). Supporting or subverting learning: Peer group patterns in four tracked schools. *Anthropology and Education Quarterly, 12,* 99–121.

Shavelson, R. J., and Stern, P. (1981). Research on teachers' pedagogical thoughts, judgments, decisions, and behavior. *Review of Educational Research, 51*(4), 455–498.

Shujaa, M. J. (1991). Does it matter what teachers think?: Teachers' perceptions of a new policy to infuse African and African American content into the school curriculum. Paper presented at the annual meeting of the American Educational Research Association, Chicago.

Slavin, R. E. (1987). Ability grouping and student achievement in elementary schools: A best evidence synthesis. *Review of Educational Research, 57,* 293–336.

Slavin, R. E. (1988). Synthesis of research on grouping in elementary and secondary schools. *Educational Leadership, 46,* 67–77.

Slavin, R. E., Braddock, J. H., Hall, C., and Petza, R. J. (1989). *Alternatives to ability grouping.* Baltimore, MD: Center for Research on Effective Schooling for Disadvantaged Students, Center for Research on Elementary and Middle Schools, Johns Hopkins University.

Slavin, R., and others. (1990). *Success for all: Effects of variations in duration and resources of a schoolwide elementary restructuring program.* CDS Report, no. 2. Baltimore, MD: Center for Research on Effective Schooling for Disadvantaged Students, Johns Hopkins University.

Spady, W. G. (1973). The impact of school resources on students. In F. N. Kerlinger (ed.), *Review of research in education.* Vol. 1. Itasca, IL: Peacock.

Turnbull, B. J. (1986). Federal and state policy. In J. Hannaway and M. E. Lockheed (eds.), *The contributions of the social sciences to educational policy and practice,* 1965–1985. Berkeley, CA: McCutchan.

Venezky, R. L., and Winfield, L. F. (1979). *Schools that succeed beyond expectations in teaching reading.* Newark: University of Delaware Studies on Education.

Vickery, T. R. (1988). Learning from an outcomes-driven school district. *Educational Leadership, 42,* 52–56.

Walberg, H. J., and Wang, M. C. (1987). Effective educational practices and provisions for individual differences. In M. C. Wang, M. C. Reynolds, and H. J. Walberg (eds.), *Handbook of special education: Research and practice.* Vol. 1: *Learner characteristics and adaptive education.* Elmsford, NY: Pergamon.

Wang, M. C., and Vaughan, E. D. (1987). *Handbook for the implementation of adaptive instruction programs: Module 4, curriculum resources for individualizing instruction.* Philadelphia: Center for Research in Human Development and Education, Temple University.

Watson, B. C., and Traylor, F. M. (1988). Tomorrow's teachers: Who will they be, what will they know? In J. Dewart (ed.), *The state of black America.* New York: Urban League.

Wehlage, G. G., Rutter, R. A., and Turnbaugh, A. (1987). A program mode for at-risk high school students. *Educational Leadership, 45,* 70–73.

Winfield, L. F. (1982). Principals' instructional behavior in inner-urban schools. Paper presented at the annual meeting of the American Educational Research Association, Boston.

Winfield, L. F. (1986a). Do Chapter 1 programs promote educational equity: A review and some comments. *Journal of Educational Equity and Leadership, 6*(1), 61–71.

Winfield, L. F. (1986b). Teacher beliefs toward academically at-risk students in inner urban schools. *Urban Review, 18*(4), 253–268.

Winfield, L. F. (1990). Restructuring schools: Organizational practices that impact school culture. Paper presented at the annual meeting of the American Educational Research Association, Boston.

Winfield, L. F. (1991a). Case studies of evolving schoolwide projects. *Educational Evaluation and Policy Analysis, 13*(4), 353–362.

Winfield, L. F. (1991b). Resilience, schooling, and development among African American youth: A conceptual framework. *Education and Urban Society, 24*(1), 5–14.

Winfield, L. F., and Stringfield, S. (1991). *A description of schoolwide projects.* CDS Report, no. 16. Baltimore, MD: Center for Research on Effective Schooling for Disadvantaged Students, Johns Hopkins University.

Yankelovich, D., and Immerwahr, J. (1983). *Putting the work ethic to work.* New York: The Public Agenda Foundation.

11

Diversifying Assessment: A Key Factor in the Reform Equation

Leonard C. Beckum

Since the publication of *A Nation at Risk: The Imperative for Educational Reform* (National Commission on Excellence in Education, 1983), education has been at the forefront of our national social and political agenda. The critical findings of that report, followed by the release of other studies, commission reports, and newspaper and journal articles decrying the failures of our nation's educational system, signaled the beginning of key policymakers' involvement in the search for ways to improve American education. State legislatures, governors, local education agencies, and numerous civic and professional organizations have been in seeming competition in their haste to propose remedies for the nation's ailing classrooms.

The public has become increasingly aware that students are not learning as much as they should, teachers are not teaching as well as they should, and institutions charged with providing education are not educating as well as they should. The proliferation of evidence pointing to the underachievement of students as a result of inappropriate programs and poorly prepared teachers has led to numerous calls for a massive reform of education, focusing on both the restructuring of elementary and secondary schools and on the preparation and training of teachers (Carnegie Council on Adolescent Development, 1989; Goodlad, 1984; Sizer, 1984; Lightfoot, 1983; Holmes Group, 1986).

Measured quantitatively and qualitatively, our educational systems are failing at their tasks. Achievement scores on standardized tests, whether compared to the scores of previous generations of American youth or whether compared to the current scores of children internationally, have been on the decline. Leaders of industry have expressed dismay over the quality of high school graduates entering the work force. The drop-out rate among minority students in our urban schools has reached as high as 50 percent (O'Neil, 1990), and the proportion of minority students going on to post-secondary education and achieving Ph.D. degrees has dropped precipitously over the previous two decades. In an interview, Albert Shanker has said that we are turning out fewer engineers, scientists, and mathematicians than are other industrial nations (Brandt, 1990). The general consensus has been that educational goals are unclear, content is amorphous, and educators are unprepared to teach this new multicultural generation.

Accordingly, the political demand for accountability has increased, putting intensive pressure on states and local education agencies, who, in an attempt to be responsive, have turned predominantly to quick, easily adopted, and relatively inexpensive instruments for measuring both student and teacher achievement levels. By 1989, most states had increased curriculum and testing requirements for students in elementary and secondary schools and had also instituted the NTE (a national teachers examination) or other, similar statewide tests for teacher certification. These new requirements were intended to make educational institutions at every level more accountable for student performance and constituted the first phase of the movement to improve schooling. However, while politicians on national and state levels were reformulating educational legislation, reformers continued to examine the educational process and to redefine the way that educational institutions should be structured in order to provide the process and content to equip all students with the skills and knowledge base necessary for success in today's competitive marketplace.

Since it is apparent that nothing short of an overhaul of the complete educational system will satisfy everyone—from parents to top policymakers—it is increasingly important for educators to refocus the discussion on reform from a piecemeal approach to a system's approach. The synthesis of design, implementation, and evaluation of effective education for students and teachers must involve all relevant contributors to the educational process. Without cooperation and collaboration, the problems inherent to the strategy of separately developing restructuring and assessment programs, which have discrete philosophies and purposes, may well undermine our ability to provide lasting and significant educational reform.

In the first phase of reform (from the mid 1980s), educators focused on cognitive issues such as the development of a core curriculum or a new emphasis on mathematics and science, longer school days, and more homework. But it soon became apparent that if schools were to become effective, the development of a new or expanded curriculum would not suffice. Therefore, the affective domain—how students learn best, why they learn, how student-teacher relationships affect learning, and different student learning styles—became another major imperative of many school reformers. Simultaneously, as methodologies to impact on the affective domain were being developed, the movement for teacher empowerment and school-based decision making grew. The emphasis on content, which started as a separate domain with the publication of the Paideia proposal (Adler, 1982), began to be integrated into the general process of school restructuring.

By the mid 1980s, common strands for successful restructuring began to emerge. Included among these were a need for orientation toward results to replace adherence to rigid regulations, school-based decision making, a problem-solving curriculum, the professionalization of teaching, and the active involvement of parents and the private sector in education.

Out of this movement and based on various underlying theories, several exploratory projects are under way, all of which share the goal of actively searching for the best way to restructure schools and educate children effectively. One of these projects is the Coalition of Essential Schools, an umbrella organization for the development of university–high school partnerships and school restructuring efforts based on the principles established in *A Study of High Schools* (National Association of Secondary School Principals and the National Association of Independent Schools, 1981–1984). The coalition currently has fifty member schools and approximately thirty-five to forty schools in six "relearning" states, that is, states whose education agencies have pledged support to the restructuring effort.

Central Park East Secondary School in New York City, which was started by Deborah Meier as an alternative school for seventh through tenth grades in the East Harlem community, is a member of the coalition. In the past several years, the school has expanded upward, adding a senior institute, and downward, adding a school for prekindergarten through sixth grade (none of the schools is larger than 270 students). Although the schools are under the leadership of Meier and work in a cooperative continuum sharing the same educational philosophy and principles, each school is organized as a separate entity with its own staff and teacher director who are free to make their own educational determinations about curriculum and assessment.

The faculty at City University of New York were interested in understanding the ways by which school faculty connected the development of the curriculum, the learning environment, and the evaluation processes. Evaluation was of particular concern, given the educational philosophy of the school and the necessity for it to operate within the framework of New York City and state testing mandates. As conveyed in an interview with the director of the prekindergarten through sixth grade at Central Park East School (personal communication, April 1989),

> When we started the school, we developed our own assessment instrument. It keeps changing . . . we've never been satisfied with assessing. . . . We've been satisfied to a certain extent with how we approach literature, language, . . . but we spend a lot of time talking about assessing, because we don't want to rely on the standardized tests as a way of assessing a child's success or failure in school. A reading test is not the way to decide whether or not a child goes on to the

next grade. . . . We have to look at the total picture—
math, science, the arts, and social skills. We have to
spend enough time understanding who the child
really is, how they learn. . . . We observe who they are
as a learner, we talk to each other; everything is
important.

The staff uses multiple processes to assess children, including lengthy staff review and observation of each child.

To do a fair evaluation of a child, you need a lot of
information. . . . We use the standardized tests because we're obligated as a public school. They don't
play a major part in assessing students . . . but I can't
tell you they don't play any part. Parents want to
know and feel comfortable with knowing what the
tests mean, because when their children leave [and go
into the real world], the tests will be used to evaluate
the child. So we give workshops and help parents to
help their children be better test takers, which is different from being better readers. This process reduces
parent anxiety. We do treat the test with integrity, but
we don't make it a central instructional focus. The
students take a practice test, the real test, and then it's
over for them. We learn from the test how the children
handle stress situations.

According to another teacher,

In the secondary school, we're wrestling through the
evaluative mechanism now in relation to our curriculum. If we say that standardized tests, New York State
Regents and Regents Competency Examinations, will
not be our determinants for evaluation and ultimately
for graduation, then what will be our determinants? If
we agree that portfolios and other long-term measures
are going to evaluate a kid, how are we going to know
that the standards will be comparable from room to

room? How will the state, the college, and the school
district be confident that what we say about a kid's
performance across the school has comparable meaning within the school system? How will a kid be sure
that the standards reflected in one classroom will be
reflected in others?

While Meier's school is but one example of emerging groups
struggling to integrate curriculum and assessment, it nevertheless
reflects one of the basic principles of the reform movement: If the
characteristics of acceptable performance are developed within a
diverse and stimulating framework, then the distinction between
curriculum and assessment will blur. This view of assessment and
its role within the curriculum is shared by researchers who state that
"teaching to the test" will not present a problem when and where
the test and the curriculum reflect the same learning goals and
methodology (O'Neil, 1990).

Only recently, evidence of growing discomfort with the appropriateness of standardized testing as the sole criterion of either
teacher or student performance has emerged on a large scale. In fact,
experts (both practitioners and researchers) such as Richard P. Mills
(Vermont's Commissioner of Education), Linda Darling-Hammond
(a professor at Teachers College), and Albert Shanker (president of
the American Federation of Teachers) are seriously questioning the
meaningful role of current testing policies. According to Mark
Tucker, president of the National Center for Education and the
Economy, "Standardized multiple-choice tests have drawn increasing fire as too simplistic, measuring the ability to recognize knowledge rather than the ability to think and solve problems, an
important skill in today's jobs. . . . If you have serious goals, you
better have serious tests" (Fiske, 1990, p. 1).

In order to accomplish the necessary synthesis of assessment
and curriculum, educators must have the freedom to diagnose their
own needs and form decisions based on these diagnoses. The National Governors Association (1989) encouraged restructuring efforts that lead to the decentralization of authority and decision
making, as well as to an emphasis on the development of accountability systems that clearly link rewards and incentives to student

performance at the building level: "Schools must have more discretion and authority to achieve results and then be held accountable for results. States must develop measures to assess valued outcomes of performance of individual schools and link rewards and sanctions to results." According to Glickman (1990, p. 41), "The message to policy makers (at district, state, and federal levels) is to hold schools accountable for achieving negotiated goals, but not to legislate how they are to achieve such results. . . . Policy makers should ease uniform standards, statewide teacher evaluation systems, and prescriptive curriculum but should not ease equal access to knowledge and documented achievement of goals."

There still exists, however, a discrepancy between the above-stated goals, on the one hand, and the day-to-day practice of policymakers, on the other, perhaps the result of a lack of communication between local and state institutions. The relationship between the setting of state standards, the relaxation of bureaucratic control, and the development of curricula that meets the needs and goals of individual schools reflects this discrepancy, often resulting in a confused agenda for the parties concerned. For example, one current New York State grant is supporting a university–high school partnership dedicated to school restructuring through school-based decision making, with a focus on the redesign of school organization, curriculum, and teaching strategies.

Philosophically, the state is committed to flexibility, individuality, and need-based content. While the state is considering the adoption of alternative assessment strategies, however, it continues to impose standardized tests in content areas without reference to local restructuring efforts. "I feel frustrated," said one professor who is leading this partnership effort at the college, "because essentially we are giving the schools dichotomous messages. We are working with the teachers, the students, and the community to help them institute the changes that will provide educational ownership of their high schools. Ironically, the state is said to be increasing the number of achievement tests in some grades, creating further likelihood of a test-driven curriculum. How do we legitimately encourage the development of a school curriculum based on the needs of the community while reality demands a curriculum based on what some test is measuring?" (personal communication).

As the above quotation indicates, while educators grapple for meaningful paths to school restructuring, assessment policies often remain confused, hovering between the lure of standardized testing procedures and the difficulties of designing and implementing other, more qualitative assessment strategies. Most frequently, the choice is made in favor of the standardized tests, resulting in the imposition of achievement standards that fail to reflect the ongoing research in both the cognitive and affective domains. Practitioners are therefore left with the problem of coping with the need for a curriculum that will satisfy two separate goals, one defined by the achievement goals of the testing process and the other evolving out of the ongoing process of reform.

Everyone encourages their communities to get involved with reform and improvement of the schools, but this involvement in the assessment process seldom occurs. Communities have been conditioned to respond to standardized test results as if the results are infallible, referring to them as "report cards" of the schools' performance without even thinking or questioning whether or not the tests are assessing what is important to the communities.

I am convinced that assessment and reform standards can and must come together, which means that we must begin to look at the components of the schooling process in a different way. Rather than using only procedures that measure students and schools laterally against each other, as if resources and starting points were the same in the neediest and most affluent school districts, I am recommending that broad goals be set, allowing room for individual growth according to different baseline data. It is important that states compare districts and schools fairly, with adequate consideration to their differing resource levels and student composition (McDonnell, 1989). The use of alternative assessments, whether portfolios, personnel profiles, or other strategies currently being explored, is insufficient unless each strategy provides a legitimate measure of progress according to the corresponding restructuring component. In essence, the school should be measured against itself with instruments that take into account many aspects of learning.

For this kind of assessment to work, individual schools must be provided with the expertise and resources necessary to make decisions that impact on budget, personnel, and curriculum (McDonnell, 1989). This approach does not preclude the establishment of broad goals and standards on a statewide or even national basis. But it does mean that the goals have to evolve with the restructuring efforts, and that we accept the fact that a period of trial and error is necessary during any period of extraordinary change. According to Shanker (Brandt, 1990, p. 111), "You need a system of self-renewal—which consists of first, knowing where you want to go and ways to find out the extent to which you've gotten there. Second, . . . giving people the power to reach the goal. And third, you need the fuel in the engine that will make them move."

Shanker echoes my own concern that both the system and the individual school must first make the commitment to change. But the system cannot make the decisions for the schools about what changes are necessary or how they should be carried out. I believe that each school should make a contract with the state, which sets out goals, timelines, and accountability procedures. In turn, the state must provide the enabling resources for the school to reach its goals.

For example, recruitment, teacher training, curriculum, student achievement, cultural diversity, learning styles, administrative procedures, community empowerment, and school decision making may all be issues for investigation or inclusion in the school restructuring process. However, what is emphasized from school to school, the priority order for change, and the speed of implementation will vary depending on motivation, need, and current resources. But whatever the plan, the appropriate strategy to measure both short-term and longitudinal growth should be developed simultaneously with each piece of the restructuring plan and implemented as part of that component and its objectives. In this process, the state would approve the restructuring and assessment plan but not predetermine it or evaluate its success outside the boundaries of the contract. According to McDonnell (1989), melding the redesign of schools with the redesign of assessment may pave the way for development of more appropriate indicator systems as potent tools in motivating schools to teach tomorrow's skills.

Along similar lines, the process of teacher education must be redefined to appropriately prepare new educators for the newly restructured schools. The growing dissatisfaction with teacher preparation and student academic performance led to the formation in

1987 of the National Board for Professional Teaching Standards. The board asked Lee Shulman and his colleagues in the Teacher Assessment Project at Stanford University to explore and identify possible prototype assessment instruments, models, and procedures (see Nelson-Barber and Mitchell, this volume). Recognition of the diversity of both assessment instrumentation and the assessment process represents a giant step in the right direction for assessing teacher preparation to teach. Assessment of teacher candidates using multiple techniques, over time and settings, with the intention of using the assessment methods to provide information for training as well as to inform the curriculum, is critical to the goal of integrating teaching and curriculum. Shulman (1987, p. 39) underscores this point:

> Our work rests on the assumption that approaches to assessment must mirror as accurately as possible the complexity and richness of teaching. It rests on a conception of teaching that differs substantially from those currently employed for such assessments as the NTE [national teachers examination] or the teacher observation systems in place in a number of states.
>
> Our work further assumes that an assessment can only be seen as a single aspect of the more general effort to improve education and the work of teachers. Thus we evaluate teacher assessment by standards that go well beyond the traditional benchmarks of reliability and validity. We ask instead whether a given approach to assessment (if taken seriously) is likely to contribute to needed changes in both the education of teachers and the settings in which they teach.

Additional vehicles being developed in California and elsewhere are the assessment center, a comprehensive field system, and the portfolio. Each of these has an instructive feature for the educational program and involves an interactive model of assessment. The hope is that candidates in these assessment settings would have an opportunity to express their thoughts about teaching as well as through curriculum rather than merely express conclusions drawn from cognitive processes conveyed through standardized tests. Each of these vehicles seeks to either evaluate directly or provide a close representation of an actual classroom setting. If schools are going through radical restructuring, then the use of familiar curricula and standardized tests are no longer appropriate vehicles for the evaluation and assessment of teachers. Recognizing this situation, researchers at regional and university centers nationwide have begun to develop alternative assessment strategies that are performance-based and reflect restructured curricula.

At my former institution, the City College of the City University of New York, we began a schoolwide reevaluation of our teacher preparation curricula and programs affecting both graduate and undergraduate students. The basic systemic approach is composed of a commitment to inquiry, curriculum planning that includes both education and liberal arts faculty, dedication to multicultural education infused throughout the curriculum, integration of and respect for the needs of the community, early clinical experiences, and a belief that excellence in content can go hand-in-hand with excellence in process. Our concerns were of necessity focused on the realization that graduates will serve a multicultural population in a volatile and evolving urban society. We realized that although many basic principles of teacher preparation may be similar to those of neighboring institutions that primarily serve suburban teacher populations, our emphases and strategies had to be quite different from theirs if we were to produce successful practitioners for city schools.

This recognition of the need for diversity and change must be but the beginning of more radical reform, which may ultimately evolve into a different way of awarding degrees and conferring credits, including a longer training period that allows for extensive work at school sites. As we moved through our review of curriculum, we are simultaneously investigating alternative evaluation procedures that will more realistically assess learning and be more predictive of classroom success. Among these methods are assessment centers, portfolios that contain goal statements, lesson plans, evaluations using videotapes, observations, and mentoring. In our case, each decision is made with the needs of our clients in mind, both those of our own student body and those of the children that they ultimately will serve.

Other teacher preparatory institutions across the country are also exploring alternative techniques for assessment and teacher training. Examples of such efforts include the design of a teacher knowledge base for application in multicultural, multilingual schools at the University of Southern California, and the development of a Personnel Evaluation and Learning Laboratory that profiles graduates at Arizona State University (Yinger and Hendricks, 1990). These initiatives and priorities, like those of the schools, are born out of the specific needs of an institution and are different according to local imperatives and resources.

It is obvious that these efforts to reformulate the educational system at every level are in their formative stages and do not yet have a clear direction. If reform is to succeed at any educational level, it is incumbent upon us to allow for flexibility in adjusting both the assessment process and the curriculum to reflect the changing knowledge base, our ongoing experience with what works, and our evolving goals. To enrich the work at individual sites, whether at the university or the school, networks must be built to facilitate the sharing of information. Although, ideally, this process would take place through face-to-face encounters, both budgets and time stand in the way of frequent meetings. The technological age, however, has given us the fax machine, electronic mail, and interactive computers. If industry can use these tools, then so must education.

If teacher educators want to be seen as equal partners with industry, then it behooves us to set goals and standards and implement changes to achieve both professional status and educational parity. If we do not assume the leadership role for education, then we will leave this most important of tasks to the political vicissitudes of states or the federal government. As educators, we must be prepared to take risks that involve uncertainty and perhaps occasional failure. But I believe we are obliged to pursue the path of excellence, holding ourselves accountable for establishing and maintaining the best possible standards for learning, achievement, and assessment.

References

Adler, M. J. (1982). *On behalf of the members of the Paideia group, the Paideia proposal: An educational manifesto.* New York: Macmillan.

Brandt, R. (1990). Restructuring schools: A conversation with Al Shanker. *Educational Leadership, 47*(7), 111–116.

Carnegie Council on Adolescent Development. (1989). *Turning points: Preparing American youths for the 21st century.* Report of the Task Force on Education of Young Adolescents. New York: Carnegie Council.

Elmore, R. F. (1987). *Early experiences in restructuring schools: Voices from the field.* Washington, DC: National Governors Association.

Fiske, E. B. (1990). But is the child learning? Schools trying new tests. *New York Times,* Jan. 31, p. 1.

Glickman, C. C. (1990). Open accountability for the 90s: Between the pillars. *Educational Leadership, 47*(7), 38–42.

Goodlad, J. I. (1984). *A place called school: Prospects for the future.* New York: McGraw-Hill.

Holmes Group. (1986). *Tomorrow's teachers: A Report of the Holmes Group.* East Lansing, MI: Holmes Group.

Lightfoot, S. L. (1983). *The good high school: Portraits of character and culture.* New York: Basic Books.

McDonnell, L. M. (1989). *Restructuring and the American schools: The promise and the pitfalls.* New York: ERIC Clearinghouse on Urban Education. (ED 314547)

National Association of Secondary School Principals and the National Association of Independent Schools. (1981–1984). *A study of high schools.* Boston: Houghton Mifflin.

National Commission on Excellence in Education. (1983). *A nation at risk: The imperative for educational reform.* Washington, DC: Government Printing Office.

National Governors Association. (1989). *Results in education.* Washington, DC: National Governors Association.

O'Neil, J. (1990). Piecing together the restructuring puzzle. *Educational Leadership, 47*(7), 4–10.

Shulman, L. S. (1987). Assessment for teaching: An initiative for the profession. *Phi Delta Kappan, 69*(1), 38–44.

Sizer, T. R. (1984). *Horace's compromise: The dilemma of the American high school.* Boston: Houghton Mifflin.

Yinger, J. R., and Hendricks, M. S. (1990). An overview of reform in Holmes Group institutions. *Journal of Teacher Education, 41*(2), 21–26.

12

Restructuring for Diversity: Five Regional Portraits

Sharon S. Nelson-Barber
Jean Mitchell

In this chapter, we discuss the theoretical and practical implications of the use of an instrument developed for teacher assessment in the education of minority teachers and of teachers of minority students in a variety of institutional, community, and cultural settings. Our fundamental question is, How can the education and testing of teachers be used to increase the humanity as well as the utility of education for all peoples? Our aim here is not to fully and definitively answer this question but rather to provide discussion and recommendations that do justice to the importance of the questions.

Part of our central thesis is that context matters, that there are significant differences in our lives, cultures, and settings that make a difference to education. We therefore describe in some detail the context of the development of the instrument in question—teacher portfolios—and the settings in which the work with them

Note: The authors acknowledge the contributions of all Teacher Education Consortium participants: Raymond Barnhardt, Vicki Dull, Elinor Ellis, John Geiger, William Gumlickpuck, Esther Ilutsik, Dorothy Jordan, Jerry Lipka, Anecia Lomack, Bickley Lucas, John McBride, Amadita Muniz, Cynthia Onore, Deborah Pomeroy, Ferdinand Sharp, Nancy Sharp, and Howard Swonigan.

was carried out, placing special emphasis on the impact of testing on teacher education programs. We then summarize a set of common themes that emerged from the work in these rather different settings and our discussions surrounding this work. From these themes, we derive implications for teacher education and a set of recommendations. These themes and the implications and recommendations extrapolated from them are not unique to the project described here; some of them have been noted many times over by other researchers and teachers. We trust that the material bears repeating once again, and we hope that schools as institutions will become more responsive to it as the ideas become more fully entrenched in the mainstream of educational thought.

Problem of Fair Testing

The challenge of designing assessments to significantly reduce the cultural bias that has adversely affected the standardized test performance of many minority group members is a compelling issue confronting educational research today. In a report on the effects of competence testing on the supply of minority teachers, Smith (1987) contends that existing tests are excluding thousands of minority candidates from the teaching profession and, if these trends continue, could decimate the ranks of minority students entering teaching in the near future. This 1987 projection is apparently becoming a reality, for 1988 statistics indicate that minorities represent only 5 percent of the teaching force. Meanwhile, it is estimated that minority students comprise at least 40 percent of the public school population (Catterall and Cota-Robles, 1988).

The outcomes of state-mandated tests have forced many schools of education to rethink the content and form of their teacher training programs. This reconsideration is particularly evident at minority colleges vulnerable to funding cuts and department closures based on student pass rates. Redesigns of curricula to correspond to the demands of teacher testing programs have enabled more students to enroll in these institutions and ultimately to pass the tests required for licensure; however, such adjustments do not address the more subtle problems of misunderstanding and misinterpretation that have made these tests a disproportionate barrier to nonmainstream students.

Recent exploratory research suggests that many teachers who are successful with nonmainstream students have developed teaching repertoires that extend beyond those offered by their teacher training programs. Indeed, many of the pedagogical strategies and interactive behaviors that characterize successful teaching in nonmainstream classrooms differ markedly from strategies and behaviors held to be models of "good practice" in the education literature and in teacher preparation courses (Delpit, 1986; Foster, 1989; Heath, 1983; King and Ladson-Billings, 1990; Nelson-Barber and Meier, 1990; Swisher and Deyhle, 1987). Often, "what works" in these classrooms has become "second-nature" due to the teachers' shared cultural identity or experience with students. What comes out in their teaching is the notion that a priori conceptions of subject matter often do not work unless they are conveyed and organized within the context of local values and expectations about teaching and learning. The teachers in question have highly specialized skill in tailoring content, using local vernacular, and building relationships with students—a skill that can be the most critical element in a teacher's success in diverse settings. The absence of teachers who bring these special perspectives and sensitivities to the classroom can only intensify the failure of many school districts to educate their growing populations of minority students.

In response to the challenge posed by the nation's changing demographics and the need to increase the pool of minority teachers, teacher assessment practitioners have attempted to develop instruments that are sensitive not only to the testing minority teachers but also to the criteria relevant to teaching in multiple cultural settings for all teachers. Clearly, many of the issues that impact teacher assessment are also salient in teacher education, which suggests an important reciprocal relationship between the two. On the one hand, teacher evaluation has the potential for discovering methods used by skilled and inventive teachers and making them available for more general use. Also, instruments developed for teacher evaluation can often be adapted for teacher education. On the other hand, in order to implement new instructional methods, teacher education will need ways of evaluating whether or not its students have grasped these approaches. Thus, much of what we have learned from our work in teacher assessment is relevant to teacher education.

New Modes of Assessment

The work of the Teacher Assessment Project (TAP), at Stanford University, offers a promising approach to the dilemma of handling cultural issues in testing. Unlike existing multiple-choice tests and teacher observation procedures, TAP has developed performance-based methods for assessing teacher competence that are devised to capture the complex and multidimensional aspects of teachers' thinking and acting. Specifically, TAP has developed procedures for teacher assessment that ask candidates not only to simulate teaching activities at an assessment center but also to document various teaching activities within the contexts of their own class-rooms. These assessments attempt to situate teachers' thinking and acting within circumstances attributable to the subject matter being taught, the grade level of the learner, and the sociocultural context of the school. These efforts were intended to tease out aspects of teacher knowledge that are tacit or that may have become routin-ized; at the same time, they were intended to minimize biases and reveal strengths that might not have appeared in other tests for teachers. Presumably, when the activities of assessment allow teachers to provide evidence and justification for their actions based on their unique teaching experiences, they also offer them more realistic opportunities to perform as well on the tests as they do in their own classrooms.

Still, new assessments will fail to admit culturally diverse conceptions of teacher effectiveness if those who evaluate the evidence are unable to accurately interpret candidate responses and performance. Similarly, educators cannot teach methods found to be effective with nonmainstream students if they are unaware such methods exist. Ultimately, the questions become, What counts as evidence of competence? What are the criteria on which candidate performances are judged?

If assessors and educators lack knowledge about cultural diversity, they can only fall back on their own taken-for-granted knowledge and assumptions about "goodness" or "appropriate-ness." If they are unable to recognize excellence when it is demonstrated, assessment processes could fail to account for, and teacher education could fail to promote, the very factors that contribute most significantly to success for many poor and minority students. Unless we make concerted efforts to record and formalize the vast store of knowledge about cultural influences on teaching and learning, the kinds of teacher behaviors and practices that work most effectively in nonmainstream settings not only will continue to go unnoticed but also will be discouraged. For example, prospective teachers are frequently cautioned against becoming too personal with their students and are advised to maintain professional distance. However, for many poor and minority students, this is exactly the wrong advice since the quality of personal relationships with teachers is one of the most significant factors in their academic success (see, for example, Delpit, 1988; Foster, 1989; Kleinfeld, 1974; Ladson-Billings, 1990; Nelson-Barber and Meier, 1990). Ways in which teachers recognize, acknowledge, and understand how cultural factors create diverse instructional and learning needs is a primary concern of the work reported below.

Tapping Cultural Diversity in Assessment

Beginning in May 1988, TAP actively collaborated with several teacher education programs that serve diverse populations in New York, Florida, Texas, Ohio, and Alaska. This group, known as the Teacher Education Consortium, began using items developed by TAP as a way to stimulate approaches to teacher preparation and assessment that were specifically attuned to the circumstances of each institution. By seeking to identify factors relating to teaching success that go unrecognized by current evaluation systems, the consortium expected to increase our understanding of the ways in which standards and evaluative measures fail to capture teachers' culturally appropriate forms of excellence. The consortium also explored the extent to which these phenomena might be built into the curricula and experiences of those preparing to be teachers. The institutional portraits below sketch the widely different concerns in each of these nonmainstream settings.

City College of New York

The City College of New York (CCNY), located in the heart of Harlem, is one campus within the City University of New York (CUNY) system, which serves the five boroughs of New York City. The School of Education at CCNY, the oldest school of education in the city, is surrounded by school districts that are among the most disadvantaged in Manhattan and the Bronx. As part of an overall commitment to serve the needs of this urban, migrant, poor, and culturally diverse population, in which a majority of the students are minority, the School of Education manages a number of programs that prepare students to teach urban minority youth. The school is charged with providing training that both addresses the day-to-day challenges of teaching and reflects the exceptional conditions likely to constitute the bulk of its students' teaching experience. Some of those conditions include a public school system that is multilingual, multicultural, and densely populated (high schools can serve five thousand students) and serves a homeless population of more than ten thousand students. These circumstances, along with the consequences of societal disorganization and inequity and the deficiencies of the public schools, place a heavy burden on traditional teacher education, which is ill-equipped to address the unique needs of these students and their settings. If, as one CCNY professor stated, a teacher's knowledge base must include sensitivities ranging from "awareness of some of the devastating student living conditions to the subtle differences between Bronx and Brooklyn English," then the strategies of teaching and the understandings of what it means to be a teacher in New York City take on new meanings.

To become more knowledgeable about the characteristics and needs of nonmainstream students and how to incorporate that knowledge into their current program, the School of Education began to scrutinize the interrelationships among beginning teacher knowledge, student particulars, and requisites for teaching in multicultural, multilingual settings. Assessment of the skills associated with these relationships is a very salient concern in light of CUNY's planned systemwide reforms for teacher education. Since New York

State has adopted the National Teachers Examination as a standard for teacher certification, CUNY is considering using the test as an entry and progress criterion for undergraduates in teacher education (Board of Trustees Task Force on Education Programs and Curriculum Impact, 1987). CUNY teacher educators never questioned the need for rigorous progress and exit standards; rather, they voiced concern that traditional test and measurement strategies, which embrace a general standard and ignore individual differences, fail to elicit the potentially rich contributions of their students. They are "strongly convinced that prospective teachers should be identified early and encouraged and supported throughout the teacher preparation program rather than denied access through early exclusionary testing" (City College of New York, 1987, p. 9).

Invited to devise a provisional plan that might better address the particular circumstances of each campus, the School of Education began to build a case for its curriculum and assessment needs for an experimental group of students. Entering into a relationship with TAP as a developmental effort, CCNY decided to focus on onsite documentation through portfolio development because this mode of assessment seemed most in keeping with the school's inquiry-based approach to teacher education. Key issues of concern were ways that portfolios might be used to evaluate students for entrance into, progress through, and exit from CCNY teacher education; ways that education and liberal arts faculty might work together to develop portfolio materials within the context of required coursework; and ways in which field experiences outside of supervised student teaching might be documented.

Some education faculty had used student portfolios in the past and characterized the process as "massive paper collection." TAP suggested that using a small experimental group of students and a narrow focus for the activities might offer them a greater opportunity for success. Also, since faculty teams were particularly interested in capturing specific cultural or idiosyncratic features of their student teachers' performances, these were included in the portfolio specifications, including clear indicators of what behaviors to expect, what these behaviors look like when observed, and what activities in particular elicit these behaviors.

Florida Agricultural and Mechanical University

The College of Education at Florida A&M University (FAMU), a well-established black institution, is primarily responsible for training black teachers for the State of Florida. Historically, its programs have produced many qualified educators for the Florida public schools. However, the lure of other professions and the Florida State Board of Education's highly centralized and regulated teacher testing program, which now requires the Florida Teacher Certification Examination (FTCE) for certification, have led to a steady decline in the number of blacks in teacher education. The seriousness of the problem was underscored in 1983 with the failure of 80 percent of FAMU graduates to pass the FTCE, which resulted in the loss of six state-funded teacher education programs at the university. A potential source of "bias" in such tests is that students have few opportunities to learn what is to be assessed (Calfee, 1983; Fisher, 1983; Popham, 1983). Therefore, the FAMU College of Education began a campaign to reevaluate its teacher education programs and its relationship with arts and science faculty, since both must share the blame when education graduates fail to pass a test of reading, writing, and mathematics (Florida Agricultural and Mechanical University, 1987, 1988).

To ensure that its education students are adequately trained and properly prepared to meet certification requirements, teacher education admission requirements have become far more strict. Standards are now defined on an entire battery of tests: the Scholastic Aptitude Test, the American College Test, the College Level Academic Skills Test, and a simulated FTCE, a traditional teacher-made test tapping reading, mathematics, professional education, and essay skills.

Although FAMU is making every attempt to ensure that its students meet the standards mandated by the Florida State Board of Education, it has concerns about this testing:

First, the College of Education, like the School of Education at CCNY, is committed to motivating and engaging those students who may not have achieved the required minimum scores for admission to teacher education programs, but who exhibit determination and potential. This commitment, however, requires a more highly organized program of support and advisement than exists at present.

Second, faculty must take immediate steps to structure class tests along the same lines as the simulated FTCE. At present, faculty do not tailor coursework to the competencies tested. Consequently, students repeatedly sit for exams without benefit of remedial help, which may account for many students' repeated lack of success on this test as well as on the FTCE.

Third, the college's deepest commitment is the development of quality educators for multicultural settings. Currently, the state emphasis on the FTCE effectively restricts attention to maintaining the pass rates of the college's students. Consequently, little time can be spent trying to better understand educational practices that are more effective in the multicultural settings in Florida in which their graduates will most likely be placed. In essence, emphasis on this paper-and-pencil exam serves to maintain the status quo by drawing energy from creative exploration of more effective approaches.

FAMU wanted to initiate internal approaches to assessment that might better serve their goals, as well as help the state reexamine how its certification goals are accomplished. FAMU faculty explored with TAP possibilities for using forms of portfolio documentation with preservice teachers, ranging from the tracking of student progress and remediation or on-site mentoring linked to college courses, to student development of their own cumulative work pieces or portfolios for reflection on their classwork. Faculty were particularly interested in the long-term effects of processes of documentation and reflection on the students. For example, though compiling evidence about one's instructional planning and teaching outcomes might be stimulating, what happens after preservice teachers complete the coursework? Do reflective reviews of one's own work really move preservice teachers to improve their pedagogical or management skills? Do they really help students build self-esteem?

To begin to address these issues, FAMU faculty developed a system for documenting the effective performance of fifteen preservice teachers in contiguous elementary-level theory and practice courses. Of the thirty undergraduate students enrolled in spring 1989, fifteen received traditional training in planning and organizing for teaching, presentation of subject matter, the theories undergirding the two, communication, principles of classroom management, and testing. The remaining fifteen constructed portfolios to document their development in these areas. During the second phase of documentation in fall 1989, all students moved to a public school setting, where students constructing portfolios prepared field entries according to faculty specifications. A large block of time was set aside for a faculty member to spend time in the field with these preservice teachers, observing as well as participating in planning along with the classroom teacher. The plan included following these students through their internships and their first year of teaching.

The main objectives of this project were (1) to place preservice teachers in a position of accountability at an early period of their training, exposing them to strategies of assessment early on in order to make them "assessment aware"; (2) to develop an awareness of self as an instrument; (3) to help preservice teachers improve their teaching and control of the instructional environment by reviewing past performances; and (4) to produce strong professional teachers who are secure and have self-esteem.

University of Texas-Pan American

Situated about six miles north of McAllen, Texas, and a fifteen-minute drive from the Mexican border, the University of Texas-Pan American (UTPA) boasts the largest enrollment of bilingual Latino American students in the United States. According to a number of faculty members, UTPA's predominantly Mexican American student body is highly motivated, with most of these students representing the first generation in their families to attend college. The university, however, is located within one of the most economically depressed areas in the United States, with a majority of families at or below the poverty level. Due to these socioeconomic circumstances, language differences, cultural and ethnic influences, and life experiences in general, many students come to the university underprepared for the demands of higher education and need a great deal of help and support.

To handle these challenges, UTPA maintains an open admissions policy that allows any student with a high school diploma or equivalent to enroll. Entering freshmen are required to take the American College Test and/or the Scholastic Aptitude Test, but results are used to determine proper course placements rather than university admission. Admission to teacher education requires that students have at least a 2.0 grade point average and at least state-required minimum scores on the Pre-Professional Skills Test (PPST).

Traditionally, UTPA has had one of the largest teacher training programs in the state of Texas, particularly for bilingual-bicultural teachers, graduating up to four hundred Latino teachers per year. However, lately, fewer than twenty Latino American teachers have graduated from UTPA each year. This drastic reduction in the potential minority teaching force is the direct result of a series of legislative changes enacted by the state of Texas in the areas of educator competence and student assessment.

Beginning in 1984, the state formalized its concern about student achievement in the public schools by imposing strict regulations, including a number of tests, to ensure that all educators accept responsibility for student mastery of the curriculum. For instance, the Texas Educational Assessment of Minimum Skills measures student achievement and helps districts address the effectiveness of their instructional programs, the Texas Teacher Appraisal System taps the classroom competencies of practicing teachers, and students seeking a degree in education are now required to pass the PPST prior to entry and again prior to graduation from schools of education (Pan American University-Valley Schools, 1988).

Schools of education in Texas began to develop programs to facilitate student preparation for teaching and to improve student test performance as measured by the current assessments. For example, an introductory course for prospective teachers at UTPA has been revised to include diagnostic-predictive testing in the three areas covered by the PPST—mathematics, reading, and writing. Although there are state-mandated limitations on the availability and use of "remedial" courses at the university level, the diagnostic features of the tests used identify areas of need, and small group instruction or tutorials are available to complement instruction in general education courses. To ensure that students are given opportunities to learn skills that are tapped by the PPST, various departments have restructured their programs and courses based on careful analysis of the content of relevant PPST exams. For students who previously have failed the PPST, a three-week series of classes is offered prior to administration of the test. In these courses, students receive direct instruction designed to prepare them for the content and the general demands associated with each test area (Texas Education Agency, 1987).

In 1989, even more restrictions were introduced to the already heavily test-laden repertoire in Texas. Students in public institutions of higher education are now required to complete the Texas Academic Skills Program, a criterion-referenced test devised to measure sophomore exit abilities. In other words, to continue in a program of higher education beyond the sophomore year, students must pass yet another test. One can imagine the effect this might have on potential student enrollment beyond the junior college level.

Another complication was the state order for schools of education to devise a radically new approach to the preparation of teachers by 1991. Now, rather than working toward degrees in education, students are expected to use hours formerly devoted to teacher education to complete coursework within liberal arts programs. Essentially, all education course work has been reduced from thirty to eighteen hours, with only twelve hours spent in education classes and six hours in student teaching.

In response to a system that places great emphasis on accountability through paper-and-pencil testing, UPTA is concerned about issues of quality and access. Public universities can always attempt to increase student pass rates by teaching to the tests; however, without a deeper understanding of specific cultural or idiosyncratic features of their students—differences in worldview, which distinguish how students make sense of the world and, in turn, how they might approach tasks and so forth—it is unlikely that faculty will be able to forge the kinds of connections needed to capitalize on their students' special talents. In this case, the strategy of teaching to the test is unlikely to be successful in increasing pass rates. Deeper understanding will be required of both students and faculty.

UTPA faculty need to be sensitive to influences of culture, ethnicity, socioeconomic circumstances, life experiences, and language, which require a special level of involvement.

The School of Education at UTPA wants to include knowledge about community context and about cultural and language diversity in its standards for teacher education. Faculty members are constructing a student exit profile that includes student test scores but also requires students to demonstrate competence in tailoring teaching to a particular linguistic and cultural context. The UTPA team believed that collaboration with TAP could help guide the development of a comprehensive response to current legislation and lead to the revision of state education agency requirements. As an initial step toward improving the assessment results in their teacher education program, faculty hoped to adapt some of TAP's assessment techniques and materials to the special needs of bilingual and multicultural teacher and pupil populations.

A team of education faculty worked to pilot-test documentation strategies using an instructor-made system for students. Because the placement files of prospective teachers tend to be very similar, portfolios can offer beginning teachers additional opportunities to demonstrate their understandings and capabilities. Thus, UTPA students were asked to view the portfolio as a mechanism to provide prospective employers with evidence of their teaching skills and experiences.

Ohio Group

This group, composed of Wright State University, University of Dayton, Central State University, and the Dayton Public Schools (DPS) system, approached TAP with their interest in becoming involved in the national effort to develop alternative means of teacher assessment. This group wanted to become familiar with the scope of our work and to explore how our findings might best be transformed via an assessment center in their geographical area. They were particularly interested in discovering ways in which assessment might better focus on the context of learning, particularly in multiethnic classrooms; whether different criteria might apply to different geographical, social, and cultural group settings; whether excellent teaching looks different across groups; and whether certified teachers who function competently in one context are able to do so in other contexts. Although TAP assessment center prototypes could have served as starting points in the design of exercises for their center, in view of the issues outlined above the group was advised to consider other modes of assessing teachers. They opted to pursue the on-site documentation of teaching skills through portfolio development.

Of particular concern to the universities was the need to ensure that their teacher education programs prepare trainees to meet the challenges of an urban student population that is considered as a whole to be at risk. DPS, concerned about providing their students with the best possible education, wanted to understand more about both the children enrolled in their system and the specialized skills that teachers might need to be most effective with these students.

DPS are nearing the end of a five-year intervention-prevention program at the induction level of teacher education, using their veteran teachers as mentors. Currently employing about seventeen hundred teachers, with about half expected to retire in the next five years, DPS view this collaboration as a wonderful opportunity to work closely with the universities in developing the skills of teachers new to the district. In this context, work with portfolios is seen as a way to help these teachers become reflective practitioners.

Operating from the perspective that portfolio development would be growth-enhancing and stimulating for beginning teachers, each institution planned to introduce the portfolio as a document used to mark the beginning of one's professionalization as a teacher. The undergraduate institutions intended to pilot-test the use of portfolio documentation with manageable samples of entry-level teacher education students, and in some cases with student teachers. Students matriculating in a number of courses would compile performance evidence drawn from their own coursework or field experiences, select items to best illustrate their personal and professional growth, and organize these materials within categories based on the knowledge dimensions created by TAP: professional responsibility, command of subject matter, content-specific pedagogy, class organization and management, and student-specific pedagogy. Students would then reflect on why these selected items contributed to their growth over the year. They would be free to contribute any additional items in support of their work.

DPS intended to pilot-test the use of portfolios as one aspect of a professional growth plan for its twenty-four or twenty-five entry-year teachers and their designated mentors. After being trained in the use of portfolios as professional development tools, mentors and entry-level teachers would provide process- and problem-oriented documentation of their teaching, with the mentors' portfolios serving as models for the entry-level teachers. As a reflective tool, documentation entries would provide a means for mentor teachers to become more knowledgeable about and responsive to the unique needs of their students. Student teacher entries would, in turn, focus on the needs of the students that they were teaching. Use of these entries would concentrate on how to accommodate these needs in current educational programs. Overall, the Ohio group is exploring whether this kind of comprehensive model for developing portfolios is a useful tool in helping both prospective, entry-level and practicing mentor teachers provide evidence of professional growth.

University of Alaska

The task of training teachers to meet the educational needs of students in a diversely populated state, roughly one-fifth the size of the continental United States, presents major challenges for the Education Department of the Rural College at the University of Alaska, Fairbanks (UAF). Although teachers in Alaskan cities combat problems similar to those that arise in any multicultural urban setting, most of Alaska is composed of small rural villages of one hundred to three hundred predominantly American Indian or Alaskan Native peoples. Many of these villages maintain the languages, subsistence lifestyles, and cultural traditions of their forebears. One village of 100 people might serve only 15 students in a single K–12 school, with one teacher responsible for grades K–6 and another for 7–12. Severe weather conditions and limited road systems often necessitate the use of correspondence programs that allow teachers only monthly contact with students. The fact that a single school district serving approximately 545 students may cover over sixty-six thousand square miles further underscores the unique problems of education delivery in this state.

Teachers often stay in these small communities only two years or less. Most of these teachers are non-native, which, in and of itself, does not mean that they cannot be effective; however, most of these individuals also are non-Alaskan, and many come from urban areas in the lower forty-eight states. Unless these teachers have trained in local programs, they come to Alaskan rural classrooms with little preparation for the extreme differences in language, culture, and lifestyle, and little sense of the specialized knowledge that could enable them to better respond to the needs of their students. Although these teachers come with the best of intentions, their teaching is often frustrated by problems of interpretation, implicit assumptions of which they are not aware, and a lack of shared experience and values with students. The chronic teacher turnover that results takes an obvious toll on student success as well as student perceptions about the importance of education.

Context sensitivity is a major emphasis of UAF's education programs. The need for teachers to adapt to extreme situations and develop interpersonal relationships with individuals very different from themselves is central to their program. There are a number of indications that native community-based expectations about good teaching do not always match school-based or literature-based expectations. For example, often culturally appropriate verbal admonitions about behavior can be more effective than those punishments (detention, suspension) so familiar to graduates of mainstream schooling (Delpit and Nelson-Barber, 1991; Locust, 1988). To what extent, then, should native teachers adapt to the current educational system and to what extent should the system learn more about what native teachers know and do? Questions of this kind are similar to those faced by TAP with respect to what effective teaching looks like in varying contexts and who should define it.

The cross-cultural educational development program trains native teachers on-site in their communities. Because only 2 to 3 percent of the teaching force in village schools are native, a particular emphasis of this program is the empowerment of teacher trainees to effect educational change in their communities while protecting and enriching the quality of their lives and culture. In these circumstances, student teachers need to, and do, develop skills that go beyond the curriculum of traditional teacher education programs. Traditional teacher education programs and assessment could then capitalize on the skills demonstrated by these native teachers (Booker, 1987). Construction of an additional set of community-determined standards into teacher education and evaluation could help to ensure that certified teachers are knowledgeable and prepared for placements in rural Alaska.

The Teachers for Rural Alaska Program prepares prospective outside and non-native teachers for rural multicultural settings, specifically, small rural high schools in Eskimo and Indian villages. For many of the trainees, this experience represents an initial exposure to the realities of rural life and native culture. According to Kleinfeld and Noordhoff (1988, p. 3), "These schools demand highly competent faculty—teachers who can teach a wide range of academic subjects to high school students of enormously varied achievement levels and teachers who can create trust between the public school and a minority community wary of the western cultural domination that the school symbolizes." The focus of the program is therefore to bridge differences between prospective teachers and community members, while preparing individuals who are reflective and are able to tailor their teaching to a particular context.

A key feature of the program is the critical appraisal of one's own teaching. From the outset, students are encouraged to reflect on their teaching—to think about the appropriateness or relevance of their educational goals, strategies, or approaches and how to respond sensitively to their teaching situations. Students are expected to develop an extensive repertoire of educational strategies and images of teaching: not simply to know seven or eight different strategies but to be able to perform seven or eight different strategies as various situations dictate.

The importance of defining ways in which people are attuned to context and culture and of incorporating native perspectives within Alaskan teacher education curricula is an immediate concern given the current move to put into place an assessment center for Alaskan administrators. According to native principals, who already are few in number, these new procedures typically assess prospective native principals negatively because the ways in which they display themselves, approach decision making, and approach working in the community, while culturally acceptable, are not in keeping with the performance expectations of the evaluators. UAF is committed to increasing the number of exemplary native teachers as well as to training non-native teachers to teach effectively in native settings. In so doing, its education programs are devised to prepare individuals to move across cultural boundaries and to adapt their behaviors to the contingencies of the environments in which they are situated. The Rural College therefore wanted to learn more about new approaches to teacher assessment that might be put into place at the national level, especially if nationally certified teachers who met the assessment criteria would be qualified to move into any contextual situation. Variables of culture and community, because they are embedded in shared experience, may not be important for mainstream teachers working in mainstream classrooms; however, they can be extremely important for teachers and students who do not share experience.

UAF, therefore, used portfolios developed by TAP to document the willingness of teachers to immerse themselves in the community environment—to know the kinds of information needed to make informed decisions about particular instructional situations, to know how to go about acquiring this information or to which sources to turn outside the school. The purpose of the documentation was threefold: to further the participants' professional development as teachers, to assess that development, and to document for outsiders the existence and relevance of factors crucial to success in this cultural setting.

Themes Emerging from Consortium Members' Use of TAP Materials

After one year of involvement, consortium members reported their reactions to the use of TAP materials in their programs: how these materials have fit into their existing programs and what, if anything, they have learned about teacher education of and for minority students in the course of adapting and using these materials. Though a single year is a brief period in the use of any innovative approach, and we have yet to fully examine these initial findings, certain themes have emerged quite clearly from consortium members' responses.

The need for direct involvement of student teachers with the communities from which their nonmainstream students are drawn was the most notable theme running through the reports. Although this theme is not new—the need for field experience is an agreed-upon aspect of teacher preparation in any setting—consortium members go beyond recommending the usual student teaching experience with nonmainstream students to recommending specific forms of community involvement by student teachers. Suggestions ranged from service as volunteers in the community to visits to students' homes and activities with students outside of school.

Agreement is high that a teacher needs to understand students' whole-life experiences in order to understand their school life, and that the kind of understanding required is the kind that only comes from direct personal involvement. When teachers have radically different backgrounds from their students, they need more extensive involvement with the students' environment than when backgrounds are largely shared. Further, there is evidence to suggest that teacher effectiveness in nonmainstream classrooms is associated with the teacher defining his or her role as extending beyond the classroom into the home or community (see, for example, Collins and Tamarkin, 1982; Delpit, 1986; Heath, 1983; Meek, 1989; Phillips, 1983). Agreement is nearly as high that mere exposure to the living conditions and culture of students is not enough; guided reflection on the field experience is necessary to assimilate it into the student teachers' active professional repertoires. Various approaches have been taken to elicit this reflection and assimilation. For instance, Wright State University reports that they have found a three-step process necessary to develop reflective teachers: (1) active involvement, (2) research and writing or discussion, and (3) formulation of teacher action, with support for that action. Several consortium members recommend a problem-posing/problem-solving approach with their student teachers. TAP materials, particularly the portfolios, were mentioned several times in the reports as useful instruments for eliciting reflection and breaking mind-sets that student teachers often have regarding school, themselves, or nonmainstream students and contexts.

Among those matters considered important for teachers, language and nonverbal communication and interaction were the most consistently mentioned. This theme makes sense when we consider that education is about understanding, and understanding rests on language and nonverbal communication. One of the arguments for the importance of direct experience as opposed to didactic teaching is that only through interaction can student teachers develop awareness of language and interactive differences. However, this is also the most powerful argument that exposure is not enough, that guided reflection is essential: People are notoriously unaware of nonverbal communication cues and interactive styles, though they respond to them all of the time. It is all too easy for a person to feel something is wrong in interactions with people of a different background without becoming aware of what is causing this feeling. In such cases, the experience can actually be detrimental rather than helpful to prospective teachers (for example, Wolcott's [1967] work in a Kwakiutl village and school). In order to avoid such missteps and to capitalize on the field experience, extensive guided reflection and support is required.

It is clear from consortium members' responses that the task of teaching nonmainstream students to become teachers shares some of the challenges and requirements of teaching nonmainstream students in K–12. That is, some of the knowledge and understanding that student teachers need to enhance their effectiveness is the very same knowledge and understanding that teacher educators must have in order to effectively develop a pool of nonmainstream teachers. Several members mentioned the importance of establishing personal relationships with their student teachers, of developing their self-esteem, and of being aware of how cultural differences affect the acquisition and expression of knowledge, all of which are recurrent themes in the literature on minority education (for example, Gee, 1989; Locust, 1988; Michaels, 1986; Spindler, 1988; Taylor and Lee, 1987; Valencia, 1984).

Related to the need for developing self-esteem among minority students, some members also noted a need for addressing personal growth as a part of developing their students' professional growth. This need makes sense in light of the often-noted importance of the self as an instrument in teaching (Lortie, 1975), an area too few teacher education programs address explicitly. Whether it is an area of more concern to minorities than to mainstream teachers is a question for future research to address.

In accord with the relationship between teaching minorities in K–12 and teaching minority teachers, several members noted that teacher educators often lack expertise in cultural issues and experience with the communities from which their students are drawn. They are thus not realistically prepared to deal with the issues raised here, though they may be aware of them and have the best of intentions. Concerning the criteria that might be used to determine whether students have acquired the kinds of knowledge and skills required in their setting, Cynthia Onore, a CCNY faculty member, notes that "at the core of this question are questions about the match between the classrooms we run and the classrooms our students are running or will run. If we are mixing messages by not practicing what we preach, then we can't really assess whether our students have acquired the skills and knowledge they might need. Certainly, this can be acknowledged to be a problem in human resources: where are we to find those who themselves have the requisite expertise, both scholarly and experiential, to disseminate the desired skills and knowledge?" (personal communication, April 19, 1991).

It is not surprising that concern over the impact of standardized testing on their students was a theme running through several members' reports. The fear is that even as they are trying to articulate and document the variations in practice that are effective with minority students, use of these tests locks in mainstream assumptions, methods, and approaches as the only officially acceptable practice, thereby excluding many minority students from teaching. This fear parallels a concern with the impact of standardized paper-and-pencil tests on nonmainstream students in K–12.

A final theme was concern with a variety of political issues. Are schools being used to preserve social inequities? If so, is this deliberate or a side effect of apparently benign policies? In light of the recent rash of criticism directed at the American school system from all sides, members of the consortium noted that we presently prepare student teachers to preserve the status quo, to operate within it, rather than to challenge it or to develop new ways of operating. In line with this observation, several members recommended that issues of racism and multiculturalism be explicitly addressed in teacher education classes.

Implications for Teacher Education

What implications do findings gleaned from such diverse settings have for teacher education in general? We consider the implications in relation to two primary objectives: (1) to better prepare all teachers, of all backgrounds, to teach the full spectrum of students in today's classrooms and (2) to increase the pool of qualified minority teachers. Although these two objectives focus our attention in different directions and yield somewhat different sets of recommendations, they also interact in interesting ways. For instance, preparation of teachers is itself a teaching task; therefore, as noted above, recommendations for the instruction of minority students also apply to the preparation of minority teachers.

Our first recommendation is backed by theory, by empirical experience, and by common sense, an unusual confluence of agreement for the field of education: effectively prepare teachers to deal with the subtle yet profound issues of communication, the behavior of students, and their responses to student behavior. These issues exist both in the area of general human interaction that affects classroom organization and order and in the area of intellectual functioning that affects the teaching of subject matter. These two areas are not independent in any teaching environment, but evidence indicates that their interaction is more salient in classrooms with minority students than it is with conventional mainstream students (Delpit and Nelson-Barber, 1991).

Given the fact that these issues generally operate automatically and outside of consciousness, and given that the goal of teacher education must be not only to increase student teachers' understanding of these phenomena but also to expand their own repertoires of perception and behavior with respect to them, direct exposure to students who represent cultural groups outside the prospective teacher's experience is vital. To know intellectually that such phenomena exist, to understand the basis for them in theory, and to be able to see them in action and modify one's own behavior in response to them are very different things. The one (intellectual knowledge) can be achieved in a traditional classroom setting through reading, lecture, and discussion; the other (leading to behavior modification) can be achieved only through direct exposure to the phenomena in question in such a form that the phenomena are highlighted. Thus, our recommendation is that student teachers be given the opportunity to acquire experience with students from backgrounds different from their own. The challenge, in a sense, is to make the fish aware of the water; that is, the student teacher must become aware of phenomena so much an unquestioned part of one's social environment that he or she is not normally aware that they exist.

Although this direct exposure is essential, it is not, generally speaking, enough. Prospective teachers also must assimilate the experience that they gain in ways productive for teaching, and this task is where the teacher education classroom can make an essential contribution. It is through reflection on their experience that prospective teachers are able to incorporate it into their professional personae; it is through reflection that they are able to fully understand and deal with their own reactions as human beings to the new and disorienting experiences to which they have been exposed. But this reflection must be aided and supported. Each individual needs the insights and reactions of others, both those of other student teachers who are going through the same process and those of persons who have a more mature perspective on these matters through longer study and experience. It is the responsibility of teacher educators to establish a setting and foster a process that elicit productive reflection on and assimilation of the cross-cultural experiences to which the student teachers will be exposed. The setting that we recommend is a seminar populated by student teachers who are all completing the cross-cultural phase of their training. If at all possible, the professor leading the seminar not only should be well versed on the relevant anthropological and sociological research but also should have cross-cultural experience in his or her own background. We are essentially recommending the cultivation of a cohort group in the presence of a mentor.

At this point, we join the two goals mentioned above—a larger pool of qualified minority teachers and better preparation of all teachers, of all backgrounds, to teach the full spectrum of minority students—in support of a common recommendation: members of as many different minority groups as possible should be included in each cohort group. Clearly, this practice serves to increase the pool of minority teachers. But we also believe that individuals from diverse backgrounds have a special contribution to make to the cohort as members process their various cross-background experiences.

First, having grown up in environments other than the mainstream of American society, they know these environments first-hand and thus are not only sources of first-hand information about them but also sources who are undergoing a similarly disorienting experience and presumably are sensitized to the needs and feelings of their fellow student teachers. Second, in a sense, most minority people have already undergone and, if they have made it to the position of student teacher, have survived and dealt with a cross-cultural experience. That is, they have not only learned their own culture but also to a significant extent have learned the mainstream American culture. Thus, they may be somewhat ahead in the process of becoming familiar with the types of cultural differences to which teachers must become sensitive and could therefore serve as resources and models as well as fellow learners in the cohort group. Third, however knowledgeable particular members of a minority group are about their own culture, there are other groups in this diverse society who are as unfamiliar to them as the groups are to most mainstream of suburbanites. Minority people thus have nearly as much to learn from the whole adventure as do those raised entirely within the mainstream culture; they thus need to be included in the cross-cultural experience for their own development as teachers. It is instructive to all involved to see first-hand that each different group or subculture presents new and unfamiliar experiences no matter how broad one's prior background.

Another group who can make a contribution to the seminar is teachers who have already undergone a similar experience. These might be student teachers who are further along in their preparation, or they might be certified teachers from the community who would serve as teaching assistants in return for a stipend or college credit. The value of these people as role models is clear.

Teacher education institutions are not fully prepared at this time to provide all of the resources necessary to develop cohort groups such as we have sketched here. First, the research community has only begun to address questions involving the impact of culture on education. While much important, fascinating, and suggestive research has been done (Barnhardt, 1982; McDermott and Gospodinoff, 1981; Mohatt and Erickson, 1981; Scollon and Scollon, 1981; Spindler, 1965), a great deal more needs to be done before we can be confident about the results.

Second, the research that has been done often remains unassimilated into the education knowledge base; education has historically turned to psychology for insight into educational processes and has only recently begun to pay attention to relevant work of anthropologists and sociologists. Similarly, educational research based on anthropological or sociological models and methods is a relatively recent tradition; it has started to pay dividends (Gee, 1989; Heath, 1983; Michaels, 1986; Spindler, 1987; Wells, 1986), but one of the primary lessons learned from this research is just how much more needs to be learned (and will always need to be learned; see, for example, Goldenberg and Gallimore, 1989).

Third, most teacher educators themselves have not been educated in a multicultural fashion and thus lack the requisite cross-cultural background. Many teacher educators, of course, have the requisite background. Some are members of minority groups, others are nonminority teacher educators who have a history of teaching minority students. Many of these individuals have participated in research on the impact of culture on schooling (Hollins, 1982; King and Ladson-Billings, 1990; Meier, 1985; Calfee and Nelson-Barber, 1991). However, to be effective, cohort groups such as we are recommending must be kept manageably small, and each group will need a properly qualified professor to lead it. People with both the requisite experience and the requisite scholarship are as yet too scarce to populate these classrooms nationwide.

For all of these reasons, it will be necessary for the teacher education community to bootstrap their operations to the desired level. This need applies, incidentally, to whatever approach people decide on to deal with the challenges of adequately educating our diverse population, as the limitations of research and of experienced professors apply regardless of the program to be undertaken. During this bootstrapping phase, it might be possible to develop innovative ways to use teachers, researchers, and community people in teacher education, for instance, by having teacher education classes conducted by a team of these people rather than by a single professor of education. Perhaps the pressures to respond to the changing demographics of America will lead to a profitable mixture of hitherto all-too-separate branches of educational endeavor.

The setting that we recommend, then, is a seminar composed of as diverse a mix of students as possible, fueled by exposure to practical cross-cultural experience, and supported by leaders with both expertise in research regarding the interaction of culture and education and some form of direct cross-cultural experience. What of the process? What recommendations can we make with regard to a process designed to foster growth in knowledge and understanding of the interaction of culture and education, and the integration of that knowledge and understanding into professional personae? We make no pretense of offering a comprehensive or exhaustive set of recommendations. Rather, we offer only a few suggestions based on our own work.

Several consortium members noted the importance of personal growth to their students' professional growth. We suggest that the importance of this interrelationship holds for all developing teachers, and that therefore the teacher education process should foster personal growth. Effective teaching requires at least a modicum of wisdom; wisdom is an attribute of the whole person, not just of the professional persona. Further, education is about the lives of persons and is a significant part of the socialization process in this society; it often has to do with very basic issues of life. Since education cannot and should not be divorced from life, professional growth cannot and should not be separated from personal growth for teachers.

A nearly universal concern among members of our consortium was how to handle minority students who have suffered from the mismatch between their past schooling and their own experience within their cultural group. The better teacher education as a whole meets the goal of recruiting minority persons into teaching and into mainstream teacher preparation programs, the more it will need to practice what it preaches with regard to the education of minority group members.

Another of the more consistent findings of the research is that relationships among teacher and students at a personal level are more valued by minority students than they are by mainstream white students. That is, the relationship factor has greater impact on purely academic learning with minority students than it does, overall, with nonminority students (Delpit, 1988; Foster, 1989; Nelson-Barber and Meier, 1990). Therefore, the students who we are preparing as teachers must be trained in a way that emphasizes relationships. We have referred to seminars as part of a process of forming cohort groups partly for this reason. Teachers need to be able to connect with their students; it is within this connectedness that many people, especially minority people, can most comfortably focus on and learn about academic subjects. Further, such connectedness is essential to the other kinds of learning that people want and expect from schools, such as learning of self-discipline, learning how to function as a person in a democratic society, and learning what fosters self-esteem. Therefore, teacher education must model this kind of education. It is not enough to tell student teachers that they must relate to their students in a more personal way, or to send them out to field settings to practice relationships with students. Rather, it is necessary for teacher educators themselves to be as involved with the student teachers as they are asking the student teachers to be with their own students.

One of the most powerful influences on teachers' style of teaching is the kind of teaching experienced as students (for example, Feiman-Nemser and Floden, 1986); if we want to influence student teachers to teach in new ways, we must use those ways in teaching them. Moreover, it is precisely in this area of teacher-student relationships that cultural differences in style and manner of expression, even in substance, are likely to be most apparent and important. Therefore, there can be no one, recommended way of accomplishing the desired state. But we cannot ask our student teachers to meet this challenge with their students if we cannot meet it with them.

Another reason for recommending a more personal, more connected and connecting process than is usual in college classrooms for this teacher preparation experience is that the kind of cross-cultural experience advocated here will be disorienting for many people and will raise feelings in them that must be dealt with if their professional development is to proceed on course. Teaching under any circumstances raises intense feelings, especially in beginning teachers, but the kind of experience that we are advocating should prove to be even more intense and challenging to personal equilibrium than a similar experience in an entirely familiar setting. This challenge is indeed one of the intended effects of the experience; we want the students to be shaken out of their usual ways of perceiving human interactions so that they will become open to seeing new ways. For both moral and purely pragmatic reasons, however, we are obliged to help them deal with these feelings and integrate them into a new equilibrium. The classroom process must encourage students to talk about their feelings and to support and encourage others to do so. This kind of interaction can only happen in an atmosphere of trust, which takes time to develop. It is the basis of our recommendation of cohort groups: groups of student teachers who are together for extended periods of time, engaging in similar experiences and sharing the personal and professional growth process central to the formation of excellent teachers.

It is possible that the use of portfolios in some form may contribute to this process. It is all very well and good to urge people to deal with feelings, to integrate new experiences, to develop trust, but there must be a vehicle and a catalyst that make these goals achievable. Portfolios can serve as a vehicle and a catalyst. They provide a more detailed record of experiences than unaided memory and thus provide better material for discussion. The act of producing the portfolio may help to objectify the experiences and thus make them easier to talk about. And the act of making the portfolios involves thinking about the experiences and therefore entails some of the reflection and integration that we want to encourage. Several consortium members mentioned the potential of the portfolios for this kind of catalyzing of personal and professional development.

Part of the potential of portfolios in this application is their flexibility; what is to be included in a portfolio can be tailored to the situation in which the student is working as well as to the particular professional expertise or understanding that we want the student to develop. Further, once the portfolio has been produced, its subsequent uses can vary. Portfolios could be shared among the members of the seminar, they could be used as a point of take-off for one-on-one interactions between the professor and the student, or particular elements could be used as beginning points for discussion within the seminar. They could even be used as summative evaluation instruments; that is, they could be part of the criteria for passing one's teacher education courses and receiving one's degree. However, the intended purposes of the portfolios should be made clear to the students before they begin work on them.

Summary

Our work with minority educators in five settings produced many research findings, such as the need for teachers who will teach in unfamiliar contexts to have practical fieldwork experience outside the school, the special importance of the teacher-student relationship to the academic learning of many minority students, the role of nonverbal and paralinguistic communicative cues in teacher-student communication, and the significance of personal growth and self-esteem to professional development for prospective teachers. Given these results, and the urgency of better preparing all teachers to teach students from backgrounds unfamiliar to them, we have recommended that fieldwork in minority communities be incorporated at an early stage in teacher education programs. In order to get full benefit from these experiences, we recommend the development of cohort groups and the strong utilization of seminars staffed by knowledgeable and appropriately experienced faculty and assisted by a variety of other personnel. These seminars should be structured to maximize both challenge and support of the students: challenging them to expand their interpersonal understanding and communicative skills and supporting them through the turmoil that these experiences can produce. The portfolio, an instrument developed for use in teacher testing, may prove very useful in stimulating reflection on both field experiences and classwork—reflection that is essential to assimilation of new perspectives into a teacher's professional persona. Much work remains to be done with portfolios to understand how to tailor this very flexible instrument to meet the needs of diverse applications.

Conclusion

Whatever process is used, in whatever setting, and developed through whatever skill and wisdom, no teacher education program will be able to fully prepare its student teachers to deal with all of the different situations in which they might find themselves during a teaching career. Not only do we not know enough about any one group to definitively guide teaching, but we could not even teach our students all that we do know about a given group. The best we can hope to do is give our budding teachers a start on a lifelong learning process, a foundation of personal security on which to build. We can hope to sensitize them to the need to continue learning about the students that they encounter, and we can point them in the direction of where to look and what to consider in order to learn what is necessary in each setting. If we can accomplish this much, we will have done our duty to them, and to the students that they will be teaching.

We have to this point been concerned with the diversity among students and teachers. Our final point has to do not with the differences that exist among human groups but with the commonalities. Not all groups have the same values, but all groups have values that are worthy of respect and that have worked to make that group a viable social entity. We do not all want the same things, but we do all have wants and can come to understand each others' needs. We do not all love the same things or love them in the same way, but we do all love. We may speak different languages, but the same capacities that allowed us to learn our own language and to understand others within our own group can be used to understand someone who speaks another language, from another group. We do not all learn in the same way, nor are we all interested in learning the same things, but we do all learn. All students respond to attention, though we may have to learn slightly different ways of giving it in different situations. All education must, to maintain integrity, reach both the differences and the similarities of students. In a cross-cultural situation, the reach is more difficult; but we believe that it may be correspondingly more rewarding for the teachers.

References

Barnhardt, C. (1982). Tuning-in: Athabaskan teachers and Athabaskan students. In R. Barnhardt (ed.), *Cross-cultural issues in Alaskan education*. Vol. 2. Fairbanks: Center for Cross-Cultural Studies, University of Alaska.

Board of Trustees Task Force on Education Programs and Curriculum Impact. (1987). *Preliminary recommendations of the Board of Trustees task force on education programs and curriculum impact*. New York: City University of New York.

Booker, J. (1987). *Program review: Alaska rural teacher training corps and cross-cultural education development program, 1970–1984*. Fairbanks: Center for Cross-Cultural Studies, University of Alaska.

Calfee, R. (1983). Standards, evidence, and equity: Implications of the 1983 Debra P. decision. *Educational Measurement: Issues and Practice*, pp. 11–12.

Calfee, R., and Nelson-Barber, S. (1991). Diversity and constancy in human thinking: Critical literacy as the amplifier of intellect and experience. In E. Hiebert (ed.), *Literacy for a diverse society: Perspectives, programs, and policies*. New York: Teachers College Press.

Catterall, J., and Cota-Robles, E. (1988). The educationally at-risk: What the numbers mean. Paper presented at the invitational conference Accelerating the Education of At-Risk Students, Stanford University.

City College of New York. (1987). *Response to the Board of Trustees task force report*. New York: School of Education, City College, City University of New York.

Collins, M., and Tamarkin, C. (1982). *Marva Collins' way*. Los Angeles: Tarcher.

Delpit, L. (1986). Skills and other dilemmas of a progressive black educator. *Harvard Educational Review*, 56(4), 379–385.

Delpit, L. (1988). The silenced dialogue: Power and pedagogy in educating other peoples' children. *Harvard Educational Review*, *58*(3), 280–298.

Delpit, L., and Nelson-Barber, S. (1991). *Rethinking issues of context and culture for the new teacher assessments.* Unpublished manuscript.

Feiman-Nemser, S., and Floden, R. (1986). The cultures of teaching. In M. Wittrock (ed.), *Handbook of research on teaching.* (3rd ed.) New York: Macmillan.

Fisher, T. (1983). Implementing an instructional validity study of the Florida High School Graduation Test. *Educational Measurement: Issues and Practices*, pp. 8–9.

Florida Agricultural and Mechanical University. (1987). *A proposal to the Florida Department of Education: Reinstatement of program approval.* Tallahassee: College of Education, Florida Agricultural and Mechanical University.

Florida Agricultural and Mechanical University. (1988). *College of education, self-study.* Prepared for the Southern Association of Colleges and Schools. Tallahassee: Florida Agricultural and Mechanical University.

Foster, M. (1989). "It's cookin' now": A performance analysis of the speech events of a black teacher in an urban community college. *Language in Society, 18*(1), 1–29.

Gee, J. (1989). Literacy, discourse, and linguistics. *Journal of Education, 171*(1).

Goldenberg, C., and Gallimore, R. (1989). Teaching California's diverse student populations: The common ground between educational and cultural research, "student diversity." *California Public Schools Forum, 3*, 41–56.

Heath, S. B. (1983) *Ways with words: Language, life, and work in communities and classrooms.* Cambridge, MA: Cambridge University Press.

Hollins, E. (1982). The Marva Collins story revisited: Implications for regular classroom instruction. *Journal of Teacher Education, 33*(1), 37–40.

King, J., and Ladson-Billings, G. (1990). The teacher education challenge in elite universities: Developing critical perspectives for teaching a democratic and multicultural society. *European Journal of Intercultural Studies, 1*(2), 15–30.

Kleinfeld, J. (1974). Effective teachers of Indian and Eskimo high school students. In J. Orvik and R. Barnhardt (eds.), *Cultural influences in Alaska Native education*. Fairbanks: Center for Northern Educational Research, University of Alaska.

Kleinfeld, J., and Noordhoff, K. (1988). *Final report to the Office of Educational Research and Improvement, U.S. Department of Education*. Fairbanks: Teachers for Rural Alaska Program, University of Alaska.

Ladson-Billings, G. (1990). Culturally relevant teaching: Effective instruction for black students. *College Board Review, 155*, 20–25.

Lortie, D. (1975). *School-teacher: A sociological study*. Chicago: University of Chicago Press.

Locust, C. (1988). Wounding the spirit: Discrimination and traditional American Indian belief systems. *Harvard Educational Review, 58*(3), 315–330.

McDermott, R., and Gospodinoff, K. (1981). Social contexts for ethnic borders and school failure. In H. Trueba, G. Guthrie, and K. Au (eds.), *Culture and the bilingual classroom*. Rowley, MA: Newbury House.

Meek, A. (1989). On creating "ganas": A conversation with Jaime Escalante. *Educational Leadership, 46*(5), 46–47.

Meier, T. (1985). The social dynamics of writing development: An ethnographic study of writing development and classroom dialogue in a basic writing class. Unpublished doctoral dissertation, Graduate School of Education, Harvard University.

Michaels, S. (1986). Narrative presentations: An oral preparation of literacy with first graders. In J. Cook-Gumperz (ed.), *The social construction of literacy*. New York: Cambridge University Press.

Mohatt, G., and Erickson, F. (1981). Cultural differences in teaching styles in an Odawa school: A sociolinguistic approach. In H. Trueba, G. Guthrie, and K. Au (eds.), *Culture and the bilingual classroom*. Rowley, MA: Newbury House.

Nelson-Barber, S., and Meier, T. (1990). *Multicultural context a key factor in teaching: Academic connections*. New York: College Board.

Pan American University-Valley Schools. (1988). *Pan American University-valley schools consortium operative plan*. Edinburgh, TX: Pan American University-Valley Schools.

Phillips, S. (1983). *The invisible culture: Communication in classroom and community on the Warm Springs Indian reservation*. White Plains, N.Y.: Longman.

Popham, W. (1983). Task-teaching versus test-teaching. *Educational Measurement: Issues and Practices*, pp. 10–11.

Scollon, R., and Scollon, S.B.K. (1981). *Narrative, literacy, and face in interethnic communication*. Norwood, NJ: Ablex.

Smith, G. (1987). *The effects of competency testing on the supply of minority teachers*. A report prepared for the National Education Association (NEA) and the Council of Chief State School Officers (CCSSO). Washington, DC: NEA and CCSSO.

Spindler, G. (1965). *Education and culture*. Troy, MO: Holt, Rinehart & Winston.

Spindler, G. (1987). *Interpretive ethnography of education*. Hillsdale, NJ: Erlbaum.

Spindler, G. (1988). *Instrumental competence, self-efficacy, linguistic minorities, schooling, and cultural therapy*. Stanford, CA: Center for Educational Research, Stanford University.

Swisher, K., and Deyhle, D. (1987). Style of learning and learning of styles: Educational conflicts for American Indian/Alaskan Native youth. *Journal of Multilingual and Multicultural Development, 8*(4), 345–360.

Taylor, O., and Lee, D. (1987). Standardized tests and African-American children: Communication and language issues. *Negro Educational Review, 38*(2–3), 67–80.

Texas Education Agency. (1987). *Texas Education Agency annual performance report of institutions approved for teacher education*. Austin: Texas Education Agency.

Valencia, R. (1984). *Schooling that limits: Intelligence testing and the educability of Chicano school children*. Santa Cruz: University of California, Department of Education.

Wells, G. (1986). The language experience of five-year-old children at home and at school. In J. Cook-Gumperz (ed.), *The social construction of literacy*. New York: Cambridge University Press.

Wolcott, H. (1967). *A Kwakiutl village and school*. Troy, MO: Holt, Rinehart & Winston.

Name Index

A

Adler, M. J., 217, 227
Afflerbach, P., 186
Akinsanya, S. K., 84, 91
Allington, R. L., 185–187, 193, 207–208, 211
Anderson, J. A., 101, 108, 134, 135, 143, 157
Anrig, G. R., 96, 108–109
Apple, M. W., 64, 78
Applebome, P., 109
Arbeiter, S., 125, 133
Arends, R. I., 13, 14, 16, 148–149, 158, 160
Ashburn, E. A., 8, 12, 13, 40, 49, 62, 164
Au, K., 261
Austin, J. S., 142, 157

B

Babco, E. L., 121–122, 133
Backus, J. M., 134, 157

Bair, J. G., 111
Baker, G. C., 153, 157
Banks, J. A., 14, 20, 46, 47, 49, 59, 63, 77, 148, 157
Banks, W. C., 25, 30, 37
Baptiste, H. T., 147, 157, 158
Baptiste, M. L., 147, 157, 158
Baratz, J. C., 95, 96, 109
Barber, W. L., 20
Barnes, H. L., 45, 48, 59
Barnhardt, C., 253, 258
Barnhardt, R., 229n, 258, 261
Barr, R., 193, 208
Barton, A. H., 183, 208
Beckum, L. C., 15, 215
Bellamy, D. D., 136, 137, 157
Bennett, C. I., 84, 90
Berends, M., 192, 209
Berkson, I. B., 2
Berliner, D. C., 12, 20, 212
Billups, S., 200, 208
Blackwell, J. E., 87, 90
Blum, R. E., 196, 208
Booker, J., 245, 259

263

Bowles, S., 47, 59
Boykin, A. W., 25, 30, 31, 37
Braddock, J. H., 8, 20, 192, 196,
  202, 208, 212–213
Brand, D., 119, 132
Brandt, R., 216, 223, 227
Brookins, C. C., 82, 91
Brookover, W. B., 194, 208
Brophy, J. E., 82, 90
Brown, B. F., 5, 20
Brown, C. I., 1, 138, 157
Brown, T. J., 104, 105, 109
Buber, M., 56
Buckley, C. W., 10, 14, 134
Buckum, L. C., 10
Bunting, C. E., 187, 208
Burstein, N. D., 27–28, 37, 103, 109,
  134, 135, 148, 150, 157–158
Butler, J. A., 196, 208
Byers, H., 83–84, 90
Byers, P., 83–84, 90

C

Cabello, B., 27–28, 37, 103, 109, 134,
  135, 148, 150, 157–158
Cabezas, A., 116, 132
Calfee, R., 236, 253, 259
Carmichael, S., 4, 20
Carr, C. T., 59–60
Carter, D. J., 109
Carter, L. F., 186, 208
Castro, R., 96, 97, 102, 109
Catterall, J., 230, 259
Cazden, C. B., 26–28, 37, 47, 59, 90
Chan, S. Q., 119, 132
Chang Miller, M., 96, 111
Chapa, J., 95, 109
Chickering, A., 158
Chinn, P. C., 9, 64, 78, 112, 122,
  126, 132
Christensen, P., 178, 180
Clark, R., 25, 37
Clemson, S., 13, 14, 16, 160
Coates, J. F., 79, 90
Cogan, J., 46, 59
Cole, M., 9, 20
Coleman, J. S., 190, 208
Collins, M., 247, 259
Comer, J. P., 200, 208

Conant, J. B., 163, 165, 180
Cook-Gumperz, J., 261
Cooper, C. C., 96, 109
Corcoran, T. B., 182, 183, 193, 197,
  208–209
Cota-Robles, E., 230, 259
Coulson, J., 59–60
Crystal, D., 115, 116, 132
Cuban, L., 46, 60, 160, 180

D

Darling-Hammond, L., 190–193,
  195, 196, 209, 220
Dash, R., 109
Davidoff, S. H., 199, 209
Davis, S. M., 83, 90
Dedrick, R. B., 182, 196, 210
Delpit, L., 231, 233, 244, 247, 250,
  255, 259–260
Dewart, J., 213
Dewey, J., 2
Deyhle, D., 231, 262
Dornbusch, S., 119
Dreeben, R., 193, 208
Drucker, P. F., 51, 60
DuBois, W.E.B., 3, 4
Ducharme, E., 42, 60
Dull, V., 229n

E

Eagle, D., 59–60
Eastman, G., 209
Ebel, R. L., 210
Eder, D., 209
Ellis, E., 229n
Elmore, R. F., 146, 158, 227
Endo, R., 132
Epstein, J. L., 182–184, 194, 209
Erickson, F., 73, 74, 77, 253, 261
Escalante, J., 14, 69, 82–83
Etzioni, A., 54, 55, 60
Evans, C. S., 46, 60
Evertson, C. M., 192, 209

F

Fallon, D., 57, 61
Feiman-Nemser, S., 255, 260

Feistritzer, C. E., 41, 60
Fenstermacher, G. D., 51, 60
Fernandez, R. R., 94, 95, 109
Finley, M. K., 190, 191, 209
Fisher, T., 236, 260
Fiske, E. B., 98, 100, 101, 109, 220, 227
Fleming, J., 134, 143, 158
Floden, R., 255, 260
Foster, M., 231, 233, 255, 260
Franklin, A. J., 37
Freire, P., 70, 78
Frymier, J., 60

G

Galambos, E. C., 96, 109
Gallimore, R., 253, 260
Galluzzo, G. R., 148–149, 158
Gamoran, A., 192, 209
Garcia, J., 46, 60
Garcia, P. A., 109–110
Gardner, H., 51, 60
Garibaldi, A. M., 14, 23, 30, 38, 95, 110
Gay, C., 148, 158
Gay, G., 14, 20
Gee, J., 248, 253, 260
Geiger, J., 229n
Giles, R. H., 5, 20
Gilmore, P., 90
Gintis, H., 47, 59
Glatthorn, A. A., 199, 210
Glickman, C. C., 221, 227
Goebel, J., 46, 60
Goldenberg, C., 253, 260
Gollnick, D. M., 5, 13–14, 20, 63, 64, 78, 147, 157, 158
Goodlad, J. I., 21, 45, 46, 60, 81, 90, 165, 180, 212, 216, 227
Goodwin, A. L., 33, 38, 110
Gordon, E., 182–183, 210
Gospodinoff, K., 253, 261
Grant, C. A., 14, 18, 20–21, 31–32, 38, 49, 51, 52, 62, 65, 78, 158
Grant, C. S., 147, 158
Green, T. F., 49, 60
Greene, M., 8, 47, 55, 56, 60
Greenwood, P., 8, 21
Griffin, P., 9, 20

Grubis, S., 86, 91
Gumlickpuck, W., 229n
Guthrie, G., 261
Guthrie, J. W., 194, 210

H

Haberman, M., 161–162, 180
Hale-Benson, J. E., 25, 38, 86, 90
Hall, C., 196, 202, 212
Hallinan, M. T., 192, 210
Hamilton, C. V., 4, 20
Hare, B. S., 184, 210
Hargreaves, D. H., 190, 192, 210
Harris, L., 91
Haskins, R., 209
Hawley, W., 182, 210
Heath, S. B., 231, 247, 253, 260
Heathers, G., 192, 210
Hendricks, M. S., 16, 226, 228
Henkelman, J., 13, 14, 15, 160
Herman, J. L., 111
Hicks, E., 64, 78
Hiebert, E., 259
Hilliard, A. G., 25–26, 31, 38, 81, 90
Hirano-Nakanishi, M., 116–117, 132
Hodgkinson, H. L., 38, 50, 60, 79, 90
Hollins, E., 253, 260
Hoopes, D. S., 83, 90
Howey, K. R., 41, 42, 44, 45, 48, 60
Hsia, J., 116–117, 125–126, 132
Hubbard, J. L., 25, 30, 37
Hutchinson, L., 59–60
Hymes, D., 90

I

Ilutsik, E., 229n
Ima, K., 121, 133
Immerwahr, J., 197, 214
Irvine, J. J., 10, 12, 31, 38, 79, 81, 84, 91
Itzkoff, S. W., 2, 21

J

Jarratt, J., 79, 90
Jenkins, M., 143, 158

Jiobu, R. M., 116, 132
John-Steiner, V., 90
Johnson, D. J., 91
Johnson, D. L., 115, 124, 132
Johnson, D. W., 30, 38, 54, 61
Johnson, R. T., 30, 38, 54, 61
Johnson, W. R., 161–162, 180
Johnston, P., 186, 193, 207–208, 210
Jones, B. F., 184, 210
Jordan, D., 229n
Joy, J., 96, 111
Joyce, B., 165, 180

K

Kaestle, C. F., 186, 210
Kallen, H., 2
Karweit, N., 207–208
Katz, L., 49, 61
Katz, M. B., 5, 21, 47, 61
Kawaguchi, G., 116, 132
Keating, P., 190, 211, 212
Keddie, N., 192, 210
Kerlinger, F. N., 213
Kerr, D., 163–165, 180
Kilmann, R. H., 83, 91
Kim, B.L.C., 115, 132
King, J., 231, 253, 260
Kitano, M. K., 132
Kleinfeld, J., 86, 91, 233, 245, 261
Kohn, A., 53, 54, 61
Kohut, S., Jr., 148, 150, 158

L

Ladson-Billings, G., 231, 233, 253, 260, 261
Lane, D. S., 80, 91
Lanier, J., 42, 61
Laskey, T. J., 109
Law, S. G., 80, 91
Leacock, E., 192, 210
LeCompte, M. D., 80, 91
Lee, D., 248, 262
Lee, V. E., 182, 196, 210
Lester, J., 3, 21
Levin, D. U., 6, 22
Levin, M. J., 115, 124, 132
Lieberman, A. F., 158
Lightfoot, S. L., 91, 216, 227

Lipka, J., 229n
Lipton, M., 192, 211–212
Little, J. W., 42, 61, 196, 210
Lockheed, M. E., 213
Locust, C., 244, 248, 261
Lomack, A., 229n
Lomotey, K., 82, 91
Long, R. C., 132
Lortie, D. C., 164, 180, 249, 261
Lucas, B., 229n
Lujan, H. D., 121, 132
Lytle, J. H., 199, 211

M

McBride, J., 229n
McCarthy, C., 64, 78
McDermott, R., 253, 261
McDiarmid, G. W., 17, 21, 27, 28, 38, 45–46, 52, 61, 86, 91
McDonnell, L. M., 7, 21, 222–223, 227
McGill-Franzen, A., 185–187, 208, 211
Macias, R. F., 107, 110
McKay, E. G., 94, 107, 110
McLaughlin, M. W., 8, 21, 146, 158
McPartland, J. S., 8, 87, 92
McQuater, G. V., 25, 30, 37
MacRae, D., 209
Madden, N., 207–208
Madden, R. L., 206, 211
Madrid, A., 101–102, 110
Maeroff, G. I., 184, 211
Majetic, R. M., 124, 132
Mann, D., 8, 21
Manning, J. B., 8, 181, 196, 200, 211
Mason, E. J., 96, 110
Meek, A., 247, 261
Mehan, H., 26–28, 37, 47, 59
Meier, D., 218
Meier, T., 231, 233, 253, 255, 261
Melendez, S. E., 100, 110
Metz, M. H., 50, 61, 182, 192, 211
Michaels, S., 248, 253, 261
Middleton, E. J., 96, 110
Mills, J. R., 10, 14, 134, 140, 141, 143, 149, 151, 152, 154, 155, 158–159
Mills, R. P., 220

Minatoya, L. Y., 121, 132
Mingle, J. R., 87, 92
Minow, M., 65, 78
Miracle, A. W., Jr., 193, 212
Mitchell, J., 9, 15, 224, 229
Mohatt, G., 253, 261
Montero-Sieburth, M., 49, 61
Mungo, S., 134, 135, 159
Muniz, A., 229n
Munoz, D., 100, 110
Murray, F. B., 57, 61

N

Nee, V., 116, 132–133
Nelson-Barber, S., 9, 15, 224, 229,
    231, 233, 244, 250, 253, 255, 259–
    261
Nettles, S. M., 199, 211
Nieves-Squires, S., 100, 110
Noddings, N., 55–57, 61
Nomura, G. M., 132
Noordhoff, K., 245, 261

O

Oakes, J., 9, 21, 25, 31, 38, 69, 78,
    190, 192–193, 211–212
O'Connor, T., 71, 78
Ogbu, J., 83
Olivas, M., 100, 110
Olsen, N. L., 196, 208
O'Neil, J., 216, 220, 227
Onore, C., 229n, 249
Ornstein, A. C., 6, 22
Orvik, J., 261
Ouchi, W. G., 55–57, 61

P

Padilla, R. V., 111
Paine, L., 50, 51, 61–62
Paisano, E. L., 115, 124, 132
Parker, D. H., 50, 51, 62
Parker, W. C., 96, 110
Parrett, W., 86, 91
Pate, G. S., 136, 159
Pearson, C. S., 110
Peck, M. S., 55, 56, 62
Peng, S. S., 122, 133

Perry, W., 44, 62
Pestalozzi, J., 56
Peters, T. J., 182, 212
Petrovich, J., 100, 110
Petza, R. J., 196, 202, 212–213
Phillips, S., 247, 262
Pierson, E. M., 199, 209
Pomeroy, D., 229n
Popham, W., 236, 262
Purkey, S. C., 57, 62, 183, 194, 195,
    212
Pusch, M. D., 83, 90

R

Ramist, L., 125, 133
Raths, J., 49, 61
Reynolds, M. C., 37, 48, 59, 62, 213
Roberts, J. I., 84, 91
Rodman, B., 95, 111, 180
Rodriguez, A. M., 106, 111
Rosenbaum, J. E., 190, 192, 212
Rowan, B., 193, 212
Rumbaut, R. G., 121, 133
Rutter, R. A., 199, 213

S

Sahol, C., 147, 158
Sanchez, J., 99, 100, 111
Sanders, J., 116, 132–133
Sarason, S. B., 8
Saxton, M. J., 83, 90
Schlechty, P. C., 15
Schuhmann, A. M., 93, 103, 111
Schwartz, F., 192, 212
Scollon, R., 253, 262
Scollon, S.B.K., 134, 143, 159, 253,
    262
Sedlacek, W. E., 121, 132
Serpa, R., 83, 90
Shade, B. J., 86, 91
Shanker, A., 216, 220, 223
Sharp, F., 229n
Sharp, N., 229n
Shavelson, R. J., 189, 212
Shavlik, D., 110
Shinagawa, L., 116, 132
Shor, I., 70, 78
Shujaa, M. J., 184, 212
Shulman, L. S., 12, 180, 224, 228

Sing, B., 113, 133
Singer, E. A., 91
Sizer, T. R., 202, 216, 228
Slaughter, D. T., 91
Slavin, R. E., 30, 38–39, 53–54, 62, 192, 196, 202, 204, 206–208, 212–213
Sleeter, C. E., 18, 21, 32, 38, 49, 51, 52, 62, 65, 78, 147, 158
Smith, B. S., 138, 150, 159
Smith, G., 230, 262
Smith, G. P., 96, 111
Smith, J. B., 182, 196, 210
Smith, M. S., 57, 62, 183, 186, 194, 195, 210, 212
Snyder, T. D., 119, 133
Soldier, L. L., 84, 92
Soltis, J., 51, 60
Sorensen, A. B., 192, 210
Spady, W. G., 190, 213
Spindler, G., 248, 253, 262
Standley, N. V., 136, 137, 147, 159
Starr, J., 73, 78
Stein, P. R., 138, 157
Stern, P., 189, 212
Stilwell, W. E., 96, 110
Stringfield, S., 214
Sue, D. W., 120, 133
Sue, S., 120, 133
Sukuki, B. H., 133
Sumida, S. H., 132
Suzuki, B. H., 116, 119, 122, 125
Swisher, K., 231, 262
Swonigan, H., 229n
Sykes, G., 180

T

Tamarkin, C., 247, 259
Taylor, F. M., 190
Taylor, O., 248, 262
Thomas, G. E., 87, 92
Tikunoff, W. J., 104, 106, 111
Tippeconnic, J. W., III, 143, 159
Touchton, J., 110
Traylor, F. M., 213
Trueba, G., 261
Tseng, W., 133
Tucker, M., 220
Turnbaugh, A., 199, 213
Turnbull, B. J., 185, 213

V

Valencia, R., 248, 262
Vaughan, E. D., 196, 213
Velez, W., 94, 95, 109
Venezky, R. L., 186, 187, 213
Vetter, B. M., 121–122, 133
Vickery, T. R., 200, 213

W

Walberg, H. J., 186, 213
Wang, M. C., 186, 196, 213
Warren, D., 180
Washington, B. T., 3
Waterman, R. H., 182, 212
Watson, B. C., 190, 213
Webb, M. B., 95, 111
Wehlage, G. G., 199, 213
Weinstein, C. S., 164, 180
Wells, G., 253, 262
Wilder, P. E., 184, 208
Wilkerson, D. A., 6, 22
Wilkinson, L. C., 69, 78
Willis, M. G., 25, 39
Wilson, B., 197, 209
Wilson, R., 109
Winfield, L. F., 8, 181, 184, 186, 187, 190, 197, 199, 213, 214
Winkler, K. J., 112, 122, 133
Winnick, L., 115, 133
Wittrock, M. C., 61
Witty, E. P., 95, 96, 111
Wolcott, H., 248, 262
Wong, G. Y., 9, 112
Wong, J., 133
Wong-Fillmore, L., 106–107, 111
Woodson, C. G., 3, 4

Y

Yankelovich, D., 197, 214
Yates, J. F., 37
Yinger, J. R., 16, 226, 228
Yoa, E. L., 80, 92
Young, M.F.D., 210

Z

Zapata, J. T., 112, 133
Zeichner, K. M., 45, 46, 48, 62
Zimpher, N. L., 8, 12, 13, 38, 40–42, 44, 45, 48, 49, 60, 62, 164

Subject Index

A

Abell Foundation, 203
Ability grouping. *See* Grouping; Tracking
Academic foundation courses, 149
Academic support systems, 141, 147–148
African American colleges, 100, 140, 236. *See also* White teacher candidates at predominantly African American colleges
African Americans: communication style of, 85; competency tests of, 124; failure of schools to meet needs of, 184; instructional approach for, 30; learning style of, 86; personal presentation style of, 84–85; in teacher education programs, 161; views of education for, 3–4
Alpha Study, 139–141, 147, 153
American Association of Colleges for Teacher Education

(AACTE), 5; minority teacher recruitment and retention symposium sponsored by, 18; study of teacher education programs by, 163
American College Test, 125, 239
American Indians, 140
Arizona State University, 226
Asian Indians. *See* Asian/Pacific Americans
Asian/Pacific Americans: academic support at university level for, 128–129; attending predominantly black colleges, 140; career goals and choices of, 121–122; competency tests and, 124–126; Confucian values in, 118–121; credit for education coursework and teaching experience overseas for, 130; demographic profile of, 112–118; identification and recruitment of, 127–128; incentives and financial aid for, 129–130; need for native teachers of, 126–

127; programs to enhance social and communication skills in, 130–131; in teacher education programs, 122–124, 161
Aspira Five Cities High School Dropout Study, 94
Assessment: alternative methods of, 221–223; integration of curriculum and, 218–222; proficiency in, 30–31; of teacher education programs, 225–226; through use of standardized tests, 220, 222, 225, 249. *See also* Teacher assessment
At-risk students, 80–83

B

Baltimore City Public Schools, 203
Beta Study, 141–142, 147
Bicultural instruction, 5
Bilingual education: for Asian students, 126–127; competency needed for, 106–107; legislation supporting, 5; undergraduate-level, for Hispanics, 100. *See also* Limited English proficient (LEP) children; English as a second language (ESL)
Bilingual Education Act, 5
Black Collegian Research Consortium, 139
Black Power, 4
Blacks. *See* African Americans
Boricua College, 100
Brown University, 202
Brown v. *Board of Education*, 3–4

C

California Basic Educational Skills Test (CBEST), 124, 125
California State University, Los Angeles, 122, 128
Career choices, 121–124
Career information, 127
Carnegie Corporation, 57
Celebrations, 15

Central Park East High School (New York City), 202, 218–220
Central State University, 241
Ceremonies, 15
Certification tests. *See* Teacher competency tests
Chinese Americans: Confucian values among, 118–121; family income of, 116. *See also* Asian/Pacific Americans
City College of New York (CCNY), 225, 234–235
City University of New York (CUNY), 218, 234
Civic organizations, 35–36
Class. *See* Social class
Classroom culture, 26–27
Classroom management, 31–32
Coaching teams, 173
Coalition of Essential Schools Project, 202, 217–218
College enrollment: among Hispanics, 93, 95, 96; decline in minority, 216
Colleges and universities: academic support for Asian students at, 128–129; African American, 100; incentives for recruitment of minorities by, 129–130; recognition of overseas teacher education coursework by, 130; responsibilities of, 76–77; restructuring teacher education in, 13–17. *See also* Schools, colleges, and departments of education (SCDEs); Graduate schools of education
Comer Process, 200
Communication: analysis of oral and nonverbal, 69; awareness of differences in, 248; benefits of courses in, 71–72; need for cross-cultural skills in, 11; programs to enhance Asian Americans' skills in, 128–131; style of African American, 85. *See also* Language use; Nonverbal communication
Communities: importance of caring, 8, 54–57; interaction of re-

structured schools and teachers with, 9–10; involvement in assessment process, 222
Community organizations, 35–36
Competency tests. *See* Teacher competency tests; Standardized tests
Competition, 52–54
Comprehensive Student Support Services (CSSS), 200
Confucian values, 118–121
Contact theory, 138
Cooperation: competition and, 52–53; definition of, 53–54
Cooperative Integrated Reading and Composition program, 204–205
Cooperative learning, 30, 69
Cooperative teaching, 201–202
Cross-Cultural Experience Program (Carnegie Foundation), 138
Cuban Americans. *See* Hispanics
Cultural conflict: examples of, 84–86; in higher education, 142; in Hispanic community, 100–101
Cultural differences: as barrier to success for Hispanics, 100; student performance and, 27–28
Cultural diversity: restructuring to accommodate, 142–143; schools, colleges, and departments of education as models of, 86–88; teacher assessment and understanding of, 232–233; and teaching and learning process, 86; techniques for accommodating, 155–156; understanding dynamics of, 64, 65; understanding of, 25–26; value of, 51. *See also* Diversity
Culture: explanation of, 182; implications of, 83–84; social class versus, 25–26; study of white, 154; understanding and teaching classroom, 26–27. *See also* School culture
Curriculum: areas for restructuring, 148–151; effect of change in,

46–47; as focus of early reform, 217; inequalities in, 192–193; integration of educational assessment and, 218–222; proposals for change in, 48; reflection of diversity in, 70. *See also* Teacher education curriculum
Curriculum design: based on concept of global education, 49; to improve student learning, 201

D

Dayton Public Schools, 241
Decision making: in cooperative teaching approaches, 201; impact of shared, 194–195; teacher involvement in, 8
Departments of education. *See* Schools, colleges, and departments of education
Dialects, 71
Discrimination, 65
Diversity: appreciation of, 50–52; development of emphasis on, 182–183; effective teaching and information regarding, 104–105; grouping to accommodate, 192; past attempts at dealing with, 184–191; reconceptualizing teacher education toward, 46–50, 58; restructuring to accommodate, 1–2, 7–10, 142–143, 246–250; school-home-community linkage programs that accommodate, 199–200; school organization programs that accommodate, 198–199; student learning programs that accommodate, 200–203; teacher candidate recruitment and, 44–45, 75–76; types of, 51. *See also* Cultural diversity
Doctoral degree holders, 87
Doctoral programs: decline in minority students in, 216; minority representation among, 76. *See also* Graduate schools of education

Dropout rate: among Hispanics, 93–95; among minority students, 216

E

Education: Asian parental involvement in, 119; need for reforms in, 215–216; varying views of content and delivery of, 72
Education Consolidation and Improvement Act (1981), 185, 186
Education faculty: knowledge and experience in cultural issues of, 249; as minority role models, 129; need for retraining of, 13; profile of, 42, 87; recruitment, promotion, and tenure of, 80; working with white minorities, 153–156
Education for All Handicapped Children Act of 1975, 185
Education restructuring: to accommodate diversity, 7–10, 142–143; considerations and recommendations for, 143–144; evolution of goals for, 223; exploratory projects in, 217–221, 225–226; historical antecedents to, 27; role of state in, 223; systems approach to, 217; teacher competency needed for, 10–12, 14–15
Educational assessment. *See* Assessment
Educational attainment: of Asian/Pacific Americans, 117; of Hispanics, 94–96
Educational foundations, 71
Elementary and Secondary Education Act (ESEA), 185
Elementary schools: example of restructuring program in, 203–206; results of tracking in, 193; teacher assignments in, 190–191
Emergency School Aid Act, 5
English as a second language (ESL), 100. *See also* Limited English proficient (LEP) children; Bilingual education

Ethnic Heritage Studies Act, 4
Ethnic studies, 66, 67, 73
Exchange programs, 72
Exemplary Schools Project, 203

F

Faculty. *See* Education faculty
Family involvement, 199–200, 204
Family relations: in Asian Americans, 119–120; Confucian philosophy and, 118–121; Hispanic, 98–100. *See also* Parents
Field experiences: integration of cultural dynamics throughout, 67–68; in minority schools, 83; for nontraditional minorities, 150–151; to prepare for educating Hispanics, 103; during preservice teacher education, 33–34, 227; types and benefits of, 150
Filipino Americans, 116. *See also* Asian/Pacific Americans
Financial aid: for Asian students, 123, 129–130; for Hispanic students, 98; to increase minority representation in doctoral programs, 76; recruitment success due to, 176
Florida Agricultural and Mechanical University (FAMU), 236–238
Florida Teacher Certification Examination (FTCE), 236, 237
Foreign language courses, 71–73
Fort Valley State College, 137
Future Teacher Institutes, 127

G

Gender: restructuring curriculum to reflect, 66–68; understanding dynamics of, 64, 65, 73
Global education, 49
Graduate schools of education: Hispanic enrollment in, 95, 96; restructuring of, 15–16. *See also* Colleges and universities; Doctoral degree holders; Doctoral programs

Grouping: alternatives to, 201–202; impact of, 192, 193; in restructured schools, 7–8. *See also* Tracking

H

Hampton University, 16
Harding Middle School (Iowa), 202
Hawaiian Americans. *See* Asian/ Pacific Americans
High school graduates, Hispanic, 93, 94
Hispanics: attending predominantly black colleges, 140, 141; competency tests of, 124; failure of schools to meet needs of, 184; methods for recruitment and retaining, 96–102, 107; preparation for teacher candidates to educate, 102–103, 107–108; profile of, 93–95, 97–98, 107; teacher competency needed to educate, 103–107; in teacher education programs, 161
Holmes Group: influence of, 7, 8, 16; professional development school concept developed by, 17
Hostos Community College, 100

I

Incentives: for recruitment of minorities, 129–130; for white teacher candidates at predominantly black colleges, 140. *See also* Financial aid
Indians (Asian), 116. *See also* Asian/Pacific Americans
Inner-city schools. *See* Urban schools
Instruction: cross-cultural conflict in, 152–153; culturally responsive strategies for, 83; importance of effective planning and organization of, 28–30; key skills needed before engaging in, 29
Intelligence, 51

Internships, in UMCP-MCPS program, 172–173, 177

J

Japanese Americans: Confucian values among, 118–121; family income of, 116. *See also* Asian/ Pacific Americans
Johns Hopkins University, 203, 206
Johnson City School District (New York), 202
Joplin Plan, 204

K

Kean College, 100
Kettering Foundation, 5
Kindergarten programs, 204
Korean Americans, 118–121. *See also* Asian/Pacific Americans

L

Language use: by African Americans, 85; differences in, 51, 248; effective teaching and, 105, 106. *See also* Limited English proficient (LEP) children; English as a second language (ESL); Bilingual education; Communication
Latin Americans. *See* Hispanics
Learning: cultural context of, 81–83; programs to improve student, 200–203. *See also* Cooperative learning
Learning community, 2
Learning style: of African Americans, 86; cultural influences on, 68–70; of Hispanics, 101
Limited English proficient (LEP) children: Asian bilingual teachers for, 127; competency need for education of, 105–107. *See also* English as a second language (ESL); Bilingual education
Linguistics courses, 71–72

M

Maplewood Middle School (Minnesota), 202
Mastery learning model, 202
Mathematics: approach to teaching, 69; Asian American students and, 125–126; UMCP-MCPS program support in, 174
Metropolitan Life Foundation, 18
Mexican Americans. *See* Hispanics
Miami-Dade County School District program, 198–199
Minorities: benefits of study of, 70–71; competency tests and, 96; recruitment of candidates from, *See also* Recruitment; individual minority groups
Minority students: at-risk, 80–83; culturally relevant education for, 4; effective teaching strategies for, 81–83; inequalities in curriculum for, 192–193; reasons for failure of, 26; underrepresentation in education programs, 122
Minority teachers: goal of increasing pool of, 252; need for, 126–127; as role models, 126; training in mainstream culture for, 252
Montgomery County Public Schools (MCPS), 167
Motivational techniques, 32–33
Multicultural awareness, 174–175
Multicultural courses: effectiveness of, 27, 102; expansion of training beyond, 107–108; views regarding, 66–67
Multicultural education: approaches to, 66–67; early views of, 2–3; elements of implementation of, 65; essential nature of, 63–64; legislation supporting, 4–5; results of inadequate, 80; standards of review related to, 6–7
Multicultural seminars: effect of, 27; recommendations for, 254, 255

N

National Board of Professional Teaching Standards, 224
National Coalition for Cultural Pluralism, 5
National Council for Accreditation of Teacher Education, 63
National Governors Association, 220–221
National teachers examination: requirements for, 216; teacher assessment through use of, 224, 235; UMCP-MCPS program support for taking, 174
Native Americans, 140
Newspapers, used for minority recruitment purposes, 128
Nonverbal communication: analysis of, 69; cultural differences in, 84, 248; style of African American, 85
NTE (national teachers examination). *See* National teachers examination

O

Optimism, unrealistic, 164–165
Organizations, 89

P

Pacific Americans. *See* Asian/Pacific Americans
Paideia proposal, 217
Parents: influence of Hispanic, 98; programs to increase involvement of, 199–200; role in education, 35. *See also* Family relations
Parochialism: among teacher candidates, 41–44; challenges to, 57; role of teacher education in countering, 44–46
Personal income: of Asian/Pacific Americans, 116–117; of Hispanics, 97

Philadelphia School District, 200, 203
Philadelphia Schoolwide Projects model, 199
Portfolios. *See* Teacher portfolios
Pre-Professional Skills Test (PPST), 124, 239, 240
Preschool programs, 204
Preservice teacher education. *See* Teacher education
Principals, 195
Professional organizations, 89
Project 30 (Carnegie Corporation), 57
Project SEED, 69
Public Law 94-142, 185
Public schools: alternatives to traditional, 6; demographic shifts in populations in, 181; responsibilities of, 56
Puerto Ricans. *See* Hispanics

R

Race: implications of, 84; restructuring curriculum to reflect, 66–68; understanding dynamics of, 64, 65, 73
Rand Corporation, 8
Reading programs, 204–205
Recruitment: of Asian candidates, 127–128; of Hispanic candidates, 96–102; of males, 177; of nontraditional minority individuals, 160, 162; of teacher candidates from diverse backgrounds, 44–45, 75–76; of white students for predominantly black colleges, 137, 140
Religious organizations, 35–36
Research About Teacher Education (RATE) Project, 163–165
Restructuring. *See* Education restructuring
Rituals, 15
Rochester Educational Council, 16
Role models: faculty members as, 129; minority teachers as, 126

S

SCDEs. *See* Schools, colleges, and departments of education
Scholarships. *See* Financial aid
Scholastic Aptitude Test: Asian Americans and, 119, 125; as requirement for admission to teacher education programs, 236, 239
School culture: benefits of changing, 194, 206–207; consistent policy enforcement and, 195; effect of assignment of teachers on, 189–191; effect of discretionary efforts of teachers on, 197; explanation of, 182–183; impact of cooperation and coordination on, 195–196; impact of shared decision making on, 194–195; inequality in curriculum and, 192–193; teacher beliefs and, 187–189, 193
Schools: accountability of, 221; administrative structures of, 79–80, 185–187; clinical experiences in, 33–34; cooperation and coordination of programs within, 195–196; failure to meet needs of diverse student body in, 183–184; features of urban, 182, 183; policy enforcement in, 195; preservation of social inequities through, 249–250; trend toward minority-operated, 4. *See also* Urban schools; Public schools
Schools, colleges, and departments of education (SCDEs): climate for Hispanics in, 98–99; dilemmas facing, 79–80; as models of cultural diversity, 86–88; need for restructuring of, 13–15, 23, 88–89; restructuring necessary within, 135
Science: Asian American students and, 125–126; focus on higher achievement in, 8
Secondary schools: availability of career information in, 127; re-

sults of tracking in, 192–193; teacher assignments in, 191

Seminars. *See* Multicultural seminars

Site-based management, 7, 199

Slaves, former, 3

Social class: culture versus, 25–26; restructuring curriculum to reflect, 66–68; understanding dynamics of, 64, 65, 73

Standardized tests: assessment of student and teacher performance through use of, 220, 222, 225, 249; community responses to, 222; decline in scores on, 216; teaching to, 240

Stanford University, 224, 232

State University of New York at Buffalo Research Institute on Education for Teaching, 16

Student achievement: effect of cultural differences on, 27–28; relationship between expectations and, 104; teacher beliefs and, 187–189

Students: access to knowledge by, 187; demographic shifts in population of, 181; evaluation of interactions between teacher candidates and, 74–75; personal relationships between teachers and, 233; profile of, 79; programs to improve learning by, 200–203. *See also* Minority students

Success for All program, 203–206

Support systems: in UMCP-MCPS program, 173–174, 176; for white teacher candidates at predominantly African American colleges, 141, 147–148

T

Teacher assessment: at City College of New York, 234–235; cultural diversity and, 233; fair testing issues in, 230–232; at Florida Agricultural and Mechanical University, 236–238; new modes of, 232–233; at Ohio Group, 241–243; performance-based methods of, 232; standardized tests as method of, 174, 216, 220, 224, 225; at University of Alaska, 243–246; at University of Texas-Pan American, 238–241

Teacher Assessment Project (TAP): overview of, 224, 232, 233; themes emerging from use of materials provided by, 246–250; work with City College of New York, 235; work with Florida Agricultural and Mechanical University, 237; work with Ohio Group, 241, 242; work with University of Alaska, 244, 246; work with University of Texas-Pan American, 241

Teacher beliefs: access to knowledge resulting from, 193; content of, 187–188; patterns of, 188–189

Teacher candidates: assessment of, 224–225; attempts to establish global perspective in, 47–49; attitudes toward minorities of, 80; decline in number of minority, 161; exposure and interactions between students and, 74–75, 250–251; impact of cultural background of, 69; parochialism among, 41–44; profile of, 40, 43, 164; readiness of, 165; retention of Hispanic, 98–102; self-examination of prejudices of, 73. *See also* White teacher candidates at predominantly African American colleges

Teacher competency tests: Asian Americans and, 124–126; emphasis on, 96; minority performance on, 230; passing rates for, 124; requirements for, 216; sensitivity to testing minorities, 231. *See also* Teacher assessment

Teacher-control model, 27

Teacher Corps, 6, 15

Teacher education: conclusions regarding, 18–19; elements of restructuring, 10–18; need for clinical experiences during, 33–34; recommendations for, 250–257; requirements for multicultural, 63; restructuring of, 24–25, 36–37, 162–163, 223–224; role in countering parochialism, 44–46, 48–49; role of home, community, and school collaboration in, 35–36; role of U.S. Teacher Corps in, 6

Teacher Education Consortium, 229n, 233, 246. *See also* Teacher Assessment Project (TAP)

Teacher education curriculum: Hispanic studies in, 101; reconceptualization of, 88–89; restructuring of, 66–68, 81–83; teacher competency testing and, 230; UMCP-MCPS, 171–172. *See also* Curriculum

Teacher education programs: Asian/Pacific Americans in, 122–124, 161; example of redesigned, 167–175; example of reevaluation of, 225–226; handling of diversity by, 52; inadequacies of, 13–14, 165–166; organized around themes, 166, 177; percentage of minorities in, 161; to prepare for educating Hispanic students, 102–107; RATE study of, 163–165; recruiting and retaining Hispanics for, 96–102; requirements for, 17–18; revision of, 24–25. *See also* UMCP-MCPS alternate teacher education program

Teacher portfolios: development of, 229–230; examples of use of, 235, 237, 238, 242–243, 246; as means of assessment, 235

Teachers: changes needed for preparation of, 12–13; competency needed for, 10–12, 14–15, 24–25; cooperation and coordination among, 196; development of reflective, 247–248, 251; discretionary efforts by, 197; elements of

effective, 81–83; encouragement of initiative and autonomy among, 196; inequalities in assignment of, 189–191; number of Hispanic, 94, 95; participation in decision making by, 194–195; personal relationships between students and, 233; profile of, 41; relationship between achievement and expectations of, 104

Teachers for Rural Alaska Program, 245

Teaching: cooperative approaches to, 201–202; cultural context of, 9, 83–86; cultural influences on, 68–70; development of vocabulary for, 14; elements of effective, 81–83; recognition of overseas experience in, 130

Team teaching, 201

Technology, 8

Temple University, 203

Tests. *See* Standardized tests: Teacher competency tests

Textbooks, 34–35

Tomas River Center, 101

Tracking: alternatives to, 201–202; inequalities produced by, 9, 191–193; trend away from, 8

Tutors, reading, 205

U

UMCP-MCPS alternate teacher education program: administration and management of, 175; background of, 167–168; recruitment and selection in, 168–169; strengths of, 176–177, 179; structure and processes of, 170–175; training program features in, 169–170; weaknesses of, 177–178

Undergraduate education, critical nature of, 23–24

U.S. Teacher Corps, 6

Universities. *See* Colleges and universities; Schools, colleges, and departments of education; Graduate schools of education

University of Alaska, 243–246

University of Dayton, 241
University of Maryland College
    Park/Montgomery County Pub-
    lic Schools Collaborative, 16–17.
    See also UMCP-MCPS alternate
    teacher education program
University of Maryland College
    Park (UMCP), 167
University of Missouri at Colum-
    bia, 16
University of Southern California,
    226
University of Texas-Pan American
    (UTPA), 238–241
Urban schools: features of, 182, 183;
    teacher assignments in, 190–191

V

Vietnamese Americans, 118–121.
    See also Asian/Pacific
    Americans

W

Washington Elementary School
    (Utah), 202

White teacher candidates at pre-
    dominantly African American
    colleges: academic support sys-
    tems for, 147–148; Alpha Study
    of, 139–141; Beta Study and,
    141–142; cross-cultural conflict
    in instruction for, 152–153; cur-
    riculum for, 148–151; enroll-
    ment of, 140; expectations and
    experiences of, 137–139; institu-
    tional policies to accommodate,
    146–147; learning environment
    for, 151–152; mission and goals
    in providing for, 145–146; over-
    view of, 134–136; profile of, 147–
    148; restructuring to accommo-
    date, 143–145, 156; staff develop-
    ment to accommodate, 153–156
Wright State University, 241, 247

X

X-roster classes, 191

Z

Zen Buddhism, 56